PROMOTING PURPOSEFUL DISCOURSE

PROMOTING PURPOSEFUL DISCOURSE

Teacher Research in Mathematics Classrooms

Edited by
Beth Herbel-Eisenmann
Michigan State University, East Lansing, Michigan

Michelle Cirillo
Iowa State University, Ames, Iowa

NCTM®
NATIONAL COUNCIL OF TEACHERS OF MATHEMATICS

Library of Congress Cataloging-in-Publication Data

Promoting purposeful discourse : teacher research in mathematics classrooms / edited by Beth Herbel-Eisenmann, Michelle Cirillo.
p. cm. — (Teacher research in mathematics classrooms)
Includes bibliographical references.
ISBN 978-0-87353-621-9
1. Mathematics—Study and teaching—United States. 2. Mathematics teachers—In-service training—United States. 3. Curriculum planning—United States. I. Herbel-Eisenmann, Beth A. II. Cirillo, Michelle.
QA13.P76 2009
510.71—dc22

2009004999

The National Council of Teachers of Mathematics is a public voice of mathematics education, providing vision, leadership, and professional development to support teachers in ensuring equitable mathematics learning of the highest quality for all students.

Printed in the United States of America

Contents

Foreword

Edward A. Silver

IN THE past two decades, our profession has seen an explosion of interest in *discourse* as a feature of precollege mathematics classrooms. Whether focused specifically on discourse, or more generally on the notions of mathematical communication and conversation in mathematics classrooms, the strong interest in this aspect of mathematics education is evident in published research papers, in the texts and syllabi associated with teacher preparation courses, and even in such policy documents as the frameworks of state curricula.

In some ways this dramatic growth of professional interest in discourse is not surprising. Although mathematics classrooms have long been places where students learned (or, more commonly, failed to learn) alone and in silence, communication and discourse have had a central place in reformers' vision of desirable mathematics teaching portrayed in early NCTM *Standards* documents (NCTM 1989, 1991). In contrast with the conventional view of mathematics teaching as a transmission of knowledge from the teacher to the students in a classroom, these documents suggest an alternative vision of mathematics classrooms, in which students engage with mathematical ideas and actively construct their understanding. In the conventional version of classroom mathematics, the chief tasks of teaching are transmitting knowledge and ascertaining that students have acquired accurate versions of the transmitted knowledge. In contrast, in the reform-inspired vision of mathematics classrooms, the role of the teacher is diversified to include posing worthwhile and engaging mathematical tasks; managing the classroom intellectual activity, including the discourse; and helping students understand mathematical ideas and monitor their own understanding. Thus, the new role envisioned for mathematics teachers is one closely tied to issues of communication.

Professional Standards for Teaching Mathematics (NCTM 1991) identifies six standards for teaching mathematics, of which one is "the teacher's role in discourse." To elaborate this standard, many aspects of a teacher's role in discourse are identified: "posing questions and tasks that elicit, engage and challenge each student's thinking; listening carefully to each student's ideas; asking students to clarify and justify their ideas orally and in writing; deciding what to pursue in depth from among the ideas that students bring up during a discussion; deciding when and how to attach mathematical notation and language to students' ideas; deciding when to provide information, when to clarify an issue, when to model, when to lead, and when to let a student struggle with a difficulty; and monitoring students' participation in discussions and deciding when and how to encourage each student to participate" (p. 35).

Interest in communication is both more widespread and more central to efforts to reform mathematics education than ever before. Nevertheless, realizing that communication is a central issue for mathematics education is necessary but not sufficient to ensure more frequent use of communication-rich mathematics teaching than has been typical in the past. As Anna Sfard so cleverly put it, "There is more to discourse than meets the ears" (Sfard 2002, p. 13). Even though interest in, and commitment to, communication in mathematics instruction are high, many teachers may struggle with the challenges of implementing these ideas to create the new version of mathematics instruction that occurs in classrooms that are true discourse communities.

As we have come to learn in the past two decades, teaching mathematics with a focus on discourse is a complex, multifaceted undertaking. Mathematics teachers must know, for example, when to simply present information and when to withhold it; when to provide explanations and when to elicit them from students; when to supply notation and language for shared use in the class and when to encourage students to invent symbols; and when to encourage students to speak freely and when to monitor their ideas and challenge them to justify their thinking. As Peg Smith and I noted some years ago, *Professional Standards for Teaching Mathematics* (NCTM 1991) "provides a wonderful image of a 'last stop' on a long journey—classrooms as mathematical discourse communities—but it says little about the various paths along which teachers might travel to arrive there or about the challenges they may encounter along the way" (Silver and Smith 1996, p. 21).

To make progress as a field in realizing the vision of communication-rich mathematics classrooms, mathematics educators must understand not only that challenges are inevitable but also that those challenges will usually not have a single, clear, correct resolution but rather, will present multiple, sometimes confusing or seemingly contradictory, options to consider. As a field we need to understand much more about how the myriad embedded issues play out in classrooms and how they can be managed in ways that let teachers accomplish their instructional goals and that promote students' learning. In our common endeavor to build the knowledge we need to make progress, mathematics teachers who are trying to create classroom discourse communities are essential partners of researchers into communication and discourse in mathematics classrooms.

In this book, the reader will find valuable examples drawn from the work of teachers who have taken seriously the ideas of communication, conversation, and discourse as essential elements of mathematics teaching and learning in the classroom. In each chapter we are privileged to gain access to one teacher's encounter with an important facet of mathematics classroom discourse. In these detailed portraits of teaching, we see how discourse issues and challenges interact with the core work of mathematics teaching: posing problems for students to work on in class, supporting students' productive engagement with mathematical tasks, sharing with students the intellectual work of doing mathematics in the classroom, and analyzing and discussing students' solutions. Incredible richness is found in these chapters—a richness of detail about teaching that is often absent in academic treatments of discourse issues.

Beyond the value of the individual contributions, a special contribution is made by the collective work. Throughout this volume we glimpse a project that engaged teachers in studying and improving teaching. This book offers an all-too-rare portrayal of teachers actively engaged, both individually and collectively, in analyzing mathematics teaching with the goal of improving it.

In this book we also find a valuable example of how mathematics teaching might be improved over time. In the United States, teaching is not commonly treated as an enterprise that can be improved through collective inquiry. Teaching is typically viewed as an individual chore, with each teacher figuring out what works best for him or her. This view appears to doom us to mediocre mathematics teaching forever, depending as it does on whatever teachers can figure out on their own. This view ignores the fact that teachers can improve their practice by carefully studying what they do, learning how they can do it better, and sharing their experiences with others in the field. By engaging all teachers in studying teaching, the profession as a whole can improve, and in turn, the learning opportunities of students in all classrooms can improve. What makes this book even more remarkable is that the teachers who contributed to this work are secondary school mathematics teachers, a cohort often viewed as uninterested in, and unresponsive to, calls for the reform of mathematics teaching.

Mathematics teaching is a complex, intellectually demanding practice. Improving this practice is equally complex. Mathematics teaching will improve only through the persistent, focused work of teachers who not only do it but also study what they do with an eye toward improving it over time. Researchers and scholars can be partners with teachers in this work, but I would argue that the locus of improvement will likely be the teachers themselves and not the scholars. The editors of this book have provided a paradigm for the profession in how collective inquiry might be organized and orchestrated toward the improvement of teaching.

Reprising the metaphor of the long journey evoked earlier, this book demonstrates what can be accomplished if teachers commit to the value of making the journey, understand that challenges and dilemmas await them along the way, and join with colleagues locally and in the larger mathematics education community. This book offers valuable guidance for the profession—the kind that points to the details of teaching that matter, that does not diminish the intellectual challenge of this work, and that invests in teachers to lead the profession toward improvement.

References

National Council of Teachers of Mathematics (NCTM). *Curriculum and Evaluation Standards for School Mathematics.* Reston, Va.: NCTM, 1989.

———. *Professional Standards for Teaching Mathematics.* Reston, Va.: NCTM, 1991.

Sfard, Anna. "There Is More to Discourse Than Meets the Ears: Looking at Thinking as Communicating to Learn More about Mathematics Learning." *Educational Studies in Mathematics* 46 (2002): 13–57.

Silver, Edward A., and Margaret S. Smith. "Building Discourse Communities in Mathematics Classrooms: A Worthwhile but Challenging Journey." In *Communication in Mathematics: K–12 and Beyond,* 1996 Yearbook of the National Council of Teahers of Mathematics (NCTM), edited by Portia C. Elliott and Margaret J. Kenney, pp. 20–28. Reston, Va.: NCTM, 1996.

Acknowledgments

The research collaboration described in this book began in fall, 2004. When we began this work, the time commitment was small, but it grew as we embarked on the study groups and, eventually, the action research projects. This activity, although professionally and personally rewarding, did not happen without the support of our families and friends. We are grateful to them for their encouragement and understanding.

We would like to thank the many people who provided guidance and substantive feedback on our work. Those conversations contributed to the project and helped us in writing this book. We are grateful to the members of the Advisory Board for the project, Thomas Cooney, David Pimm, Barbara Jaworski, Catherine O'Connor, and Margaret Smith. We appreciate their ongoing support, feedback, and guidance. Discussions with David Wagner, Mary Schleppegrell, Corey Drake, and Jay Lemke gave us insight into the professional development work and our analytic methods. The process used at the writing retreat, which supported the teacher-researchers in writing the first drafts of their chapters, was designed with guidance and input from Laura Apol and Tom Bird. We thank all these people for their advice and guidance.

We are grateful to Jerilynn Lepak, Karen Marks, Gwendolyn Lloyd, Amy Roth McDuffie, and Tom Bird for their feedback on earlier drafts of some chapters. Finally, we would like to thank the people at NCTM who helped this book come to fruition: Ken Krehbiel, Joanne Hodges, Myrna Jacobs, Ann Butterfield, Randy White, David Barnes, and the members of the Educational Materials Committee.

This material is based on work supported by the National Science Foundation under grant number 0347906 (CAREER: Discourse Analysis: A Catalyst for Reflective Inquiry in Mathematics Classrooms; Beth Herbel-Eisenmann, principal investigator). Any opinions, findings, and conclusions or recommendations expressed in this material are those of the authors and do not necessarily reflect the views of the National Science Foundation.

SECTION 1

Introduction

CHAPTER 1

Introduction to the Project, the People, and the Reflective Activities

Beth Herbel-Eisenmann

THE BELL rings and the teacher is standing at the board, chalk still in hand after writing $3x = -9$. She points to the board and asks, "What is the value of x?" Immediately, hands go up and she calls on one of the students sitting in the middle of the room. "Negative three," says the student. "That's right, good job, Samantha," replies the teacher. The teacher erases the board and begins to explain how to solve equations of the type $ax + b = c$, and the class continues.

This example is fairly typical of most of my school mathematics experiences. In it, the teacher selects the task, the teacher asks students what the answer is (Initiates), the student provides an answer (Responds), and the teacher provides feedback (Evaluates) before moving on to the next problem. This Initiate-Respond-Evaluate (IRE) sequence (Mehan 1979; Sinclair and Coulthard 1975) is one of the most common ways that teachers and students interact in mathematics classrooms (Stigler and Hiebert 1999). Another version of the interaction could have included the question "How did you get negative three?" The student might have said that she had to do the same thing to both sides, so she divided $3x$ by 3 and -9 by 3 and ended up with $x = -3$. Alternatively, she might have said something like, "I know that $3x$ means three times something and I know that the three times something has to give me negative nine. The number times three that gives me negative nine is negative three, so x must be negative three." The quantity (number of words) and quality (mathematical significance) of each student's responses is quite different. And each provides a window into how a student thinks about the structure of the problem, playing an important role in formative assessment.

In response to these different solutions, the teacher has many different options for her response. For example, she may reply, "Why do you need to divide *both* sides by three?" or "How do you know the answer is negative three and not three?" or "How can we check to see whether negative three is correct?" Other alternative responses might include "So, you think x is negative three. Did anyone get something else?" or "How many of you agree with Samantha? How many of you disagree with Samantha? Would someone who disagrees please explain what he or she thinks about this problem?" or "How does this problem compare with the set of problems we did yesterday when we graphed equations of the form $y = ax + b$?" Again, each of these potential responses offers different learning opportunities for the students. In fact, I have included only a small set of possible responses—many others are possible.

My current interest in mathematics classroom discourse makes me look back on my own classroom experiences as a student, a student teacher, and a classroom teacher and wish that I had known that such alternatives were possible. I wish someone or something had challenged me to think about *why* those alternatives should be considered and used in my classroom. I wish I had considered how each of those options could have helped me engage my students in a kind of mathematics that was not just about short, correct responses to procedural questions, but rather about understanding how and why big mathematical ideas work; about connecting these ideas; and about learning to read, write, and speak in mathematical ways (for example, using mathematical arguments and justifications). Because I did not have such opportunities, I did not question my use of the familiar IRE sequence nor did I consider how that sequence might be restricting my students' views about what it means to know and do mathematics.

Undoubtedly, part of a teacher's role is helping students speak, read, and write mathematically, because all these fluencies are required to be a full participant in the mathematical community. As a beginning mathematics teacher, my only model for what to do with language consisted of writing vocabulary words on the board, followed by recording detailed definitions. Students were then asked to commit these words and definitions to memory and use them appropriately in class and on their homework, quizzes, and tests. This model is the only one I had observed for my entire mathematics education.

Reflecting and Connecting with Practice

- What was your experience like when you were a student of mathematics? What about this experience worked well for you? What did not work well for you? What effect did this experience have on most of your classmates and peers?
- What in your preservice teacher education or professional development conformed to your actual experience? What might have challenged your thinking about that experience?
- What information were you given about language development? What information were you given about interactions with your students?
- Which of the examples above sound most like your classroom interactions?

When I started graduate school and enrolled in a class on classroom discourse, I was overwhelmed with all the information that was available. I soon realized that language involved much more to be concerned with than simply learning vocabulary and definitions or even asking whether I used "high-level" questions. I came to understand that for at least four reasons, classroom discourse was something that needed more careful and thoughtful attention in mathematics education. These four reasons are that—

1. mathematics is a specialized form of literacy;
2. spoken language is a primary mode of teaching and learning;
3. the particular context in which language is used plays a role in what is appropriate to say and do; and
4. language is intimately related to culture and identity (see Herbel-Eisenmann, Cirillo, and Skowronski [2009] for further articulation of these reasons).

Once I understood the significance of classroom discourse to students' social and mathematical experiences in school, I wanted to better understand the significance of such information for practicing teachers.

After taking a position at a university, I was fortunate to find a group of secondary school mathematics teachers who were interested in such an endeavor. During the years that we have worked together, we have all come to believe that classroom discourse involves a great deal that we had not considered. Also, we did not realize how our discourse patterns could invisibly undermine the goals we have for our students.

Reflecting and Connecting with Practice

- What does the word *discourse* mean to you? What might be some reasons for you to increase your awareness of the patterns in your own classroom discourse?
- As a classroom teacher, what are you currently doing in your interactions with students? How much do you talk? How much do they talk? Who talks more?
- How are you helping students gain skills in speaking, reading, writing, and listening to mathematics?

In this book, we share parts of our story from an ongoing collaboration, which has involved myself (Beth), eight secondary school mathematics teacher-researchers (Angie, Darin, Jean, Jeff, Joe, Lana, Patty, and Tammie), and two graduate students (Michelle and Katie, who worked with us for two years) who were also former secondary school mathematics teachers. By making the distinction between university researchers and teacher-researchers, we do not mean to diminish the role of teacher-researchers but to distinguish between particular professional contexts and different roles in the project. We do so only to identify the fact that we are employed by different institutions and have different expectations and requirements in our positions.

Over the past four years, we have worked together to consider alternative ways to interact with students and some of the reasons that underlie the ways that we interact with students. Through a series of learning and reflective activities, we believe that we have transformed our thinking and our classroom practices. We see this book's central focus as what the teacher-researchers believe they have learned and are working on related to their classroom discourse. When the teacher-researchers wrote their chapters, they focused on sharing with other mathematics teachers the insights they had gleaned through their experiences in the project. Our primary audience is mathematics teachers, mathematics specialists, and educators of mathematics teachers.

In this introductory chapter, I present some background information about the project, the people, and the learning and reflection activities we engaged in. *I emphasize that the subsequent chapters rely on the information in this chapter and in chapter 2, in which I define relevant technical language and include information about classroom discourse.* At the end of each description of learning activities, we provide some prompts for others to use as they engage in the activities that we did—either individually or with colleagues. As will become apparent in subsequent chapters, doing these activities as a group led to more powerful results. So, if possible, we suggest inviting others to join you in trying some of these activities. However, we also believe that the information in this book can be helpful to any mathematics teacher interested in carefully considering his or her classroom discourse.

The People and the Project

In this section, I describe the broader goals and phases of the project to briefly give the reader some background. One of the objectives of the project was to consider how ideas and concepts from the literature on classroom discourse could be used to engage classroom teachers in cycles of action research that could improve secondary school mathematics teaching and learning. For our purposes, action research was considered systematic inquiry into one's own practice for the purpose of learning about and changing one's practice to better support students' learning. Another objective was to better understand how we can use our discourse practices more consciously to better support our goals for teaching mathematics. The university researchers' roles in the project were organized into three phases:

1. collecting and analyzing baseline data about each teacher-researcher's classroom discourse at the beginning of the project;
2. organizing meetings of a study group that focused on literature on classroom discourse, discourse in the mathematics classroom, and action research; and
3. supporting teacher-researchers through cycles of action research.

The teacher-researchers wrote daily and weekly reflections during the classroom observations, attended all the meetings that their schedules allowed, selected readings and discussed them, designed and completed ongoing cycles of action research, wrote reflective journals throughout all the phases of the work, and shared findings and reflections at professional conferences. We emphasize the teacher-researchers' admirable openness in inviting us into their classrooms and their even greater courage in exposing their practices to others through the chapters they contributed to this book. Furthermore, we highlight that this kind of exposure of one's practice and thinking deserves careful consideration and respect as readers make their way through this book.

When looking for teachers who might be interested in doing this work with us, we purposely tried to find people of different genders, from different kinds of environments, with different experiences and backgrounds, and with different curriculum materials and professional development experiences. This kind of diversity in a teacher-research group is important because it generates information that is useful for teachers who work in many kinds of settings. The teacher-researchers in the group taught in different kinds of communities (rural, urban, and suburban) and in different kinds of schools (e.g., magnet school for talented and gifted students, designated Title I school). Jeff (for the second half of the project), Joe, and Lana taught in high schools, and the remainder of the teacher-researchers taught in middle schools. The percent of students in each of these schools who were living in poverty also varied. (The percent of students eligible for free and reduced-price lunches ranged from 12 percent to more than 65 percent.) The number of years the teacher-researchers taught mathematics ranged from four to twenty-three years, with all but Darin and Joe (who was a first-year teacher when he joined the project) having taught for ten or more years (as of the 2007–2008 school year). Angie, Darin, and Tammie all had elementary teaching certification and could teach up to eighth grade; the others were certified to teach mathematics in seventh through twelfth grade.

The teacher-researchers used different types of curriculum materials and had been involved in different professional experiences. Angie, Jean, and Tammie were working in schools that had used curriculum materials funded by the National Science Foundation (NSF) for more than ten years. (NSF-funded curriculum materials are those developed with funding from NSF to embody the ideals put forth by the National Council of Teachers of Mathematics [NCTM 1989]). Jean was also a pilot teacher for the NSF-funded curriculum program that she used. The rest of the teacher-researchers taught in schools where more conventional curriculum materials were adopted and used. Outside this project, all the teacher-researchers participated in professional development mandated by the district, and half had master's degrees. Most of the teacher-researchers attended state conferences for mathematics teachers, and some were active in the National Council of Teachers of Mathematics (NCTM) at the regional and national levels. Darin was unfamiliar with NCTM prior to the project. Jean and Jeff were certified by the National Board, and Jean and Angie had received the Presidential Award for Excellence in Mathematics and Science Teaching.

Given this diversity, we think it is important to emphasize that all the participants believed that they had learned about themselves as teachers, their students as learners, and the ways they interact with their students. They had also developed a vision of better teaching as a result of reading, discussing, reflecting on, and using ideas from discourse literature. All the teacher-researchers had volunteered for the project, stating that their purpose was to continue to improve their teaching.

Learning about, Reflecting on, and Changing Classroom Discourse

As a group, we began the project by reading and discussing the discourse standards that appear in *Professional Standards for Teaching Mathematics* (NCTM 1991, p. 34):

> The discourse of a classroom—the ways of representing, thinking, talking, agreeing, disagreeing—is central to what students learn about mathematics as a domain of human inquiry with characteristic ways of knowing. Discourse is both the way ideas are exchanged and what the ideas entail: Who talks? About what? In what ways? What do people write, what do they record, and why? What questions are important? How do ideas change? Whose ideas and ways of thinking are valued? Who determines when to end a discussion? ... Discourse entails fundamental issues about knowledge: What makes something true or reasonable in mathematics? How can we figure out whether or not something makes sense?

We have revisited this quotation throughout the project and have found it powerful because it raises issues about mathematical content and processes and about social issues in the mathematics classroom. We also appreciated its reminder that our values, our perceptions of what it means to know and do mathematics, and our roles as authorities are important. The discourse standards also include information about what the roles of teacher, student, and technology should entail. Although the discourse standards provided some interesting information and suggestions, we realized that the description does not say much about how to achieve those standards. Therefore, we have been working together to learn about, discuss, reflect on, and become more purposeful about our classroom discourse.

Reflecting and Connecting with Practice

- How does this information about "discourse" compare with the definition you wrote earlier? Read the discourse standards. What other information would you now add to your definition?
- Which aspects of the discourse standards do you think you already attend to or include in your practice? Which aspects had you not thought about and want to consider further?

In the following sections, I describe some of the learning activities over the past four years that helped us reflect on and change classroom discourse:

- discussing analyses of the baseline data;
- creating mappings of "what is closest to my heart in my teaching";
- participating in a study group on classroom discourse, mathematics classroom discourse, and action research;
- identifying a performance gap; and
- engaging in cycles of action research (which included watching video-recordings of classroom practices).

Because the collaboration has taken place over four years and the learning activities did not occur consecutively in the order listed above, the description of these learning activities is not linear or chronological. Rather, several strands of overlapping activity came together later in the project (and will come together later in the chapter). Thus, the transition from the description of one activity to the next does not necessarily indicate a movement forward in time. Rather, each description presents a thread of activity, describing its course to the point at which the threads are woven together to show how they helped the teacher-researchers' action research projects to take shape. For the bigger picture of these activities, we provide a timeline overview in figure 1.1.

Collecting and Considering Baseline Data

Each teacher-researcher allowed one of the university researchers to observe and videotape a typical week of his or her teaching four times during the school year (about every other month) during the first year of the project (2005–2006 school year). After collecting these data, the university researchers did some quantitative and qualitative analyses.

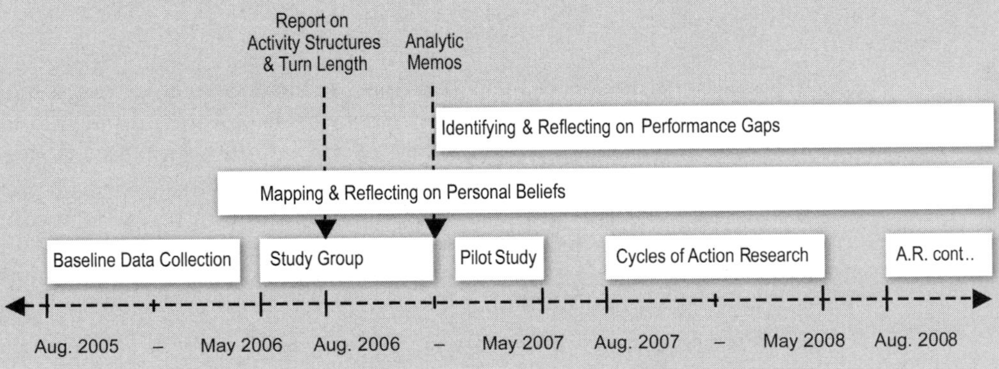

Fig. 1.1. Overview of timeline for activities

We were not sure what information might be interesting or useful to the teacher-researchers, because the literature reports few instances of this kind of reciprocal work. So we offered many different kinds of analyses of their discourse practices. We include some of the detail about the analyses here for two reasons:

1. Some of the ideas we describe here appear in the chapters written by the teacher-researchers.
2. Some of the analyses of the baseline data presented aspects of classroom discourse that the teacher-researchers had not considered before the project, and for some of the teacher-researchers, this information helped them focus their action research projects.

Reflecting and Connecting with Practice

- Choose one class to focus on and two lessons in which you are doing something that is fairly typical in this class. Either set up a video camera or ask a colleague or student to run the video camera for you. If you have access to a microphone, it may help you better capture what your students say. If you do not have access to a video camera, try audiotaping the lessons. Watch your videotapes or listen to your audiotapes, and write down all the things you notice about yourself and your students.

Our first level of coding the baseline classroom data consisted of creating timelines of the various "activity structures" that occurred.

Lemke (1990, pp. 2–4) wrote the following about activity structures:

> A [classroom] lesson is a social activity. It has a pattern of organization, a *structure*. Events of specific kinds tend to follow one another in a more or less definite order.... People have to do something to get it started, to enact one kind of event after another, and to bring it to a close.... All social activities are like this.... In real life you never know for sure what is coming next, but if you can recognize that you are in the midst of a patterned, organized kind of social activity, like a lesson ..., you know the probabilities for what is likely to come next. All social cooperation is based on participants sharing a common sense of the structure of the activity: of what's happening, what the options are for what comes next, and who is supposed to do what. A lesson has this kind of *activity structure.*

Lemke's work occurred in science classrooms, however, so the university researchers used a modified version of his definitions to code the data. For example, we kept track of when the teacher was doing "classroom business," "setting up" or "going over" an activity, doing a "demonstration," or giving a "lecture." We also kept track of when the class was doing "warm-up problems"; "going over homework"; engaging in "small-group work," "seatwork," or "whole-class work"; or when they were doing "boardwork." These codings allowed us to create pie charts of the percent of time spent on each kind of activity. We also used a computer program to do a word count of the length of each turn: for each week, comparing the number of words spoken by each teacher-researcher with the number of words spoken by the students in the classroom.

Reflecting and Connecting with Practice

- Watch your videotapes or listen to your audiotapes again, but this time pay attention to the activity structures. What kinds of activity structures do you use in your classroom? In what order do you progress through your activity structures? How do you transition from one activity structure to the next? How much time do you typically spend on each of these activity structures? How might this duration vary from day to day?

The university researchers gave each teacher-researcher a binder with the foregoing information. We briefly discussed some of the things we found in this analysis. In particular, the teacher-researchers were interested to know that, as a group, they spent almost 25 percent of their time going over homework. We also talked about the fact that students were expected to interact differently in many of these activity structures. For example, when the teacher-researchers conducted "classroom business," they typically wanted their students to sit quietly and listen carefully to what they were saying. When their students worked in small groups, however, the teacher-researchers wanted students to talk to one another, explain their thinking, ask one another questions, and so on. None of these different expectations were apparent to the teacher-researchers before we talked about students' participation in the different activity structures. The teacher-researchers wondered whether all their students understood the implicit rules for how to interact in each of these participation contexts.

The teacher-researchers were also quite shocked to discover how many words they spoke in comparison with their students. Across the data set, the mean length of a teacher-researcher's turn was 32 words. The mean length of the student's turns was 5 words. Teachers' turns ranged from 1 word to 1273 words; students' turns ranged from 1 to 268. On average, the teacher-researchers spoke about five times as many words as the students. The university researchers asked the teacher-researchers to read the information in their binders carefully so that we could discuss the findings again at our next meeting. In the meantime, to help the university researchers decide where to focus our detailed qualitative analysis of their classroom discourse, we asked the teacher-researchers to decide which of the activity structures they would like to know more about.

Reflecting and Connecting with Practice

- Given the number of activity structures you observed in your classroom videotape, how many different ways do you expect your students to interact? Do some students seem to understand these tacit rules and others not? How might you make these tacit rules more explicit to your students?
- Listen carefully during one of your videotapes. How many words do you speak? How many words do your students speak? What is the range of the lengths of your turns? What is the range for your students' turns?
- If your students only speak a few words at a time during whole-class work, when else might you provide opportunities for them to practice talking mathematically using longer turns? (For example,

longer turns might include formulating a mathematical justification or developing a mathematical generalization and explanation based on a series of explorations.)

After the teacher-researchers selected the activity structures that interested them, the university researchers did a detailed analysis of, and wrote an analytic memo about, each activity structure.[1] The first part of the memo gave an overview of the activity structure: when it tended to take place, the number of minutes spent on it each day, and the total number of minutes over the weeks. Next came a description of any patterns that appeared across the set of that activity structure. For example, when Jean did her warm-up problems, she always put the problems on the board, read them to the students, had them work on the problems in small groups, and then called on volunteers to explain how they solved each problem. Furthermore, when students explained, she always asked them what they did and why they solved the problem the way they did.

The second part of the analytic memo covered language forms the teacher-researchers used. We described whether they primarily asked questions, made statements, or issued commands by using imperatives. Describing the use of each of these forms helped the teacher-researchers better understand both their own roles and the roles that were negotiated for their students. A teacher's statement gives a sense of authority because it positions the speaker as a giver of information and the listener as someone who is a receiver of information. A command positions the teacher as someone who can tell someone else what to do. Question forms can sometimes be used to elicit information, but also have a more participatory effect, inviting the listener to respond. The university researchers also provided information about the nature of the statements, questions, and commands by identifying the most commonly used forms of questions (e.g., ones that start with what, how, and why) and commands.

Another language form was the kind of process in which the teacher-researchers were engaging students. We looked for when and how they used "thinker" verbs such as *consider* and when and how they used "doer" verbs such as *calculate* (Rotman 1988). We include more information about these processes in chapter 2. We described the kinds of

1. Our analysis was guided by systemic functional grammar (Lemke 1990; Halliday 1978; Schleppegrell 2004; Pimm 1987; Rotman 1988) as well as other discourse literature (Cazden 2001; Mehan 1979; Stubbs 1975; Dillon 1984, 1985; Wood 1998; Gee 1999; Fairclough 1995; Barnes 1969, 1976).

pronouns the teacher-researchers tended to use and when they seemed to use them. When and how *we*, as opposed to *I* and *you* are used relate to which party constructs what kind of knowledge and whether knowledge is mutually constructed or the domain of the teacher.

Finally, the university researchers described any other characteristics that we noticed when we listened to the classroom data, such as the types of words the teacher-researchers seemed to emphasize and the duration of their wait times and pauses. We mainly tried to describe patterns we saw and heard, provide percents whenever possible (e.g., the percent of questions that started with *what* rather than *why*), and provide examples from the transcripts to illustrate the discourse patterns we noticed.

After the university researchers wrote the analytic memos, we had a full-day retreat during which we explained the structure we used for the analytic memos and the reasons for focusing on particular aspects of the teachers' classroom discourse. Each teacher-researcher carefully read the analytic memos and was encouraged to comment on them with reactions, questions, and alternative interpretations. We then broke into small groups of one university researcher and two or three teacher-researchers on the basis of the grade levels the teacher-researchers taught. In the small groups, the teacher-researchers discussed what they thought of the information in the analytic memos; asked clarifying questions of the university researcher as well as one another; and provided alternative interpretations of, and reactions to, the analysis. The teacher-researchers were asked to start thinking about situations in which they saw their discourse patterns actually undermining their goals for their students and times when they thought they could use their discourse patterns more purposefully to better achieve their goals. To examine how their discourse patterns corresponded to their goals, they used a "beliefs mapping," that we had created during the previous school year and that I describe in the next section.

Creating a "Beliefs Mapping"

As part of our project meetings, we often read and discussed short articles or chapters. After the baseline data collection was completed, about nine months into the project, we read a chapter from *Connecting Mathematical Ideas: Middle School Video Cases to Support Teaching and Learning* (Boaler and Humphreys 2005). In one of the first chapters, Humphreys set the context for the reader by describing herself and her classroom. In one section, Humphreys described "what is closest to the heart" (p. 11) in her teaching. After we read and discussed that chapter, the university researchers asked each teacher-researcher, over the next month, to record any words, phrases, or pictures that came to mind that captured what was closest to their hearts in their teaching, that is, to try to capture what they believed really drove their practice. They suggested that the teacher-researchers write down things that had to do with teaching, learning, or mathematics, as well as other influences on their teaching decisions.

Reflecting and Connecting with Practice

- Over the next month, carry a set of stick-on notes with you and, as ideas occur to you, use them to write words, pictures, or phrases that you think capture what drives your instructional decision making.
- What kinds of experiences do you think are important for your students to have in your classroom? What kinds of expectations do you have for your students?
- What are some of the roles you play in the classroom, and why do you think those roles are important? What are some of the roles that students play in your classroom, and why do you think those are important? What role does your textbook play in the classroom?
- What does it mean to "know" and "do" mathematics?
- What part do students' experiences outside the classroom play in your classroom?

Over the month that the teacher-researchers were engaged in this activity, the university researchers analyzed their first two interviews, background information sheets, and two teacher-belief surveys they completed during the first year of the project. As a result, the university researchers generated a list of conjectures about what we thought the teacher-researchers might write on their stick-on notes and recorded them on a differently colored set of stick-on notes. At the next meeting, the university researchers gave the teacher-researchers large sheets of paper and asked them to arrange their stick-on notes in relation to the center of the page, which represented what was "closest to their hearts" in their teaching. The work of Cooney and his colleagues (Cooney 2001; Cooney and Shealy 1997; Wilson and Cooney 2002) and that of

Chapman (1999; 2002) influenced the decision to make the mapping a spatial representation: all these writers described teachers' beliefs as occurring in "clusters" that can be central or peripheral to the core of their beliefs.

After the teacher-researchers created the spatial representations, they wrote a journal entry that explained what they had written on their stick-on notes as well as why they had arranged the notes the way they had. The university researchers then explained that we had written conjectures on our own stick-on notes, and we asked the teacher-researchers to read them carefully and incorporate our conjectures into their mappings. We told them that the they could do one of three things: (1) if they agreed with the statement, they could place it in relation to what they had on their mapping; (2) if they thought the words were close but not quite right, they could change the wording before they incorporated the note; and (3) if they disagreed with the conjecture, they could cross it off and place it at the bottom of the paper. The teacher-researchers worked through our conjectures and then wrote another journal entry that described their reaction to our conjectures as well as explained how they positioned our stick-on notes in relation to their previous mapping. We then had a whole-group discussion about the activity, and the teacher-researchers shared how difficult they had found the task of capturing their beliefs on stick-on notes. Once comfortable with the format, the teacher-researchers found that this "beliefs mapping" helped them clarify what they believed and valued in their practice; the action research process allowed them to decide whether their professed beliefs were aligned with their classroom discourse practices.

Reflecting and Connecting with Practice

- After you have defined a set of professed beliefs, create a spatial map on a big sheet of paper. If the center of the paper is what is "closest to your heart in your teaching," how do all the things you wrote relate to the core of your professed beliefs? (If helpful, you can draw connecting lines and write connector words between the different stick-on notes.)
- Write a journal about your "professed beliefs." What do you see as the core of your beliefs? Which beliefs seem more central, and which seem more peripheral? How are the different clusterings related—or not related—to one another?

The university researchers created smaller versions of the belief mappings (see chapters 3 and 5 for examples) so that each teacher-researcher would have a version to refer to throughout the project. Lana, in particular, said that this experience was powerful for her. She came to teaching mathematics after other careers and had taken mainly mathematics requirements for her certification. To have to express her beliefs about teaching, learning, and mathematics made her realize that clarifying these beliefs would help her become a better teacher because she could now carefully examine whether she was enacting her professed beliefs. More generally, the belief mappings became a crucial reflective tool for the teachers, a point I explain further in the section on "Identifying a Performance Gap."

Participating in a Study Group

A year into the project, we began a study group on classroom discourse and mathematics classroom discourse. To learn what the teacher-researchers would find compelling, I created a library of potential readings instead of creating a specific reading list; I organized the readings according to the length of the discourse construct on which they focused. For example, some readings focused on word-length constructs such as "pronouns" (e.g., Rowland [1992, 1999]); word and phrase-length constructs such as the "hedges" used to reduce our commitment to something we say (Rowland 1995) and mathematical terms (e.g., Thompson and Rubenstein [2000]; Herbel-Eisenmann [2002]); sentence-length constructs such as "questions" (e.g., Vacc [1993]); and interaction-length constructs such as "revoicing" (O'Connor and Michaels [1993, 1996]) and "focusing and funneling" (Wood 1998; Herbel-Eisenmann and Breyfogle 2005). We also read about larger sociocultural issues, for example, ideas such as habitus (Zevenbergen 2001) and mathematics as a discursive practice (Adler 1999). The only required reading was Cazden's *Classroom Discourse* (2001), a good introduction to the topic written for a broad audience. This foundation was particularly important because the teacher-researchers typically read a wide variety of professional literature. Nevertheless, the teacher-researchers found the jargon to be a little overwhelming and amusing at first. For example, they laughed at the fact that people actually named things that we do with language, such as *hedging*. Saying "That is a linear function" sounds more certain than hedging this main statement by adding "I think" and "might": "I think that might be a linear function." As the teacher-researchers became more familiar with the terminology of discourse, however, they started to use it to comment on their own talk in the project meetings and found it an important addition to their ability to articulate what they were doing with language in their classroom discourse.

Every week from June until the middle of August 2006, the teacher-researchers selected two to four readings. We met for about four hours to discuss the readings and share a meal. The time around meals, which provided an opportunity for everyone to talk about their lives inside and outside school, was important for developing a sense of community. All our formal discussions before and after the meal began with everyone's sharing ideas that were interesting, important, unclear, troublesome, and so on, from the selected set of readings. When the discussion seemed to slow down, we would then shift to covering each article in turn to make sure that each person had a chance to talk about the aspects of each article that resonated with him or her. The discussions were often intense and went back and forth from trying to make sense of the ideas academically to trying to understand the ideas in relation to classroom practices (for a vivid illustration of these discussions, see Herbel-Eisenmann, Drake, and Cirillo [2009]).

The next sections of this chapter show how we brought together the threads of the analysis of the baseline data, the beliefs mapping, and the study group readings to identify a focus for the teacher-researchers' action research projects.

Identifying a "Performance Gap"

We read literature on classroom discourse, some of which was described above and will be further described in chapter 2, until the middle of December 2006. We then read two books written by elementary school teacher-researchers who were working in areas outside mathematics (Gallas 1995; Ballenger 1999), but who were focusing on their classroom discourse, as a segue into reading a book on doing action research. The main book that guided our work on action research was written by Hopkins (2002), but we also read other selections related to this topic.[2] After we read about and discussed these readings, each teacher-researcher picked a focus for a pilot study, allowing them to start exploring the process of action research. Many of the teacher-

2. We read a few chapters from Burnaford, Fischer, and Hobson (1996), Gallas et al. (1996), and Grant and McGraw (2006).

researchers were a little unclear about what they would be doing and how they would do it. We returned to Hopkins and began the process of identifying a *performance gap,* or the discrepancies "between behavior and intention" (p. 57). As Hopkins (2002, p. 57) pointed out, research suggests that—

1. there is often incongruence between a teacher's publicly declared philosophy or beliefs about education and how he or she behaves in the classroom;

2. there is often incongruence between the teacher's declared goals and objectives and the way in which the lesson is actually taught; and

3. there is often a discrepancy between a teacher's perception or account of a lesson and the perceptions or accounts of other participants (e.g., pupils or observers) in the classroom.

Hopkins contended that identifying a performance gap can be an important beginning point for cycles of action research.

To help the teacher-researchers identify their performance gaps, the university researchers asked them to consider our analyses of their baseline discourse, the readings that they thought were most helpful to them, the journals that they had been writing since the beginning of the project, their belief mappings, and the Hopkins book. In this way, many of the other activities in the project work came together.

We revisited the idea of a *performance gap,* and I explained that when I had originally conceptualized the project, I had anticipated that their action research projects might come from one of three sources:

1. Something that they were already dissatisfied with in their practice

2. Something that they had discovered from a reading

3. A mismatch between their beliefs mapping and their practice revealed by our analysis of their discourse or their own observations of themselves on the videotapes

After about two hours of individual reflection time, the teacher-researchers shared tentative ideas about what they might focus on in their pilot study. They asked one another questions, shared ideas, and suggested other readings that they found pertinent to the ideas. Each teacher-researcher recorded ideas in a journal entry and was asked to keep thinking about these ideas and paying attention over the next week or two to the area they might focus on.

Reflecting and Connecting with Practice

- Think about two of the areas the teacher-researchers considered when they developed their research projects: Are you dissatisfied with a particular aspect of your practice? Did you learn something in the section on classroom discourse that intrigues you? If so, watch your videotape or listen to your audiorecording and pay specific attention to that aspect of your classroom practice. What do you notice?
- Most of the teacher-researchers' action research projects grew out of the third aspect: the identification of a mismatch between their professed beliefs and what they were seeing in their classroom discourse. Spend some time revisiting your beliefs mapping, then use that information to examine the videotape or audiorecordings you have captured. Can you identify any performance gaps in your own classroom practice? If so, write a journal entry in which you reflect on the performance gaps: What seem to be some of the main issues? Who are some of the primary contributors to the performance gap? How does the performance gap affect your students?

When the teacher-researchers came together for the next project meeting, they again shared what they thought their focus would be and what data they might collect to better understand that aspect of their classroom discourse. They also shared plans for how to improve the aspect in question. For example, Lana came to the project with an interest in using technology and built on that interest (see chapter 5). Jean found the readings on revoicing to be interesting and decided she needed to better understand her own use of revoicing (see chapter 7). Patty had written "mathematics is about thinking" in her beliefs mapping but said that the interaction patterns she saw in her analytic memos and in the videos she watched focused more on students' answers and the correctness of those answers (see chapter 3).

As the teacher-researchers gained some clarity on the focus of their pilot study, most of the pilot-study time became a time to learn to operate the cameras, explore various data sources, and watch themselves on the tapes. Their days were packed with teaching, supervising, curriculum meetings, after-school mathematics team practice, and other extracurricular and district events (not to mention that all of them also had families to attend to). Thus, all our project meetings were devoted primarily to reflection time during which the teacher-researchers brought videotapes of their teaching and spent their time watching themselves and writing in their journals. The whole-group time typically consisted of talking while we ate a meal together and then a quick go-around at the end of the meeting, when the teacher-researchers shared some of the things they were noticing and some aspects of their practice they were trying to change, sometimes soliciting advice from the others in the group.

In preparing to give a presentation at the national NCTM conference in Atlanta, each teacher-researcher had to select ideas from the readings that they thought shaped their thinking about the work. They visited and revisited articles and selected an important idea about classroom discourse to share in these presentations. This preparation also helped them reexamine their understanding of those readings in the context of their action research projects. Through this process, they clarified their focuses and action research plans; this endeavor carried them through the remainder of the school year and provided an opportunity to shape their plans for the following year.

Reflecting and Connecting with Practice

- Select a performance gap that is really important to how you support your students either mathematically or socially. Make a plan for some ways to try to narrow the gap between your beliefs mapping and your classroom practices, drawing from your experience with students, the readings you have done, related professional development experiences, and discussions with colleagues.
- In some of the readings on action research that we used, the authors suggested that all teacher-researchers should transcribe a brief segment of their classroom discourse. Select a section of your videotape or audiorecording (no more than 15 minutes) that most relates to your interest in classroom discourse, and transcribe the talk. What do you notice about your classroom discourse now that you did not notice before? What is significant about what you notice, given the performance gap you identified?

Engaging in Cycles of Action Research

All eight teacher-researchers returned to the meetings in the fall of the third year (August 2007) refreshed and ready to begin again. Before the first week of school, we started with a daylong retreat during which the university researchers shared some of the analyses we had completed and articles and book chapters that were in press (Herbel-Eisenmann, Cirillo, and Skowronski 2009; Herbel-Eisenmann and Schleppegrell 2008; Wagner and Herbel-Eisenmann 2008; Cirillo, Bruna, and Herbel-Eisenmann, in press), and the teacher-researchers talked about their pilot studies. The teacher-researchers were motivated by their transcripts and videos, which reminded them of their performance gaps.

Although some facilitators of action research suggest having teacher-researchers write a focused question, we found that having each person define an area of focus worked better for us. The teacher-researchers started to volunteer to talk about how they were progressing and to share (if they were comfortable) some data from their classrooms. Almost all the meetings consisted of the teacher-researchers watching videotapes, writing in their journals, and revisiting important readings. These activities were followed by brief presentations by one or two of the teacher-researchers. They shared data, watched one another on videotape, asked one another questions, and so on. When I visited each of the classrooms in the fall, I talked to all the teacher-researchers individually and had them articulate their focus and tell me how they thought their action research projects were going. The individual debriefings seemed to be valuable as a time for some of the teacher-researchers to think about the data they were collecting and for others to choose a specific focus from the many that were interesting to them.

Reflecting and Connecting with Practice

- Using the performance gap you have identified and the plan that you have made, decide what data you might collect as evidence of change. Try to keep the data-collection plan manageable, and draw on things you already do in your practice: written assessments, occasional videotaping or audiorecording, using short surveys, observing small groups more closely, keeping a teacher journal, and so on. See the upcoming chapters written by the teacher-researchers to learn what kinds of data they collected.
- Reread some of the information on action research to make a plan for your own cycles of action research. Engage in discussions and planning with your colleagues.

A deadline to present something about their work at a regional conference in October helped the teacher-researchers become concrete about what they were doing for their beginning action research cycle and why they were doing it. I asked them to think about the one thing they had learned so far that they wanted everyone in the audience to know or understand and to shape their presentations around that idea. At the time, I had not realized what an impact the prospect of having to make a public presentation would have on the work that they were doing. During project interviews with the university researchers in the spring of 2008, however, all teacher-researchers said that the presentations made them realize that they had important things to say and that the presentations required them to be articulate and clear about their thinking. Organizing their presentations also helped them move forward on their projects.

As the teacher-researchers continued to collect data in their own classrooms, they brought data with them to every project meeting. By February, the teacher-researchers were volunteering to share their experiences and were feeling more confident about their projects. Some teacher-researchers made dramatic changes to their projects. For example, Jeff, who was trying online discussions, decided that he had so many problems with access to, and use of, technology that he changed his focus to having students take over the "going over homework" activity in the classroom at the beginning of class (see chapter 6). Other teacher-researchers clarified the ideas that they were focusing on in relation to their practice. For example, Jean, who was focusing on *revoicing* (O'Connor and Michaels 1993, 1996), clarified her distinction between revoicing productively to overrevoicing (which she called *co-opting*). This clarification then allowed her to examine when in her teaching she tended to do each of these things, making her more aware and purposeful about when and how she revoiced. Still other teacher-researchers changed their discourse patterns to support students both socially and mathematically.

In June of 2008, we met for a five-day writing retreat. After some support and guidance from literacy colleagues who taught the writing process, the university researchers set up a version of a writer's workshop that included reflection, writing, and feedback time. As a result, each teacher-researcher produced a draft of a book chapter about something they learned that they wanted to share with other mathematics teachers. After a few more rounds of writing and feedback, the teacher-researchers approved the final versions of their chapters, which appear in the subsequent sections of this book.

Reflecting and Connecting with Practice

- Try to meet regularly with a group of interested colleagues. Spend part of the time watching yourselves on videotape or listening to yourselves on audiorecordings, part of the time revisiting readings or finding new related readings, and part of the time talking to your colleagues about the ideas you are working on. Draw on one another as resources to continue shaping your classroom practice.
- After engaging in a few cycles of action research, consider doing a presentation for your colleagues or for a professional meeting to engage others in discussions about your work. Alternatively, consider writing about what you learned for a teaching journal such as *Mathematics Teaching in the Middle School* or *Mathematics Teacher.*

References

Adler, Jill. "The Dilemma of Transparency: Seeing and Seeing through Talk in Mathematics Classroom." *Journal for Research in Mathematics Education* 30 (January 1999): 47–64.

Ballenger, Cynthia. *Teaching Other People's Children: Literacy and Learning in a Bilingual Classroom.* New York: Teachers College Press, 1999.

Barnes, Douglas. *Language, the Learner and the School.* Baltimore, Md.: Penguin Books, 1969.

———. *From Communication to Curriculum.* London: Penguin Books, 1976.

Boaler, Jo, and Cathy Humphreys. *Connecting Mathematical Ideas: Middle School Video Cases to Support Teaching and Learning.* Portsmouth, N.H.: Heinemann, 2005.

Burnaford, Gail, Joseph Fischer, and David Hobson, eds. *Teachers Doing Research: Practical Possibilities.* Mahwah, N.J.: Lawrence Erlbaum Associates, 1996.

Cazden, Courtney. *Classroom Discourse: The Language of Teaching and Learning.* 2nd ed. Portsmouth, N.H.: Heinemann, 2001.

Chapman, Olive. "Inservice Teacher Development in Mathematical Problem Solving." *Journal of Mathematics Teacher Education* 2 (May 1999): 121–42.

———. "Belief Structure and Inservice High School Mathematics Teacher Growth." In *Beliefs: A Hidden Variable in Mathematics Education,* edited by Gilah Leder, Erkki Pehkonen, and Gunter Torner, pp. 177–94. Dordrecht, Netherlands: Kluwer Academic Publishers, 2002.

Cirillo, Michelle, Katherine R. Bruna, and Beth Herbel-Eisenmann. "Acquisition of Mathematical Language: Suggestions and Activities for English Language Learners." *Multicultural Perspectives,* in press.

Cooney, Thomas J. "Considering the Paradoxes, Perils, and Purposes of Conceptualizing Teacher Development." In *Making Sense of Mathematics Teacher Education,* edited by Fou-Lai Lin and Thomas J. Cooney, pp. 9–32. Dordrecht, Netherlands: Kluwer Academic Publishers, 2001.

Cooney, Thomas J., and Barry E. Shealy. "On Understanding the Structure of Teachers' Beliefs and their Relationship to Change." In *Mathematics Teachers in Transition,* edited by Elizabeth Fennema and Barbara S. Nelson. Mahwah, N.J.: Lawrence Erlbaum Associates, 1997.

Dillon, J. T. "Research on Questioning and Discussion." *Educational Leadership* 42 (November 1984): 50–56.

———. "Using Questions to Foil Discussion." *Teaching and Teacher Education* 1, no. 2 (1985): 109–21.

Fairclough, Norman. *Critical Discourse Analysis.* London: Longman, 1995.

Gallas, Karen. *Talking Their Way into Science.* New York: Teachers College Press, 1995.

Gallas, Karen, Mary Anton-Oldenberg, Cynthia Ballenger, Cindy Beseler, Steve Griffin, Roxanne Pappenheimer, and James Swaim. "Talking the Talk and Walking the Walk: Researching Oral Language in the Classroom." *Language Arts* 73 (December 1996): 608–17.

Gee, James Paul. *An Introduction to Discourse Analysis: Theory and Method.* New York: Routledge, 1999.

Grant, Maureen, and Rebecca McGraw. "Collaborating to Investigate and Improve Classroom Mathematics Discourse." In *Teachers Engaged in Research: Inquiry into Mathematics Classrooms, Grades 9–12,* edited by Laura Van Zoest, pp. 231–52. Greenwich, Conn.: Information Age Publishing, 2006.

Halliday, Michael. *Language as Social Semiotic: The Social Interpretation of Language and Meaning.* Baltimore: University Press, 1978.

Herbel-Eisenmann, Beth A. "Using Student Contributions and Multiple Representations to Develop Mathematical Language." *Mathematics Teaching in the Middle School* 8 (October 2002): 100–105.

Herbel-Eisenmann, Beth A., and M. Lynn Breyfogle. "Questioning Our *Patterns* of Questions." *Mathematics Teaching in the Middle School* 10 (May 2005): 484–89.

Herbel-Eisenmann, Beth A., Michelle Cirillo, and Kathryn Skowronski. "Why Classroom Discourse Deserves Our Attention!" In *Mathematics for Every Student: Responding to Diversity, Grades 9–12,* edited by Alfinio Flores. Reston, Va.: National Council of Teachers of Mathematics, 2009.

Herbel-Eisenmann, Beth, Corey Drake, and Michelle Cirillo. "Muddying the Clear Waters: Teachers' Take-up of the Linguistic Idea of Revoicing." *Teaching and Teacher Education* 25, no. 2 (February 2009): 268–77.

Herbel-Eisenmann, Beth, and Mary J. Schleppegrell. "'What Question Would I Be Asking Myself in My Head?' Helping All Students Reason Mathematically." In *Mathematics for Every Student: Responding to Diversity, Grades 6–8,* edited by Mark W. Ellis. Reston, Va.: National Council of Teachers of Mathematics, 2008.

Hopkins, David. *A Teacher's Guide to Classroom Research.* 3rd ed. New York: Open University Press and McGraw-Hill, 2002.

Lemke, Jay. *Talking Science: Language, Learning, and Values.* Norwood, N.J.: Ablex Publishing Corporation, 1990.

Mehan, Hugh. *Learning Lessons.* Cambridge, Mass.: Harvard University Press, 1979.

National Council of Teachers of Mathematics. *Curriculum and Evaluation Standards for School Mathematics.* Reston, Va.: NCTM, 1989.

———. *Professional Standards for Teaching Mathematics.* Reston, Va.: NCTM, 1991.

O'Connor, M. Catherine, and Sarah Michaels. "Aligning Academic Task and Participation Status through Revoicing: Analysis of a Classroom Discourse Strategy." *Anthropology and Education Quarterly* 24, no. 4 (December 1993): 318–35.

———. "Shifting Participant Frameworks: Orchestrating Thinking Practices in Group Discussion." In *Discourse, Learning and Schooling,* edited by Deborah Hicks, pp. 63–103. New York: Cambridge University Press, 1996.

Pimm, David. *Speaking Mathematically.* London and New York: Routledge & Kegan Paul, 1987.

Rotman, Brian. "Toward a Semiotics of Mathematics." *Semiotica* 72, nos. 1/2 (1988): 1–35.

Rowland, Tim. "Pointing with Pronouns." *For the Learning of Mathematics* 12 (June 1992): 44–48.

———. "Hedges in Mathematics Talk: Linguistic Pointers to Uncertainty." *Educational Studies in Mathematics* 29 (December 1995): 327–53.

———. "Pronouns in Mathematical Talk: Power, Vagueness, and Generalisation." *For the Learning of Mathematics* 19 (July 1999): 19–26.

Schleppegrell, Mary J. *The Language of Schooling: A Functional Linguistics Perspective.* Mahwah, N.J.: Laurence Erlbaum Associates, 2004.

Sinclair, John McHardy, and R. Malcolm Coulthard. *Towards an Analysis of Discourse: The English Used by Teachers and Pupils.* London: Oxford University Press, 1975.

Stigler, James W., and James Hiebert. *The Teaching Gap.* New York: The Free Press, 1999.

Stubbs, Michael. *Organizing Classroom Talk.* University of Edinburgh: Centre for Research in the Educational Sciences, 1975.

Thompson, Denisse R., and Rheta N. Rubenstein. "Learning Mathematics Vocabulary: Potential Pitfalls and Instructional Strategies." *Mathematics Teacher* 93 (October 2000): 568–74.

Vacc, Nancy Nesbitt. "Questioning in the Mathematics Classroom." *Arithmetic Teacher* 41 (October 1993): 88–91.

Wagner, David, and Beth Herbel-Eisenmann. "'Just Don't': The Suppression and Invitation of Dialogue in Mathematics Classrooms." *Educational Studies in Mathematics* 67 (February 2008): 143–57.

Wilson, Melvin, and Thomas J. Cooney. "Mathematics Teacher Change and Development." In *Beliefs: A Hidden Variable in Mathematics Education?* edited by Gilah C. Leder, Erkki Pehkonen, and Gunter Torner, pp. 127–48. Dordrecht, Netherlands: Kluwer Academic Publishers, 2002.

Wood, Terry. "Alternative Patterns of Communication in Mathematics Classes: Funneling or Focusing?" In *Language and Communication in the Mathematics Classroom,* edited by Heinz Steinbring, Maria G. Bartolini Bussi, and Anna Sierpinska, pp. 167–78. Reston, Va.: National Council of Teachers of Mathematics, 1998.

Zevenbergen, Robyn. "Mathematics, Social Class, and Linguistic Capital: An Analysis of Mathematics Classroom Interactions." In *Sociocultural Research on Mathematics Education*, edited by Bill Atweh, Helen J. Forgasz, and Ben Nebres, pp. 201–16. Mahwah, N.J.: Lawrence Erlbaum Associates, 2001.

CHAPTER 2

Some Essential Ideas about Classroom Discourse

Beth Herbel-Eisenmann

In the next four sections of the book, the teacher-researchers illustrate the importance of professional readings to their changing understanding of, and conversations about, their classroom practices. Many ideas became central to our study-group discussions and, to prepare the reader for the subsequent chapters, I define and describe many of these ideas here. The ideas presented here come from a subset of the almost fifty chapters and articles that we read together.

One way the readings seemed to influence our discussions was to help us distinguish between language that we use for *content* purposes and language that we use for *social* purposes. The first book we read and discussed, for example (Cazden 2001, p. 2), pointed out that, in such contexts as schools, "one person, the teacher, is responsible for controlling all the talk that occurs while class is officially in session—controlling not just negatively, as a traffic officer does to avoid collisions, but also positively, to enhance the purposes of education." In fact, some of the literature we read on classroom discourse made a distinction between language that is used to focus on the mathematical understandings being developed (i.e., "to enhance the purposes of education") and language that is used to control social behaviors (i.e., "to avoid collisions"). An important point is that many people attach negative associations to the word *control,* yet we realize that control is necessary in the teaching of mathematics. As teachers, we should be more concerned about careful consideration of what we control and how we control it than about control as being merely good or bad.

I use this distinction between discourse for content-learning purposes and discourse for social purposes as a way to organize the ideas from discourse literature that we discussed in the study group and that we draw on in the remainder of the book. Although we see *all* language in mathematics classrooms as serving *both* of these purposes, we also think that some language brings the learning of content to the foreground and moves social control to the background, and vice versa. For example, a statement like "This function is a linear function" is mainly about the mathematics being studied. A statement like "Please put your notebooks away so we can go to lunch" serves more strongly a social control purpose. Fuzzy areas occur between these two categories because reality rarely fits in neat categories.

Reflecting and Connecting with Practice

- What do you think of this distinction between language for content-learning purposes and language for social purposes? Where do you see these two purposes in your own discourse practices? In what instances do you see purposes that are "fuzzy"?
- Do you see more language in your classroom that focuses on the learning purposes or on the social purposes? Which of each kind of language seem to be used by you? Which of these kinds seem to be used by your students?
- As you read the next two subsections, keep track of ideas related to these two uses of language that you had not considered previously. Record your initial reactions to these ideas as well as how you think they relate to your own classroom practice.

Discourse for Content-Learning Purposes

One of the early book chapters that we read described the difference between a calculational approach and a conceptual approach to teaching (Thompson et al. 1994). Although this distinction was important to us in many of our group's discussions, Patty's work (chapter 3), in particular, was influenced by the distinction between these two approaches to teaching. Lana also used this distinction to consider her students' talk when they were using graphing calculators in class (see chapter 5). In the calculational approach, the teacher focuses primarily on what students did or how they did it, emphasizing the operations and calculations that were used to solve the problem, making little connection with the underlying mathematical concepts and their relationships. In the conceptual approach, the teacher focuses on *why* the students did what they did and *how* the processes connect with the meanings being created in solving the problem. Furthermore, in the conceptual approach, explanations and justifications are grounded in the concepts and relationships that are central to the problem. Indeed, as previous research has shown (Stein, Glover, and Henningsen 1996; Stein and Lane 1996) and the subsequent chapters highlight, the kinds of mathematical tasks that we use can help or hinder a teacher in developing a conceptual approach to teaching. A point that we talked about often was that high-level mathematical tasks are necessary but not sufficient for getting students to talk deeply about mathematical ideas.

When using high-level tasks to teach, however, maintaining a high level of cognitive demand from students is often difficult. A clear connection was evident between the different kinds of questions teachers asked about a task and whether they were teaching calculationally or conceptually. Questioning strategies, which our group talked about extensively, have been shown to be related to the development of a math-talk learning community; that is, "a classroom community in which the teacher and students use discourse to support the mathematical learning of all participants" (Hufferd-Ackles, Fuson, and Sherin 2004, p. 82). In fact, the lower-level description of a math-talk learning community described the teacher in the role of questioner using questions that tended to focus on finding the right answers.

We decided, however, that focusing exclusively on the initial question was less important than the questioning *pattern* that evolved in a longer stretch of interaction. A teacher could start with what appeared to be an open-ended question, for instance, "How can we decide which of these is mathematically correct?" but end up "funneling" (Wood 1998; Herbel-Eisenmann and Breyfogle 2005) the student's thinking with questions until the student produces the solution that matches a previously taught solution, even though other ways of thinking about a problem may exist. For example, if the teacher follows the question "How can we decide which of these is mathematically correct?" with "What does the book say about that problem?" or "What did I say about this kind of problem yesterday?" the level of thinking the students have to do is limited to recall, and the authority for determining correctness lies with the textbook or the teacher.

Through the readings, we decided that other types of questions better served the purpose of helping teachers understand students' thinking, set up alignments or oppositions of ideas to engage students in mathematical argumentation, and deflect students' ideas to require the students to make sense of one another's ideas. Many of the teacher-researchers found that a "focusing" pattern (Wood 1998; Herbel-Eisenmann and Breyfogle 2005) better supported these goals. In a focusing pattern, the questions serve to help foster better understanding of what the student is trying to say so as to help other students and the teacher understand the student's thinking. A focusing pattern can also highlight important mathematical aspects of the student's thinking to make the thinking more transparent to other students. For example, if we return to the vignette at the start of the book, focusing is apparent in such questions as "You said, 'You can just do the same thing to both sides of the equation and get negative three.' Can you say more about the 'thing' you are doing to both sides and why you can do that 'thing' to both sides?" or "How many agree with an answer of negative three? How many agree with the answer of three? How can we decide which of these is mathematically correct?" These kinds of questions help develop a math-talk community in which students' explanations become more complex and they take more responsibility for their learning. Furthermore, the highest level of math-talk learning community involves supporting students to ask one another questions rather than rely on the teacher to always do so.

As we continued to discuss how we could ask good questions, we also came to find that the timing of the questions and the pauses between them are important. Although we had all heard that "wait time" (Rowe 1974) is important, what the teacher-researchers did not know was that it is not important only to wait *after a question* is asked. An equally important (and less commonly known) time to wait is *after a student responds* to the initial question. When this second type of wait time was added, students' responses became more complex (Rowe 1986). As the teacher-researchers watched themselves on videotape, many of them were surprised to find that their perceived wait time and their actual wait time were quite different. When they tried to incorporate more wait time (both after posing questions and after students' responses), the teacher-researchers often discovered that what felt like minutes was, in reality, only about 10 seconds.

Another aspect of learning mathematics that we began to read about and discuss was related to helping students learn specific terms associated with mathematical ideas. Teaching such terminology is not an easy task, because mathematical terms envelop varied and complex meanings. An added challenge is that some mathematical terms (e.g., *point* or *negative*) are adopted from everyday language and have quite different meanings in mathematics (Pimm 1987; Thompson and Rubenstein 2000). We decided that our practices of recording vocabulary words and their definitions on the board, asking students to commit them to memory, then requiring students to use mathematical terms correctly were based on a false sense of how people appropriate and make sense of language. Instead, people learn language through experiences with objects, images, metaphors, and the like. For example, students can talk about the idea of the slope of a line in many different ways (Herbel-Eisenmann 2002). When students look at a graph, they might talk about the "slantiness" of the line. From the table, they may talk about it as "what it goes up by" (that is, the additive rate of change in the *y*-values as the *x*-values go up by one). Eventually we wanted students to connect all these ways of talking with the associated representation and with the idea of the slope of a line—it is not just a term that we memorize and use: it means something for students' everyday experiences, not just in relation to the graph, table, and equation. Being able to coordinate all these different meanings and understand that they are related to the idea of "slope" is essential to understanding complex mathematical ideas. Tammie (chapter 8), in particular, became interested in trying to help students acquire mathematical language through written text by having students write solutions to some of the problems they solved.

One way that teachers help students acquire this language is through something called *revoicing*, which has been defined as "the reuttering of another person's speech through repetition, expansion, rephrasing, and reporting" (Forman, McCormick, and Donato 1998, p. 531; O'Connor and Michaels 1993; 1996). The idea of revoicing is one that the teacher-researchers have discussed at length and remains a significant idea that we have focused on in the group. In fact, Jean (see chapter 7) focuses primarily on revoicing, but revoicing also appears in Tammie's and Angie's chapters (see chapters 8 and 9, respectively). When a student offers a response to a teacher's question, rather than evaluate the response, a teacher might rephrase the response in a more mathematically precise way. For example, if a student said, "I timesed two and three to get six," the teacher might reply with, "So, you multiplied the width of two and the length of three to get an area of six square meters?" The teacher's returning the question to the student is important because it allows the student to agree or disagree with the restatement of her idea (O'Connor and Michaels 1993, 1996). Revoicing serves many purposes, of which modelling correct use of mathematical language is only one. Revoicing allows the teacher to align students' explanations with academic content and with one another's explanations; attribute ideas to students; and ultimately positions students as competent mathematical thinkers. Other functions that O'Connor and Michael (1996, pp. 74–75) describe include—

> reformulating... in order to advance [the teacher's] agenda, changing the contribution slightly so as to drive the discussion in another direction. She may be simply rebroadcasting the student's utterance to reach a wider audience than the student reached.... By revoicing an utterance, [the teacher] further externalises and clarifies [the student's] reasoning for him, so that it more effectively communicates his explanation to the group.

One of the conclusions that the teacher-researchers reached is the importance of having students revoice one another. They have found that consistently requiring students to revoice one another helps students learn to listen to their peers. The teacher-researchers thought having students listen to one another was important because students might hear an idea in a way they had not considered previously or hear someone say something in a way that made more sense to them than the teacher's explanation (Herbel-Eisenmann, Drake, and Cirillo 2009). A recent book titled *Classroom Discussions: Using Math Talk to Help Students Learn* (Chapin, O'Connor, and Anderson 2003), which Angie writes about in chapter 9, includes a section on revoicing and other talk moves that the teacher-researchers have found helpful in their thinking about classroom discourse.

Mathematics is not just about concepts, however. We also found that we needed to consider the processes in which we were engaging students. NCTM (2000) highlights the processes of problem solving, reasoning and proving, communicating, making connections, and representing. These processes are captured in the verbs we use and the verbs that students use. Some verbs that are common in mathematics are "doer" verbs: *write, draw, build, graph, multiply,* for example. Other verbs are "thinker" verbs and require reflection from students: for example, *think about, decide, justify, reflect on, consider.* The verbs that teachers and curriculum materials use send messages to students about what mathematics *is.* Mathematics is something we do, but it is also something we think about. We found, however, that almost all the verbs used in the mathematics classrooms were "doer" verbs, sending the message that mathematics is not really about thinking. Patty (in chapter 3), in particular, has taken this concern up in the work that she is doing.

Many of the processes that we want students to use in mathematics are also used in other content areas. Such processes as mathematical argumentation, however, require words, sentences, and discourses to be put together in very specific ways that will make the text specifically mathematical. We use certain words and organize verbal mathematical arguments in ways that are quite different from the ways we structure arguments in everyday life and in other subject areas, such as social studies or English language arts. Our interactions with students help them understand what constitutes an acceptable mathematical argument. That is, *mathematical* explanations must be explanations that do more than agree with someone because she or he has high status in the classroom (Yackel and Cobb 1996). It also must be more than just a procedural description if we want students to develop a high-level mathematical argument (Kazemi and Stipek 2001). (For more about creating a context for mathematical argumentation, see Stein [2001]; Weingrad [1998]; Wood [1998].)

An underlying goal in much of the work that teachers describe in the upcoming chapters is for the teachers to empower their students to engage in, understand, and own the mathematics they study. Through the work we have done together, the teacher-researchers became aware that they could unknowingly undermine their intentions to develop their students' mathematical authority. For example, Forman, McCormick, and Donato (1998) examined authority patterns in a classroom in which the teacher was working toward the vision described in the *Standards* (NCTM 1989, 1991, 2000) documents. The authors found that, although the teacher wanted to solicit, explore, and value several strategies for solving problems, some of her discourse practices undermined this goal. They argued that the teacher asserted her authority through the use of such tacit language patterns as interrupting, vocal emphasis, repetition, and expansion. Despite the fact that three students in her class presented different and mathematically correct solution strategies, the teacher overlapped a student's explanations *only* when the student was *not* using the procedure the teacher had recently taught. This study is a clear example of the fuzzy space between mathematical purposes and social purposes. That is, by using such patterns as interrupting students, which typically control social aspects of the discourse, the teacher devalued the potential of multiple ways to solve problems. I now turn to describing some language patterns that brings social control in the classroom to the foreground.

Discourse for Social Purposes

For deep discussions about high-level mathematics to take place, the teacher-researchers knew that they needed to create a safe social environment in which students can take risks (Yackel and Cobb 1996). Although language is a primary tool for establishing routines and rules in the classroom (Voigt 1985), even the ways in which we organize our classroom can contribute to controlling how students interact. For example, by having students sit in rows and face the front of the room, we discourage them from making eye contact with one another. Yet, when we talk to others outside the classroom, we often make eye contact with people to whom we are speaking. Darin, in particular, changed aspects of his physical environment to allow students to see one another, with the goal of encouraging them to speak to one another (see chapter 4).

Another organizing routine, having students raise their hands before they are allowed to speak, is a way of controlling participation. Although teachers understandably do not want students to compete in shouting out answers, to have to raise one's hand and wait to be called on could deter students from sharing, cause them to forget the contribution they wanted to share, or even tacitly discourage them from coming up with answers: if their hands are not raised, students may think they are not responsible for coming up with a response (Lee 2006). Tammie (chapter 8) decided that requiring her students to raise their hands was stopping them from sharing ideas. She incorporated a new expectation that students would raise their hands only if they had questions; if her students wanted to share ideas, she no longer required them to raise their hands.

As discussed in chapter 1, one common language routine in mathematics classrooms is the IRE sequence. Through this pattern of interaction, teachers control not only the amount of information that students share but also who gets to speak and when. This kind of interaction is unique to classrooms and would be considered rude in everyday settings with friends, for example.

Teachers can control aspects of the classroom discourse in many other ways. Sometimes the control is blatant, for example, when a teacher launches into a ten-minute lecture about something and students sit quietly, saying nothing. At times this kind of teacher monologue is appropriate, especially if the information is "arbitrary" or information that "no one can know without being informed by others. The arbitrary concerns names and conventions which have been established within a culture and which need to be adopted by students if they are to participate and communicate successfully within this culture" (Hewitt 2001a, p. 44). For example, if students talk about slope only as the "slantiness" of a line, they will not know mathematically appropriate terminology. At some point, the mathematical terms need to be offered. When a teacher gives a monologue for that purpose, the information conveyed is controlled and student participation can be nonexistent.

Sometimes control and authority need to be shared with students, and in that scenario the interaction patterns require a more relaxed structure. Such an atmosphere is especially appropriate when students are engaging in what Hewitt (1999, 2001a, 2001b) called the "necessary" in mathematics. The "necessary" includes information in mathematics that someone can come to know if provided with appropriate experiences; it includes such things as mathematical properties and relationships (e.g., Pythagoras's theorem). Hewitt argued that many ideas in mathematics that are necessary are treated as if they are arbitrary. This set of essays, in particular, was meaningful to Joe (see chapter 10) as he worked to engage his students in practices that were less familiar to them. Again, the relationship between social control and mathematical activity becomes fuzzy.

Another way to control social behaviors includes instances when teachers tell students what to do by giving a series of commands: "Open your notebooks. Please stop talking, and turn to page 32 in your textbook." By saying such things, the teacher is directing students' behaviors and is calling on her position as a teacher, hoping that students will concede. (An important point is that this control does not just happen on its own; control is mutually negotiated between the teacher and students. Teachers, however, usually have more power in the situation.) Teachers can also employ less explicit ways to control the social behaviors in their classrooms, for example, by talking over students as they are trying to explain something (what is called *overlapping speech* in the discourse literature and "interrupting students" by the teacher-researchers; see chapter 7). Other means of control include the tone that is used, for example, replying with a sarcastic tone or repeating a student's response with a rising intonation, hinting that the response was incorrect.

Often when teachers have to direct students' behavior, they have to lessen the threat to students' "face" (Goffman 1967). In discourse studies, a theory of politeness explains how we use language to do so. The teacher-researchers found the theory of politeness to be complex but informative because it helped them understand that, by the very nature of the role of teacher, they continually posed threats to students' face when they evaluated their contributions, interrupted them, or put constraints on their freedom of action (Bills 2000; Cazden 1988). Some of the strategies used to soften evaluations of students' wrong answers include giving hints or clues that the student was incorrect, being ironic, and using rhetorical questions in place of making statements (Bills 2000). This last strategy—using questions in place of statements—sometimes becomes clear when a teacher asks the same question twice in a row. Often, when this happens, even if he or she is correct, the student will change the answer because asking a question twice often signals that the answer was incorrect (Cazden 2001). One danger in using questions to correct students' mistakes is that students may "'politely' correct [the mistake] without engaging with the reason why the correction was needed" (Bills 2000, p. 44).

Another way that politeness strategies can influence classroom discourse is through expressing approval of, or concern for, students' wants or through aligning them with the group instead of having them be viewed as an outsider. Some of the strategies that Bills (2000) found included apologies for imposing on students, using students' language, offering excuses for students' difficulties, and trying to let students know that they are part of the group. Jeff drew on some of this work as he tried to develop a stronger sense of community in his classroom (see chapter 6).

Reflecting and Connecting with Practice

- Reread the list of ideas that were new to you. Select one or two of the ideas, and read some of the articles and book chapters to learn more about them.
- After you have learned more about the ideas you have chosen, examine your classroom practice with respect to those ideas. You might want to revisit your videotape or audiotape, or may want to start paying attention to these ideas in your teaching. Either way, recording your reactions and reflections in your journal will help you make sense of these ideas.
- Invite some of your colleagues (either in your building or other mathematics teachers from other schools) to read and discuss the readings. What were their reactions and responses to the readings? How do they compare with your own?

Summary

The literature that we read and discussed furnished the basis for many of the ideas the teacher-researchers write about in their chapters. Some of the ideas bring mathematics to the foreground, for example, the distinction between calculational and conceptual discourse. Other ideas were centrally related to social control and included the ways in which we use language to be polite to students. The teacher-researchers drew on a range of the ideas discussed in this chapter, and their work illustrates the ways in which this literature transformed not only how they thought and talked about their classroom practice but also how they engaged in discourse practices with students. In subsequent chapters, the teacher-researchers articulate many ways in which their new understandings of discourse practices have helped them become more aware of, and purposeful in, their language choices.

Overview of the Remainder of the Book

This book consists of five sections, each with a somewhat different framing of the teacher-researchers' experiences. In section 2, Patty Gronewold, Darin Dowling, and Lana Lyddon Hatten share their "awareness journeys," or the journeys they experienced as they juxtaposed their beliefs mapping and videotaped aspects of their teaching with the analyses of their baseline discourse to identify their "performance gaps" (Hopkins 2002). They focus on the progress they have made over the four years; proffer images of careful, ongoing consideration of their discourse practices; and share plans for continuing the journey toward improving their discourse practices.

In section 3, Jeffrey Marks and Jean Krusi write about dilemmas, issues, and questions related to aspects of their discourse practices. These dilemmas and issues are illustrated through the use of transcripts, which are elaborated with insights that each teacher-researcher has about what they think is happening in the transcripts. Both authors raise important questions and dilemmas associated with getting students to participate more and to take greater ownership for their own mathematical sense making.

The focus of section 4 is providing images of productive discourse practices. By "productive discourse practices," we mean not only discourse practices that encourage more student participation but also practices that seem to support better mathematical learning. In particular, Tammie Cass and Angie Shindelar share some ways that they help students use mathematical language meaningfully and some language moves that help bring foundational mathematical ideas to the foreground. Although the other sections include images of productive discourse practices as well, this section makes specific practices central rather than tells a broader story about change in discourse practices.

Sections 2, 3, and 4 each end with a response chapter written by a university researcher. We invited these three people to write responses because they had written articles and books that had a significant impact on our thinking about classroom discourse. In her response to section 2, Courtney Cazden highlights some core ideas related to what she thinks teacher educators might learn from the chapters. David Pimm takes up the ideas of control, voicing, and revoicing in his response to section 3. The final response chapter appears in section 4. In that response, Catherine O'Connor discusses the important ways the teacher-researchers adjust their talk so as to engage students in mathematically rich conversations.

The final teacher-researcher's chapter appears in section 5. In his chapter, Joe Obrycki draws on data from student interviews to explain his students' perceptions of his attempts to engage them in inquiry-based mathematics. He used these data to show that, although some students struggled with, and were at first disgruntled by, the activities, they came to understand that he was actually helping them think and understand *why* mathematical formulas and theorems make sense. The students said that they thought their experiences would serve them better in future mathematics classes and in their lives outside school.

In the final section, chapter 11 synthesizes some of the main themes from the preceding chapters, and chapter 12 highlights the teacher-researcher's voices to argue that this kind of work is important for other mathematics teachers, mathematics specialists, and teacher educators.

References

Bills, Liz. "Politeness in Teacher-Student Dialogue in Mathematics: A Sociolinguistic Analysis." *For the Learning of Mathematics* 20 (July 2000): 40–47.

Cazden, Courtney. *Classroom Discourse: The Language of Teaching and Learning.* 1st ed. Portsmouth, N.H.: Heinemann, 1988.

———. *Classroom Discourse: The Language of Teaching and Learning.* 2nd ed. Portsmouth, N.H.: Heinemann, 2001.

Chapin, Suzanne H., M. Catherine O'Connor, and Nancy C. Anderson. *Classroom Discussions: Using Math Talk to Help Students Learn.* Sausalito, Calif.: Math Solutions Publications, 2003.

Forman, Ellice A., Dawn E. McCormick, and Richard Donato. "Learning What Counts as a Mathematical Explanation." *Linguistics and Education* 9 (Winter 1998): 313–39.

Goffman, Erving. *Interaction Ritual: Essays on Face to Face Behavior.* Garden City, N.Y.: Anchor Books, 1967.

Herbel-Eisenmann, Beth A., "Using Student Contributions and Multiple Representations to Develop Mathematical Language." *Mathematics Teaching in the Middle School* 8 (October 2002): 100–105.

Herbel-Eisenmann, Beth A., and M. Lynn Breyfogle. "Questioning Our *Patterns* of Questions." *Mathematics Teaching in the Middle School* 10 (May 2005): 484–89.

Herbel-Eisenmann, Beth A, Corey Drake, and Michelle Cirillo. "Muddying the Clear Waters: Teachers' Take-up of the Linguistic Idea of Revoicing." *Teaching and Teacher Education* 25, no.2 (February 2009): 268–77.

Hewitt, Dave. "Arbitrary and Necessary, Part 1: A Way of Viewing the Mathematics Curriculum." *For the Learning of Mathematics* 19 (November 1999): 2–9.

———. "Arbitrary and Necessary, Part 2: Assisting Memory." *For the Learning of Mathematics* 21 (March 2001a): 44–51.

———. "Arbitrary and Necessary, Part 3: Educating Awareness." *For the Learning of Mathematics* 21 (July 2001b): 37–49.

Hufferd-Ackles, Kimberly, Karen Fuson, and Miriam G. Sherin. "Describing Levels and Components of a Math-Talk Learning Community." *Journal for Research in Mathematics Education* 35 (March 2004): 81–116.

Hopkins, David A. *A Teacher's Guide to Classroom Research.* 3rd ed. New York: Open University Press and McGraw Hill, 2002.

Kazemi, Elham, and Deborah Stipek. "Promoting Conceptual Thinking in Four Upper-Elementary Mathematics Classrooms." *Elementary School Journal* 102 (September 2001): 59–80.

Lee, Clare. *Language for Learning Mathematics: Assessment for Learning in Practice.* New York: Open University Press, 2006.

National Council of Teachers of Mathematics (NCTM). *Curriculum and Evaluation Standards for School Mathematics.* Reston, Va.: NCTM, 1989.

———. *Professional Standards for Teaching Mathematics.* Reston, Va.: NCTM, 1991.

———. *Principles and Standards for School Mathematics.* Reston, Va.: NCTM, 2000.

O'Connor, M. Catherine, and Sarah Michaels. "Aligning Academic Task and Participation Status through Revoicing: Analysis of a Classroom Discourse Strategy." *Anthropology and Education Quarterly* 24 (December 1993): 318 35.

———. "Shifting Participant Frameworks: Orchestrating Thinking Practices in Group Discussion." In *Discourse, Learning, and Schooling,* edited by Deborah Hicks, pp. 63–103. New York: Cambridge University Press, 1996.

Pimm, David. *Speaking Mathematically.* London and New York: Routledge and Kegan Paul, 1987.

Rowe, Mary Budd. "Wait Time and Rewards as Instructional Variables, Their Influence on Language, Logic, and Fate Control: Part One—Wait-Time." *Journal of Research in Science Teaching* 11 (1974): 81–94.

———. "Wait Time: Slowing Down May Be a Way of Speeding Up." *Journal of Teacher Education* (January–February 1986): 43–50.

Stein, Mary Kay. "Mathematical Argumentation: Putting Umph into Classroom Discussions." *Mathematics Teaching in the Middle School* 7 (October 2001): 110–12.

Stein, Mary Kay, Barbara Glover, and Marjorie Henningsen. "Building Student Capacity for Mathematical Thinking and Reasoning: An Analysis of Mathematical Tasks Used in Reform Classrooms." *American Educational Research Journal* 33 (Summer 1996): 455–88.

Stein, Mary Kay, and Suzanne Lane. "Instructional Tasks and the Development of Student Capacity to Think and Reason: An Analysis of the Relationship Between Teaching and Learning in a Reform Mathematics Project." *Educational Research and Evaluation* 2 (1996): 50–80.

Thompson, Alba G., Randolph A. Philipp, Patrick W. Thompson, and Barbara A. Boyd. "Calculational and Conceptual Orientations in Teaching Mathematics." In *Professional Development for Teachers of Mathematics*, 1994 Yearbook of the National Council of Teachers of Mathematics (NCTM), edited by Douglas B. Aichele and Arthur F. Coxford, pp. 79–92. Reston, Va.: NCTM, 1994.

Thompson, Denisse R., and Rheta N. Rubenstein. "Learning Mathematics Vocabulary: Potential Pitfalls and Instructional Strategies." *Mathematics Teacher* 93 (October 2000): 568–74.

Voigt, Jorgt. "Patterns and Routines in Classroom Interaction." *Recherches en Didactique des Mathématiques* 6 (1985): 69–118.

Weingrad, Peri. "Teaching and Learning Politeness for Mathematical Argument in School." In *Talking Mathematics in School: Studies of Teaching and Learning*, edited by Magdalene Lampert and Mary L. Blunk, pp. 213–37. New York: Cambridge University Press, 1998.

Wood, Terry. "Alternative Patterns of Communication in Mathematics Classes: Funneling or Focusing?" In *Language and Communication in the Mathematics Classroom*, edited by Heinz Steinbring, Maria G. Bartolini Bussi, and Anna Sierpinska, pp. 167–78. Reston, Va.: National Council of Teachers of Mathematics, 1998.

Yackel, Erna, and Paul Cobb. "Sociomathematical Norms, Argumentation, and Autonomy in Mathematics." *Journal for Research in Mathematics Education* 27 (July 1996): 458–77.

SECTION 2

A Journey of Awareness and Change

CHAPTER 3

"Math Is about Thinking": From Increased Participation to Conceptual Talk

Patricia A. Gronewold

My teaching career began before the NCTM *Standards* (1989, 1991) were published. I relied on teaching the way I was taught, and the habits that I developed in these early years created my comfort zone. Of course I have known about the NCTM *Standards,* and over the years I have implemented different strands with various degrees of success. However, none of these attempts seemed to stay with me to form any sort of cohesive, let alone progressive, teaching. Parents and students did not seem to notice this problem as I did. In fact, I received many compliments, which led to my feeling that what I was doing was correct and good for my students. Year to year I relied on the fact that parents and students liked the way I was teaching. The discrepancy between their comfort with my teaching style and what I wanted it to be became clear at a district mathematics meeting when a videorecording of *Shea's Numbers* (Ball 1993) was played as an introduction to this project. As I watched, I knew I wanted my class discussions to resemble the one taking place in that recording.

The past four years have been a journey of reflection for me. It began with articulating my views and beliefs. The suggested readings and group discussions gave me a chance to reflect on my teaching and decide on the adjustments I thought I should make. The discourse analysis of the baseline data gave me insight into how I teach and helped me focus on what I wanted to change. Each step gave me an opportunity to reflect on how I teach and why I made the choices I made. The important things that I learned are (a) that what I say and the questions I ask influence the kind of language my students use and (b) that what I, as the teacher, emphasize is what my students emphasize.

Closest to My Heart Mapping: Examining My Beliefs

Early on our group members created a mapping of what was closest to our hearts about our teaching (see fig. 3.1). I found this exercise to be very useful in helping me focus on how I felt about teaching mathematics. What are the reasons I teach mathematics? What are the most important things I want my students to gain, and what methods are important to get them to that point?

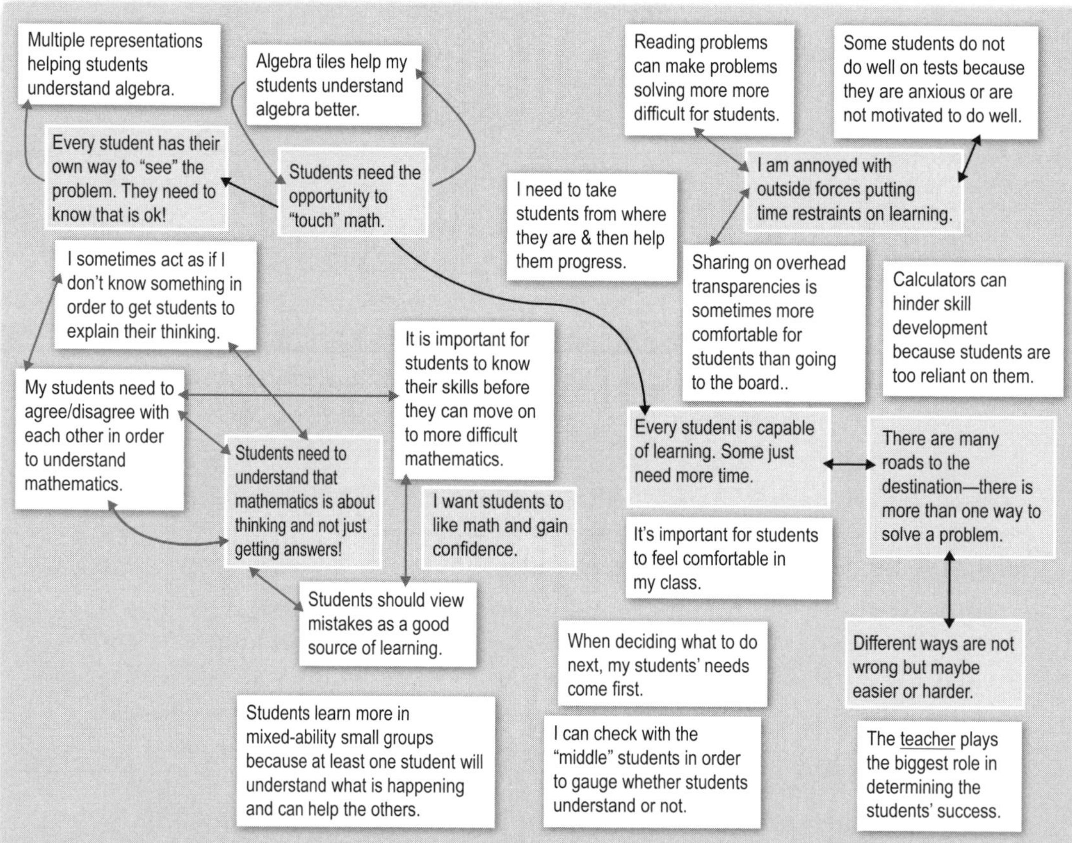

Fig. 3.1. My mapping of what is closest to my heart in my teaching

Looking at my mapping now, I cannot explain why I placed the note about skills at the very center of my mapping (i.e., "It is important for students to know their skills before they can move on to more difficult mathematics"). If I were to create a new mapping today, that note would not be anywhere near the center. The journal entry that I wrote about the mapping at the time did not even mention that note, but instead the three notes just below it:

- "Every student is capable of learning. Some just need more time."
- "I want students to like math and gain confidence."
- "Students need to understand that mathematics is about thinking and not just getting answers!"

A majority of my remaining journal entries related to these three notes. These three notes would still be at the center of my mapping, especially the note that students should understand that mathematics is about thinking. At times students get correct answers for the wrong reasons, or they do not fully understand how the mathematics works. At other times students get wrong answers when they understand the mathematics but make a simple arithmetic error. I have found that students in my classes mostly want to get *an* answer. If they get a wrong answer, too many times they assume that they do not understand and give up. When students know that mathematics is about thinking, they also know that correct answers are not the only way to show correct thinking.

Analysis of My Baseline Discourse Data

I was not surprised that the analysis of my baseline discourse data showed that the discussions in my class had an IRE pattern (Mehan 1979). I was also very aware of the fact that I did most of the talking in the classroom. At the time, I believed that I could make adjustments to change these things. One part of the discourse analysis disappointed me greatly, however. That was when I saw how frequently I emphasized *only* right answers. In the classroom episode described below, students had been using algebra tiles to do hands-on equation work.

> ***PG:*** If you need to write those on your paper, write them on your paper. If it's going to get you the *right* answer, use that tool. If you want the pieces, we'll give you the pieces. We want you to get your *answers right,* whatever it takes to get that. (11/14/05)

I would also tell students the reason for learning a procedure was to avoid making errors that would cause them to get wrong answers:

> ***PG:*** OK, you didn't listen to the question. OK? The question is, If we're not going to leave this as a minus problem because,

> when we get complicated problems and you've got minus problems all over the place, subtracts, and you've got negatives involved, you're going to end up with some *wrong answers* if you leave them all as subtract problems. Because it takes a while to really understand how all those subtract signs work together. (11/14/05)

Through the statements I was making, I undermined the message I wanted to send. I was telling my students that it was *all* about correct answers and procedures that avoid wrong answers. I did not routinely have my students look back at the reasoning behind their work.

In the analysis of the baseline discourse data, my colleagues and I also noticed that my word use and questioning style could set up an expectation that answers must be justified. The analysis showed that when students were asked *why* questions, they responded with "because...," as in the following example:

> ***PG:*** OK, it's four. Annie, why did you change your mind?
>
> ***Annie:*** *Because* if the sign is different, you have to subtract. (11/15/05)

Some students learned to justify answers even when they had not been asked a *why* question:

> ***PG:*** I guess that's what I'm asking you. Erik?
>
> ***Erik:*** Wouldn't it be positive three *'cause* two negatives times each other equals a positive?
>
> ***PG:*** OK, say it again.
>
> ***Erik:*** Uh, that instead of negative three it should be positive *'cause* two negatives times each other equals a positive in the integer rule. (1/25/06)

These examples show that what *I* say can influence how my students reply. I was interested in finding out whether I could use that influence to help my students understand that mathematics is about thinking.

My Action Research Strategy

Early in the school year, I formulated an action research strategy for how I would shift my students' focus from getting correct answers to understanding that mathematics is about thinking. After analyzing my discourse further and reviewing articles that I had liked, I determined that I would concentrate on my questioning techniques. If I wanted my students to understand the reasons behind their answers, I needed to ask them to explain their thinking. My strategy was to plan the questions that I would ask in advance. Because I wanted to see whether my words helped my students view mathematics as being about thinking, I also included thinking verbs whenever appropriate. When possible I planned follow-up questions for likely responses. I also planned to ask students whether they agreed or disagreed with their classmates. Doing so would allow me to ask them to explain and justify the comments with which they agreed or disagreed.

Having questions prepared is one thing, but I knew that questions in themselves would not be helpful unless the students had time to think and the opportunity to participate. This realization resonated with several of the articles we read that dealt with the idea of wait time (see, e.g., Rowe [1986]). I was familiar with the concept of wait time *after asking a question,* but I had not previously read about wait time *after a student responds.* Providing this wait time can allow other students to determine whether they agree or disagree with another student's response and what thoughts they want to add to the discussion. Also, students will sometimes correct their own thinking after speaking out loud if they have time to think about what they heard themselves say. The benefit to me is that I can think about how I want to respond (or not respond) to the student.

I found that the need to question my students' thinking arose at times other than during my prepared lessons. While going over students' daily work, I questioned how they determined their answers. In this next example, some students had arrived at correct answers but could not fully explain why $m\angle BKF$ measured 45 degrees.

PG: You're looking at this picture (see fig. 3.2). Twenty-one says find the measure of angle *BKF.* Find the measure of angle *BKF.* So *BKF* [points to *B, K, F*]... How could you go about figuring out *BKF*? *BKF*? Jung?

Jung: [inaudible]

PG: *FKA* [points to *F, K, A*] is ninety.

Jung: *BKF* is, like, half.

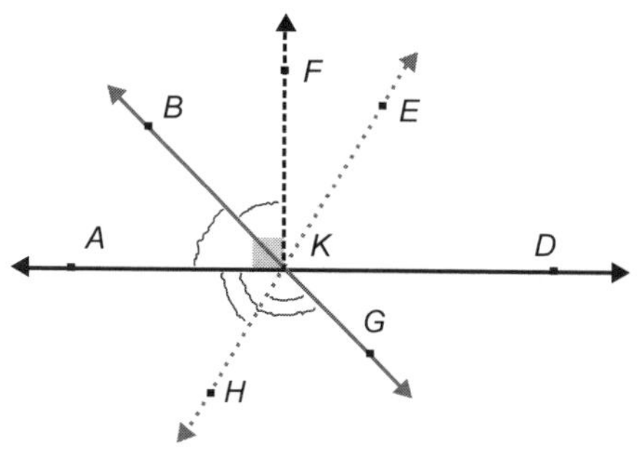

Fig. 3.2. Problem 21 from the homework assignment.

PG: He said *BKF* is ... half of that. Do you agree with him when he says *BKF* is half?

Students: Yes.

PG: Deandre? Are you agreeing?

Deandre: Yeah, because that line goes through the square.

Here, I did not specifically ask Deandre to explain his thinking, but he seemed to understand that if he agreed with someone, he needed to give a supporting explanation.

PG: Because this line [points to segment *BK*] goes through the square, so that means it's half?

Deandre: Uh huh.

PG: Everybody agrees? That's why it's half?

Marianna: Yeah.

PG: So I couldn't possibly have drawn through the square and not have it be half?

Alex: Well, you could.

I wanted students to understand that one cannot just make a decision about a diagram on the basis of how it looks. My fear was that my students might believe that when a ray *appears* to bisect a 90-degree angle, the angles are equal. I wanted to be sure they did not make decisions based on faulty assumptions about diagrams.

Julia: Not through the corners.

Here is a student who understood that the fact that the line is a diagonal makes the situation unique. I apparently did not hear this comment because I did not ask the student to explain it.

PG: I've got lots of people talking. I'm going to go with Marilyn.

Marilyn: The angle has two equal sides.

PG: Two equal sides. What do you mean by "two equal sides"?

Marilyn: [inaudible]

I wish Marilyn's comments were audible. She evidently explained what she meant, because I did not pursue it further, but her comment still did not fully explain how we knew the measure of the angles.

PG: OK. How do I know for sure that these two angles are equal [points to angle *FKB* and then angle *AKB*]? Ariana, how do I know for sure that those two angles are equal?

Ariana: [inaudible]

PG: Because of what?

Ariana: Because the line divides the square in half.

PG: OK, because the line divides the square in half [points to segment *BK*]. It's all based on that? Jack?

Jack: Because the ninety-degree angle *AKF*—there's two angles in there.

PG: OK [points to angle *AKF* and then points to angle *BKA* and to angle *BKF* at the same time]. There's two angles in there?

Jack: And one of them is half.

PG: So here I have a ninety-degree angle [points to angle *AKF*] and two angles in it [points to angles *BKA* and *BKF*], so these two are half [points to both angles *BKA* and *BKF*]?

Jack: No, I'm saying that *FKA* is ninety degrees [*PG* points to the letters *F, K, A* as student says them] and the *BKF* is forty-five degrees [PG points to letters *B, K, F* as student says them]. That one has to be half.

In looking back at the transcript, I obviously do have students who are using their reasoning skills about diagonals of squares. Unfortunately, I seemed to be very focused on what I was looking for from them, and I missed the opportunity to pursue this reasoning explicitly.

PG: OK. What I want to know is, How do you know that's [points to angle *BKF*] half? I agree forty-five is half of ninety. How do I know for sure that this one's half [points to angle *BKF*] and this one's half [points to angle *BKA*]. What in your picture guarantees me that they want me to know that those are the same, that they are half? Esmerelda?

Esmerelda: The blue line.

PG: The blue curve [points to the angle marking for angle *BKA*]. Those work just like tick marks, don't they? They are saying this angle [points to angle *BKA*] is equal to that angle [points to angle *BKF*]. (9/24/07)

Esmerelda finally shared the idea that the given diagram had the notation necessary for her to be mathematically certain that the two angles were equal to each other. We moved on because she shared the answer I was looking for.

The challenge of hearing only some of the students' contributions on the videotape made it difficult for me to determine whether a consistent change had occurred in my students' use of thinking verbs and, in general, made it difficult for me to determine what they were thinking. I shared this frustration at a project meeting and was reminded that I had liked a reflection sheet (see fig. 3.3) we had seen in one of the articles

Name________________ Date______

REFLECTION ON OUR DISCUSSION

How did you help make this discussion better?
Make a check for each that applied to you.
Then select one to write about below.

_______ I learned a math idea from someone.
_______ I taught someone a math idea.
_______ I thought about a math idea.
_______ I disagreed or questioned a math idea in our discussion.
_______ I referred to someone else's idea.

____
____
____
____

Fig. 3.3. Student Reflection Sheet (adapted from Sherin, Louis, and Mendez [2000])

we read (Sherin, Louis, and Mendez 2000). After reviewing that article, I decided to implement the reflection sheet as a way not only to receive feedback from the students but also to instill the importance of thinking and participating in class discussions. I asked students to complete a reflection sheet every couple of weeks. At the beginning of class I would tell them they would complete a reflection sheet at the end of the class. As students began independent work time, I would give each student a reflection sheet to complete and return to me before they left class that day.

In their early reflections, students gave simple responses that showed that they were able to contribute to other students' understanding, for example:

> I disagreed to the answer that Jung gave for the warm-up, then I helped him to understand the right answer. (Devin, 12/4/07)

> Devin taught me the first problem is a opposite of sign. I taught Hazel that you have to add *a* to *a* and *b* to *b* in problem 3. (Jung, 12/4/07)

These comments show that Jung confirmed Devin's statement that he helped facilitate Jung's understanding of the problem. The choice "I thought about a math idea" gave students who were not as comfortable speaking in class an opportunity to share their thoughts.

> I thought about #4, $3(x - 2) - 10 = 2$. I didn't really get it but I tried. I learned a math idea from Danielle on #4. (Chad, 12/4/07)

In a different lesson, we had a discussion in which one student divided by 10 and another multiplied by one-tenth. Carley wrote that she benefited from the discussion.

> I learned that ÷ by 10 and × by .1 are the same thing. I thought about the homework assignment when you were putting people's work on the overhead. Like I went through step by step and saw how each person got their answer. (Carley, 1/17/08)

Carley also wrote that viewing the methods used by each student to solve his or her homework helped her understand.

In the following example, Anthony admitted that he normally does not speak in class:

> I tried answering a couple of times, even though I was wrong about both answers. I listened to the whole discussion and wrote down everything on the projector. I discussed with someone, whether you could have more than two (–). Ex. –[–(n)]. I normally don't speak at all. (Anthony, 11/27/07)

I believe that the only reason Anthony spoke on this particular day was because he knew he would have to write about his participation in the discussion. He also showed a willingness to expand the concept beyond the current discussion when he shared that he discussed with another student whether you could have more than two negative signs. Had I not used the reflection sheet, I would not have been aware of what he was thinking.

Unfortunately for me, Anthony's reflection also showed that he was still focused on the fact that his answers were wrong and not on what part of his thinking was right. This concern shows that I have not been completely successful in moving my students away from focusing on correct answers to focusing on their understanding of the mathematics.

My Discovery!

As the school year ended, I reflected on the success of my strategy. I had had some success in changing my speaking and getting students to reflect on their participation in class discussions. I admit that I had difficulty preparing questions ahead of time. However, I had influenced my students, in that they came to understand through my questions that they would be expected to explain and justify their answers. They offered explanations even when they were not prompted to explain.

I also discovered that what I emphasize is what my students emphasize. After reviewing a transcript, it was suggested that I reread "Calculational and Conceptual Orientations in Teaching Mathematics" (Thompson et al. 1994). In this article the authors compared vignettes of two teachers presenting the same problem. The authors found that although both teachers pressed their students to give explanations for their solutions, they did so differently. What resonated with me was that my class discussions were very much like those of the calculational teacher in the article. In comparing the two teachers, the authors stated that the teachers were "driven by different images of their pedagogical tasks and the goals they served" (Thompson et al. 1994, p. 85). For me, the image is that of pursuing a problem to be solved. As I showed in an earlier transcript, I did not follow the discussion on the diagonal of the square because I was set on reaching my selected solution. I did press my students to explain their answers, but I accepted the explanation of the procedures they followed to calculate their answers. That acceptance perpetuated my students' idea that the most important thing is calculating correct answers, not focusing on why the mathematics makes sense. Although I no longer tell my students that all that matters is correct answers, my tendency to emphasize using correct procedures instead of articulating thinking is unfortunate. Every time I miss the opportunity to explore students' thinking and instead focus on the procedures, I implicitly send the message that mathematics is about calculating correct answers instead of thinking and making sense. Therefore, calculating correct answers and learning the procedures is what my students emphasize and value.

What Next?

Thompson and her colleagues (1994) wrote in their article, "It is important that students also appreciate that the most powerful approach to solving problems is to understand them deeply and proceed from the basis of understanding and that a weak approach is to search one's memory for the 'right' procedure" (p. 90). As I have tried to shift my students' focus to *thinking* about mathematics, I believe that this statement sums up what I mean by thinking. I want my students to have a *deep understanding* of the mathematics. My goal for next year is to begin the slow process of moving from a calculational approach to a conceptual approach to teaching. The article pointed out that making this shift not only is a challenge but can also be a bit scary. I can no longer rely solely on the activities provided in my textbook.

No matter how I change my questions, students will not think creatively if I ask about a simple problem. I also need to guard against the thought that, by simply locating and then including high-level problems, all my troubles will be solved. In the article by Thompson and her colleagues (1994), the authors noted that a good task does not guarantee that students will have a deep, meaningful discussion and understanding. That outcome is the teacher's responsibility. I will always need to be on guard against falling back into the old habits of focusing on particular procedures and correct answers, and instead I must constantly try to listen to my students' reasoning and respect their thinking.

Reflecting and Connecting with Practice

- Patty found that she focused on correct answers more often than she thought she did. Think about times in your classroom when you focus on correct answers. Why did you focus on correct answers? How often do you focus on right or wrong answers rather than on the process students went through to solve a problem? What might be some of the benefits of *not* focusing on the answer, but on the solution process?

- Patty wrote about asking "why" questions and planning questions in advance. Are these techniques a regular part of your practice? As you select your next high-level task, generate a set of solutions you think your students might come up with and plan questions for each solution that focus on getting students to say not only *what* they did but also *why* they did it. Try out the task, and use the planned questions if the opportunities arise. How did this approach seem to influence the quality of students' mathematical contributions? As you continue to use this type of questioning, what kind of support may students need to justify and explain their solutions without your having to request explanations?
- Return to the beliefs mapping you created when you read chapter 1. What verbs did you use to describe mathematical activity? When you talk to students or ask them questions, how often do you use "thinker" verbs (e.g., *reflect, think about, consider*) and how often do you use "doer" verbs (e.g., *do, write, calculate, measure*)? What impact do you think these different kinds of verbs have on students' views of mathematics?
- At least four times over the next month, ask students to respond to the prompts on the Student Reflection Sheet in figure 3.3. What do you learn about students that you did not know before? How could you use that information to support students' sharing of solution strategies?

References

Ball, Deborah L. *Shea's Numbers.* Ann Arbor: University of Michigan, 1993. Videorecording.

Mehan, Hugh. *Learning Lessons.* Cambridge, Mass.: Harvard University Press, 1979.

National Council of Teachers of Mathematics (NCTM). *Curriculum and Evaluation Standards for School Mathematics.* Reston, Va.: NCTM, 1989.

———. *Professional Standards for Teaching Mathematics.* Reston, Va.: NCTM, 1991.

Rowe, Mary B. "Wait Time: Slowing Down May Be a Way of Speeding Up!" *Journal of Teacher Education* 37 (1986): 43–50.

Sherin, Miriam, David Louis, and Edith P. Mendez. "Students' Building on One Another's Mathematical Ideas." *Mathematics Teaching in the Middle School* 6 (November 2000): 186–90.

Thompson, Alba G., Randolph A. Philipp, Patrick W. Thompson, and Barbara A. Boyd. "Calculational and Conceptual Orientations in Teaching Mathematics." In *Professional Development for Teachers of Mathematics,* 1994 Yearbook of the National Council of Teachers of Mathematics (NCTM), edited by Douglas B. Aichele and Arthur F. Coxford, pp. 79–92. Reston, Va.: NCTM, 1994.

CHAPTER 4

Reading (Articles), Writing (Reflections), and A-Risk-Metic: Working to Improve My Practice

Darin Dowling

In the fall of 2004, I had been teaching for five years and was seeking a change. I taught the way that I was taught—all direct instruction without much problem solving or practical application, working straight from the book without deviating from its order. I did not spend much time in conversation with my students about what they were thinking. I was trying to survive my first years of teaching. At first I thought the change needed to be in career choice, and I pursued that option for a while. I spent many Sundays looking through the classifieds at a wide variety of options. I have an elementary education degree with an endorsement in mathematics, so I did not have the mathematics qualifications to work in a corporate setting. I considered becoming a corporate trainer, thinking the "students" that I would be working with would want to be in the classes I was teaching and would therefore be more active participants. I also considered general labor jobs similar to the ones that I had held during my summers away from teaching. Those types of jobs consisted of physical labor that I enjoyed, and they did not involve any mental stress. But I finally realized that I did not want to leave teaching. I wanted to make changes in the classroom that would be beneficial for me and for my students. I was frustrated with what was happening in the classroom and was looking for some help.

As I sat in the library that day of the in-service meeting and watched a clip of a teacher teaching (Ball 1993), I thought that what she did during class was good for students. They were engaged and focused on the task at hand. I wanted to be able to achieve that outcome in my classroom. I knew that becoming involved in the Discourse Project might not be a magic cure-all for the frustrations that I was experiencing but hoped that it might give me some tools to use.

I did not know what "discourse" really meant at the time of that meeting. I knew it had something to do with communication in the classroom, but that was about it. I was curious to learn more about it and how it could affect students. I wondered whether I would be able to engage students the way the teacher in the videotape did. I also thought about the students that I have had in the past and wondered whether they would have responded negatively to the changes that I was considering. Such a response was a big fear of mine, but I believed that I needed to try to engage my students in mathematical conversations.

Episode 1: Before the Changes

The following transcript is from a lesson on division of fractions in January of 2006. I thought at that time that I had made some sort of progress in my teaching since 2004, but I still was not really engaging students. This transcript represents the way that interactions tended to occur in my class. I believed that I had a good rapport with the students, and I sensed that they honestly cared about what was going on in the class.

> ***DD:*** OK, there's the original problem for number 1. Now, yesterday we worked with just division of fractions. OK, we had some whole numbers in there, but we didn't have mixed numbers. So I thought we'd start with this [points to problem of dividing 3/7 by 1/4 on the projector]. Let's review what we were supposed to do with division of fractions with this problem. OK, this is our example: three-sevenths divided by one-fourth. This is what we worked on yesterday. What are you supposed to do in order to solve this problem? Mary?

> ***Mary:*** Ah, you leave three-sevenths the same and then you change the, uh, what's it called, the division sign into a multiply—so a times sign—and then find the reciprocal of one-fourth.

> ***DD:*** One-fourth, which is?

> ***Mary:*** Four.

> ***DD:*** Over one, right? OK, so now that we've done that, what do we do next? Alan?

Alan: Calculate our answers.

DD: Tell me how to get it, please. Then you can tell me the answer.

Alan: Then you multiply straight across, which three times four is twelve. Then seven, which equals one and five-sevenths.

DD: One and five-sevenths, 'cause you did what?

Alan: Reduced.

DD: You see how many times …

Alan: Seven goes into twelve.

DD: … seven goes into twelve.

Alan: Then there's five remaining.

DD: All right. OK, for the most part it seemed like there are a number of people going, "yes, yes." So as we're checking our work we're doing a lot better than what we did before, at least on our quiz, anyway. So it seems like we're making progress like we should be.

At the end of this lesson, I believed that progress was made, especially with the number of responses that I received during this part and the number of "yes" statements that were muttered.

As I watched videotapes of my classes at the beginning of this project, I could not believe that I did not have more students literally falling asleep in my class, because *I* had a hard time remaining awake for the time that I was watching the video! My class periods were filled with my providing steps to solve problems and students' repeating those steps for acknowledgement and credit. That pattern was made quite clear by my requests of students and their procedural responses, as can be seen in the preceding transcript. I had not given any importance to the thought processes behind the responses of the students. No students were really challenged in their thinking by me or a classmate. I knew at the time that this approach was not best practice, but I felt unable to make changes. I was numbed by the prospect of creating new material and coming up with new ideas.

Changing My Practice

Through reading articles and having discussions in our project meetings, I became aware of some of the opportunities for changing my practice. The other participating teachers shared insights into the readings that I might have missed if I had been trying to make those changes on my own. Also, listening to other teachers talk about their practice and the things that were happening in their classrooms led me to believe that some of the suggestions would not be too difficult to try. The group served as a great sounding board to talk about possible ideas, to discover whether anyone else had tried them out, and to discuss the possibilities of success or failure.

One of the first changes for me was the seating arrangement of students in the classroom. When I first started teaching, I set my room up the way I remembered classrooms from my days in school. I thought that I would have better control of the students if they were seated in rows facing the front of the room. I could more easily monitor behavior that way, and I did not have to worry about the students talking as much to one another. The seating arrangement also restricted students' movement in the classroom, thus assisting me in controlling their behavior (see chapter 6 for more on teacher control). I was under the impression that if the students did not have freedom, they would maintain better focus in mathematics class. I realize now that this thought was quite naïve.

I made some other physical changes in my room that I thought would help me build richer classroom discourse. The main influences behind these changes came from our project meeting discussions about our classrooms. Many of the other teachers in the project would talk about their room setups and how easy it was to have discussions during class. I thought that changing the room arrangement would be a very easy way to start making changes in my practice.

I have desks in my room, and I moved them around into groupings of twos, threes, and fours. With that change, students' movement seemed even more limited, as chair legs were now protruding in all different directions, and at times I had difficulty moving around the room to help students. But the change was beneficial to students while working on problems. They were able to talk to one another with relative ease and were able to stay on task while multiple groups were working and talking at the same time. In whole-class discussions, however, some students had difficulty seeing the speaker because their desks were facing different directions and they could not turn around in their seats. This limitation led me to try some other options.

For the 2007–2008 school year, I set the room up in four large rows—

two on each side of the room—with the desks all facing the center of the room. I could easily have students slide their desks into pairs or quads for group work with this setup, and they could return to their individual workspaces if necessary. The desks were close together, but the large open walkway down the center of the room allowed us to move around with relative ease. I placed my teacher station in the center of the room so that, when we had whole-class discussions, everyone faced the center and students could share ideas across the room, face-to-face. Overall, the arrangement tended to feel more like a place for discussion.

My teacher workstation also changed. I had previously used a traditional overhead projector, and it suited what I was doing just fine. But with the school's purchase of document projectors, I was able to change how I presented information and ideas in class. Students no longer had to write their ideas with smeary overhead pens. Now they could bring up their pencil-and-paper thoughts and present them to the class just as they had been written down at their desks or in their groups. I think that this technology change allowed students to take more ownership in the class and better represent their thinking because they could directly put their work up for all to see (see chapter 5 for more about technology and discourse). I was also able to grab interesting problems and ideas from practitioner journals or the Internet and add them to lessons with relative ease, opening possibilities for discussions.

I think that the biggest change for me was the change in the curriculum materials that I used in class. I realized that I did not like the textbook used by my district. I was not always happy with the ordering of topics, and I thought that the textbook tried to cover too much in some sections and did not really support students along the way. As a result, I tended to use a textbook that was published in the early 1980s. I thought its progression through the concepts was more fluid, and I liked the way it tended to focus on just one topic for each section. Considering the way I was teaching at the time, I thought that the older book was the better choice for my students.

I was later able to obtain a discontinued series of Connected Mathematics Project (CMP) (Lappan et al. 1998) materials from another district. I noted a huge difference between the way CMP and the textbooks I had been using presented lessons and required students to respond. The regular textbooks that I had been using would typically provide fifteen to twenty practice problems for students to work on after I explained the initial examples. The CMP materials, in contrast, required students to step away from traditional procedural responses and focus more on conceptual responses—less "step-by-step" and more "What do you think?"

I had been concerned about how I was going to create tasks for students that would engage them in the types of discussions that I saw on videotape during project meetings, but now the CMP series was doing that for me. The chapter titled "Getting to Know CMP" (Lappan et al. 1997) contained a response to the question "What is a good task?" As I read through the points (pp. 40–41), I realized that the problems in CMP were exactly what I needed. Some of the features of a good task are the following:

- Students can approach a problem in multiple ways using different solution strategies....
- The problem may have different solutions or may allow different decisions or positions to be taken or defended....
- The problem requires higher level thinking and problem solving....
- The problem promotes the skillful use of mathematics.
- The problem can create an opportunity for the teacher to assess what his or her students are learning and where they are having difficulty.

Other points were listed in that section, but the ones above really resonated with me. Also, I found comfort in knowing that I had developed a close enough relationship with the other teachers in the project that I could go to them for help and advice whenever I needed it.

At the time I received the CMP materials, my school was focusing on differentiated instruction in the classroom. I had struggled with this requirement in the past when students were not grouped by ability. If the students in the class had a wide range of abilities, my instruction reached out to the students in the middle area, and I merely helped the struggling students a little more while leaving the higher-level students to fend for themselves. CMP supported my initiative for differentiated instruction because the materials focused on discovery, problem solving, and mathematical reasoning and provided opportunities for written and verbal discussion along with differentiation and independent project options (Kathy Gavin, handout 6/23/08).

With all the visible changes happening in my classroom, some invisible changes occurred as well. My focus changed when I started using the CMP materials, because I was required to start looking at the "why" questions more than the "how" questions in my discourse with students (see chapter 3 for more on patterns of questioning). In previous years, I thought that I had done my job if students were able to restate the steps in solving a problem correctly. My idea of successful teaching would have had students saying something like, "When you divide fractions, you first find the reciprocal of the second fraction, then multiply the numerators straight across, then the denominators straight across," something that I would have expressed similarly in the previous day's direct teaching. If the students were able to repeat it, then my job was done.

The questions that the CMP materials posed and encouraged me to ask were much deeper. The CMP materials challenged students to truly think about their answers and forced them to use their information to make concrete statements about what they thought would happen in the future. The materials often asked students to draw diagrams, models, charts, and graphs to represent their thinking. Some items asked students to use a particular representation, and others left the representation for the students to choose. Each section always included a follow-up section to check for student understanding. It often required the students to think about the discussion of the previous problems as they worked to solve extensions from the lesson. I think that these aspects of CMP have led to a huge change in my teaching because they have prompted me to check for that understanding more often. The discourse that I observed during certain CMP sections was a good indicator of how much the students were learning, because they were asked to apply what was covered, not just regurgitate what specific steps were followed.

All these outcomes confirmed my belief that the selection of higher-level tasks was an area that could make a significant positive impact on my students. The problems from the textbook that I had used were not challenging enough to probe students' thinking. They were very procedural. So I needed to look at some outside sources for help. One of those was obviously the CMP materials. Other sources included *Mathematics Teaching in the Middle School* (the official NCTM journal for teachers of grades 5–9), NCTM conferences, district in-service sessions, and the other teachers in the project. The Internet has also been a great resource.

Episode 2: After the Change

My focus class for the action research phase was a sixth-grade mathematics class that included three fifth graders and a fourth grader. This group of students was not always willing to share their thoughts without some prodding. In the weeks before the interaction described next, we had worked on some problems that were followed by similar types of

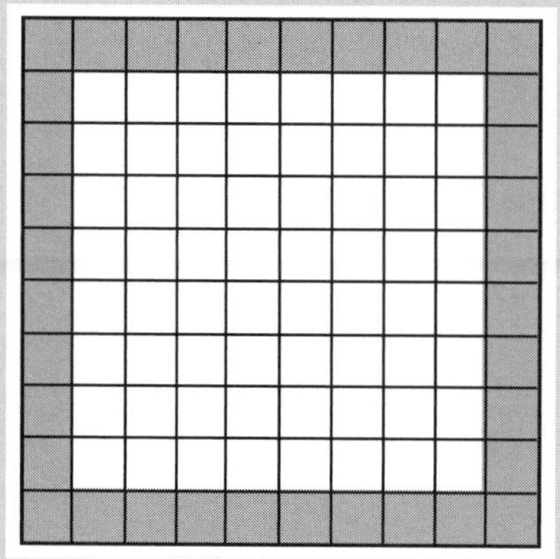

Fig. 4.1. The border problem.

discussions. The students started to become more accustomed to engaging in discussions after I presented tasks and were becoming more willing participants. The following activity is from a videotape that I watched at one of the project meetings (Boaler and Humphreys 2005). In the taped episode, the teacher (Humphreys) facilitates a discussion of the border problem. This problem involves a ten-by-ten grid of squares with the outside squares shaded to create the border (see fig. 4.1). Students are asked to determine how many squares are shaded without counting the squares. This was the second year that I used this problem in class. The transcript is from October of 2007, the first day that we worked on the problem.

DD: OK, I have a problem I'd like for you to take a look at. Without writing anything down on your paper, and without talking to anyone else in class, and without counting every single one out individually [puts up transparency of the problem]. I have a ten-by-ten square and I want to know how many smaller squares have been shaded in. While you're figuring out how many are shaded, or you're not counting them all individually—trying not to do that, anyway—think about what you thought of first. What was the first thing you thought of? When you get it, just keep your hands down, if you would please. That way you give some other people time to take a look at it and think about it. [One-minute pause] OK, would anyone like to volunteer what they were thinking about? Chrissy?

Chrissy: I was sort of thinking that all sides … um, it's ten by ten—each side has ten—but when I counted them out with the corners, when I counted them out with the corners, it wasn't all ten on all sides.

DD: OK, so you thought each side had ten, and if each side had ten, how many total squares would you have?

Chrissy: Have forty squares.

DD: Have forty squares. OK, and then you added some stuff after that. What else were you thinking?

Chrissy: Um, that there's four sides, wait …. That there's eight, like, without the corners, on each, and that with the corners there are still, um, there would only be nine. Unless you counted those.

DD: Without the corners?

Chrissy: Without the corners there was, um, eight on each side.

DD: Could you show us up there what you mean by being without the corners?

Chrissy: [moves to projector] I counted the corners, like, "one, two, three, four, five, six, seven, eight, nine, ten." Plus this one I counted "one, two, three, four, five, six, seven, eight, nine." And, um, since this corner is used by this, there's only nine up here. And that means there would have to be nine over here, and then there would be eight over here.

DD: Then eight on the side. So you have, how many are going across the bottom for you, then?

Chrissy: Um, there's ten on each side, it's just each has to use two corners. So it's not exactly ten on each side …

DD: OK.

Chrissy: …so I didn't figure out what it was, yet.

DD: OK, so initially you thought forty. So, how many are up there now? When you relooked at it?

Chrissy: Um … um [mumbles to self], eight ... um, thirty-two plus ... [full voice] Thirty-six.

DD: Thirty-six. OK. So now, another way of thinking? Jason?

I thought that a lot of positive things were happening in this lesson. The type of task that I asked the students to work on was completely different from the type in Episode 1. I asked students many different types of conceptual questions in contrast with the procedural questions in the first lesson. I was more focused on the *how* and *why* parts of their responses rather than the correctness of their answers. I think that this emphasis was evident in the way I phrased the questions at the beginning in line 10 and at the end in line 40. I was deliberate about my questioning and about making clear my curiosity about the students' thinking. I also ended the interaction with Chrissy by responding "OK," letting her know that I heard her response but not indicating that I thought her way was "right." I also asked students to explain more of their thinking or be more specific about items that they did not understand. In lines 17 and 18, I pushed Chrissy to make a clearer response.

I knew what she was trying to say, but I also knew that a lot of students in the class would be lost in her explanation. In line 24, I asked Chrissy to move to the overhead projector so that she could use the visible diagram to help with the explanation. Doing so allowed her to show on the diagram where she started with her thinking and how she proceeded around the diagram to complete her thoughts. I believed that such invitations to the front of the room also lent a new level of students' ownership over the answer and transferred the importance of the idea back to the students.

Looking at the broader picture after the changes, I noticed that because the types of questions I asked had changed, the responses from students changed as well. I would no longer say, "Nice job," and move on to the next topic. Often an answer that a student gave might lead to further explanation; it might pose a new question to the class, or it might spark a response from another student who either supported or disagreed with the original statement.

As I watched the videotape of the lesson several months after it occurred, I noticed that I had still missed opportunities to allow for students to explain their thinking and contribute responses. I also noticed that I tended to focus on particular students rather than the whole group. In this transcript excerpt, the focus was on Chrissy's explanation, but other students contributed after she did. Also, while I watched the videotape I remembered the uncomfortable feelings I was experiencing during the discussion. I think they became evident when I tried to ask a question and then stumbled and rephrased it so that I did not "funnel" (Herbel-Eisenmann and Breyfogle 2005; Wood 1998) a student into a particular answer but allowed her or him to really explain the process that she or he used to solve the problem (see lines 17–18 and 30–31).

While I am engaged in a discussion, I am constantly thinking about the many types of questions that I could possibly ask: Why did you think that, or what caused you to think that? Is there something in the problem that led you to think this way? Does anyone disagree with what was said, and why? Does anyone else have something to add? (I think that I should have asked this question before calling on Jason in line 40, because some sort of follow-up on Chrissy's response would have been good before moving on.) After each response, I am thinking of questions to use as follow-ups or ways of getting students to provide the follow-up themselves. I have an ongoing struggle in my head during the course of a discussion. At the end of a lesson I often feel worn out. I am mentally exhausted because of those internal battles, those feelings that I never really experienced with the style of teaching that I was using before. I might have felt exhausted because of a particular student's behavior, school field trip, or just from an entire day of on-your-feet teaching, but never from one class discussion.

Participating in the project and trying higher-level tasks with students has made me more aware of what is going on in students' learning and more aware of the amount of work required to encourage it.

Concluding Thoughts

I have made changes in many areas, such as classroom setup and curriculum. And through those changes I do feel a resurgence in my teaching. I believe that I am challenging myself and the students by making these changes in my practice. I am more engaged with what students are saying. I am continually listening to their ideas and conducting my own conversation with myself about what I should say, how I should say it, when I should say it, and whether I should say it at all (should I let a student take over?). The days when a lot of this type of interaction occurs are the days when I feel the most reward and, at the same time, the most exhaustion. At times when the class period has ended, I have not experienced that mythical sense of closure that mathematics teachers believe they should obtain. But often in these instances the discussion just continues the next day.

I am happy that I was not able to find another job four years ago when I was frustrated with my teaching. The changes I have made in my classroom have allowed me to gain a different outlook on teaching and have forced me to be a more active participant. I feel good after a real discussion happens in class. I enjoy the hunt for students' thinking and the search for good questions that help students share their thinking with the rest of the group. I also like the challenge of following up on a discussion that may not have been productive. I know that not every task I pose goes as planned. Now I am more concerned about how to keep it on track and bring a sense of closure that focuses on powerful mathematical ideas.

In looking back on my experience, I would encourage any teacher feeling the same frustrations that I felt to become a risk taker and to try to make these kinds of changes in his or her practice. In all honesty, teachers may not need to feel frustrated with their teaching to want to make a change. They should always be in a position to want to better their practice and try new and exciting things to benefit students. I was extremely hesitant when people offered ideas about changing what I was doing, because I did not want to leave my comfort zone. Or maybe I rejected the ideas because they were not similar to the ways that I was taught in the past, or because I did not think that I was creative enough to teach in this style or that I could maintain control of a classroom with this kind of atmosphere. But the more I thought about it and the more I learned, the more I realized that the changes were not as hard to make as I once thought. This process of improvement is ongoing because I am more aware of things that are happening in the classroom. I look forward to the changes that are yet to come.

Reflecting and Connecting to Practice

- Are you satisfied with your curriculum materials? If not, what are some of the things you can do? Think about the tasks that you use in your classroom. Do these tasks have the features of a good task? If not, how can you modify them? If they do, what can you do to extend them even more? If you have not tried engaging students in a high-level task like the Border Problem, try one and observe how your students tackle the problem.
- Both Patty (in chapter 3) and Darin (in this chapter) wrote about teaching in a manner that was similar to how they were taught. How does your experience as a student of mathematics compare with the way you now teach? Which aspects of your school mathematics experience are part of your current teaching practices? Which aspects have you chosen not to incorporate into your practice? Why?
- Darin experimented with the arrangement of the students' desks in his classroom to facilitate better interactions among students. Reflect on your classroom arrangement. Think about the advantages and disadvantages of different room arrangements. Might other possible arrangements be more conducive to higher-quality discourse?
- Maintaining control while trying out new things was a concern for Darin. Do you have a similar concern? Think of one or two things that seem a little risky but might create a powerful learning experience for your students. Take a risk, and try these ideas out.
- Darin tried *not* to say "nice job" after students' responses. What do you see as positives and negatives about giving this sort of evaluative feedback to students? What are other options for responding to students that might open up the classroom discourse more?

References

Ball, Deborah L. *Shea's Numbers.* VHS. Ann Arbor: University of Michigan, 1993. Videorecording.

Boaler, Jo, and Cathy Humphreys. *Connecting Mathematical Ideas: Middle School Video Cases to Support Teaching and Learning.* Portsmouth, N.H.: Heinemann, 2005.

Herbel-Eisenmann, Beth A., and M. Lynn Breyfogle. "Questioning Our *Patterns* of Questions." *Mathematics Teaching in the Middle School* 10 (May 2005): 484–89.

Lappan, Glenda, James Fey, William Fitzgerald, Susan Friel, and Elizabeth Phillips. *Getting to Know CMP.* Menlo Park, Calif.: Dale Seymour Publications, 1997.

———. *The Connected Mathematics Project.* Palo Alto, Calif.: Dale Seymour Publications, 1998.

Wood, Terry. "Alternative Patterns of Communication in Mathematics Classes: Funneling or Focusing?" In *Language and Communication in the Mathematics Classroom,* edited by Heinz Steinbring, Maria G. Bartolini Bussi, and Anna Sierpinska, pp. 167–78. Reston, Va.: National Council of Teachers of Mathematics, 1998.

CHAPTER 5

Talking around Graphing Calculators: A Journey through Performance Gaps

Lana Lyddon Hatten

INITIALLY, I did not consider mapping what was closest to my heart in mathematics teaching and learning to be especially important or useful. I have changed my mind about the usefulness of this mapping, and now I draw heavily on what I profess to believe to guide planning and make decisions (see fig. 5.1 for my mapping). Because I consider my beliefs important, when I am planning a lesson I now ask myself, "Will this activity in any way make students grapple with important mathematics, or will it intrigue them? Is there anything that requires them to persist? Can this lesson possibly lead to mathematics being seen as beautiful or mind-blowing (in a good way, not an 'I give up' way)? Who is driving the mathematical bus?"

My mapping also includes my belief that technology is and has been a wonderful tool both for engaging students and for managing the classroom. I decided to use technology in the classroom to motivate students and demand that they think hard and experience the wonder of mathematics. From previous experience, I knew that students' enjoyment would be high and intimidation, low. I thought I could make a good thing better by listening carefully to my students' talk when they used technology.

For me the Discourse Project has been, above all, an awareness journey. In this chapter, I share some of the journey and discuss aspects of which I have become more conscious. I also share the directions I plan to head for the next leg of the journey. This chapter is a snapshot along a path that is longer and slower than I expected. I anticipated that changing my practice by examining and then improving the talk in my classroom would involve hard work. I did not anticipate that examining

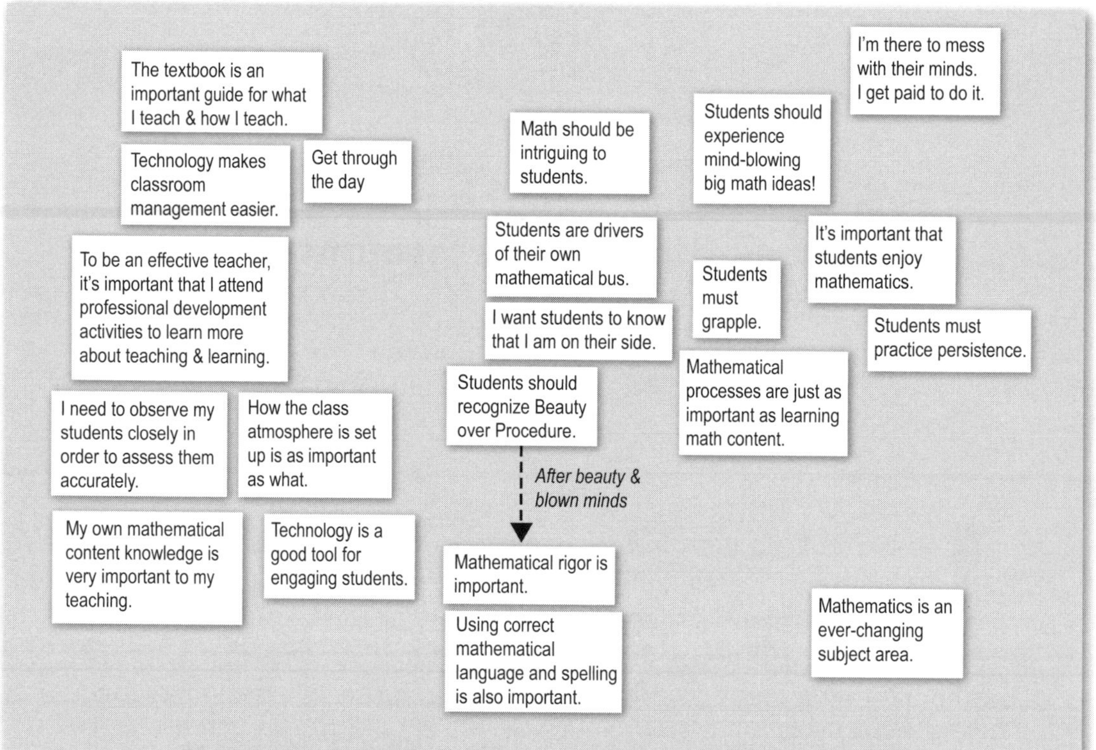

Fig. 5.1. The mapping of what is closest to my heart in my teaching

my practice in this way would require a deeper awareness of what happens in the process of learning, interacting, and knowing. I now have more strength in my beliefs, and I believe with more confidence that the course I am on is a productive one for students.

Early Awareness of My Assumptions

Early in the project (and before I purposely started to change things), I began to pay closer attention to how the graphing calculator was used and what the talk was like during its use. I noticed that what I was doing and what the students were watching were not very meaningful. Disappointedly, I noticed that the talk consisted of my telling the students which buttons to push. I had expected the use of technology to be a vehicle for students to make important and meaningful connections among different representations—algebraic, geometric, numeric, and verbal. The calculator was not granting access to big, mind-blowing mathematical ideas as I wanted it to. When the TI 84+ calculator was present, I said things like this:

> ***LLH:*** First push [STAT], choose the [CALC] menu, select [4:LinReg], type [L1], comma—the comma is above the [7] key—and to type [L1] push [2ND] and the [1] key, then type [L2]. To paste the regression equation into [Y=], go to [VARS], [Y-VARS], [1:Function], then [2:Y], and hit [ENTER].

And like this:

> ***LLH:*** To find the point of intersection on the graph, do not use [TRACE]. That is not accurate enough. Go to the [CALC] menu, which is [2ND] [TRACE]; select number [5], [INTERSECT]; hit [ENTER], [ENTER], [ENTER].

I did not perceive myself to be a teacher who just told students what to do. When I read transcripts from the baseline data collection, however, that is what I was doing. Increased awareness can be painful.

I thought about my "performance gap," as David Hopkins (2002) called it. Once I realized that the students' experiences with graphing calculators were frequently reduced to pushing the buttons that I told them to push, I quickly generalized that I often told students what to do in other contexts. What was going on here? I eventually discovered two reasons that I appeared to be a procedural teacher but did not feel like one. Both these reasons had to do with the fact that I did not want to underestimate or patronize my students. This realization was significant and powerful for me.

The first reason was that I did not wish to patronize my students by stating what I thought might be obvious to them. The students at my magnet school are identified as gifted (although not always in mathematics). If anything, I erred on the side of assuming too much understanding and independent sense-making. I believed that these students could not help but make sense of the mathematics. Making that assumption is exactly what I was doing in my keystroke pedagogy about the use of a graphing calculator. For example, I might show students how to find the intersection point of two lines on a graphing calculator but neglect to engage them in a discussion of the fact that the point of intersection is the solution to the system of equations. I assumed that students grasped the conceptual understanding; I needed only to share the particulars of how a graphing calculator could deliver a result. I believed that if they could make the graphing calculator perform, students would internalize the mathematical concept. I did not think it would happen automatically, but somehow in the act of *doing the procedure,* I assumed that students would *understand the mathematical concept.* Before I reflected on my talk about the use of the graphing calculator, I believed that students automatically made sense of the mathematics, so that the mathematics did not demand explanation, exploration, or communication.

The second reason was that I did not wish to patronize my students by giving them more time to process mathematical ideas than they needed. Because my students were gifted, I believed they would learn and understand faster than I. Before I reflected on my talk about the use of the graphing calculator, I thought that spending time in conversation might be unnecessary busy work. For example, a conversation about why every point on the perpendicular bisector of a line segment must be equidistant from the endpoints would be obvious and a waste of time. Why should students listen to classmates talk about something I assumed they already understood? I thought my students processed information so quickly that if I showed them why a concept made sense or how a procedure worked, they would hear and understand at the same time. I made this assumption out of respect for their intelligence and time. However, my assumptions about sense making and processing seemed important to challenge. By experimenting with my assumptions, I did not believe I would do any lasting damage to anyone's mathematical experience. I hoped that more students would increase their mathematical power as a result.

Increasing Awareness through Observing "Accurately"

Watching videotapes of my classroom was another activity that I was willing to do but did not initially appreciate fully. I recall my first experience of carefully reviewing a videorecording of a single class period. Reviewing this videotape helped me reflect on my practice more broadly. I remember that, during the actual class period, I believed that the lesson was cohesive and had gone well. In my immediate written reflection on the class period, I noted,

> … we answered the first homework question. It was a nice lead-in to review the chapter and introduce the quadratic formula because, before it could be solved, the equation had to be factored—which was nasty. I liked that I was able to say something like "Wouldn't it be nice to have another algebraic way if this way is or seems impossible?" (Daily Reflection, 11/21/05)

When I viewed the videotape of this class period the following summer, it clearly showed that I—not my students—was doing the work, making the connections, and giving the reasoning. They did not have the chance to do anything except listen until quite late in the class period. Although a coherent thread was present in the lesson, it was a long and boring one. (Again, awareness can be painful.) When students sang the quadratic formula, however, they became quite lively! Even though they appeared attentive up to that point, I knew that lively was better. I decided that I wanted my students to do something rather than watch me.

After I invited students to try a practice problem, I also noticed that many students were slow to begin working on it. I could understand that they had not been doing anything for most of the class period, so quite a shift would be necessary to get in gear and try to solve a new type of equation. As I watched the videotape, I wondered how, together, we could set the classroom expectations early in the semester to allow and encourage more student participation from the beginning. What I thought was happening during the class period differed dramatically from what I observed while viewing the recording afterward. This awareness moved me to a significant understanding of my teaching. I was quick to judge my teaching negatively and to be disappointed when I viewed a class period from the third-person perspective. The next small yet even more important awareness was that if my own perceptions could differ so widely between the lesson when I was teaching it and the lesson when I watched it, almost certainly both of those perceptions differed from my students' perceptions (see chapter 10 for more about students' perceptions). I suspected that an additional layer was involved in my performance gap—this one between my perceptions and my students' perceptions of a lesson. And after all, whose perceptions are the important ones?

An Evolving Practice

Once I had identified a gap between what I professed in my mapping and what I actually observed happening in the classroom, I spent a year intentionally including in each unit a richer task that required the use of technology. By "richer" I mean that the activity was not just included for the novelty of using technology. Instead, the activity was multilayered so that it was accessible to any student, and students who were working more quickly could engage with the activity more deeply. Each task also contained mathematics that related to the unit. I made this decision because I thought that using technology—which students already found engaging—would intrigue students and give them something to persist in and grapple with.

I considered the mathematical understandings that I wanted the students to gain from the activity. I began to be aware of asking the higher-level questions that I wanted students to be able to answer during the activity (see chapters 3 and 9 for more about the process of moving toward higher-level questions). I held students accountable for articulating their solutions. Previously, I had often used a whole-class discussion of an individual or small-group activity and allowed one person to speak for the entire group. But now I carefully observed small groups and made sure that each group arrived at a deep mathematical understanding. Since I have made these changes, the students have not disappointed me. I find that they are eager to express what they know or are trying to figure out. In the next three subsections, I include three examples from my classroom to illustrate the discussions that we now have in the classroom. The examples show both some ways in which my observations and reflections have influenced my classroom discourse and some of the issues with which I am still grappling.

First Classroom Example

In October of 2007, the class was in a familiar whole-class setup. I asked the class, "How long would it take an investment to reach $1800 if the initial investment was $400 and the money doubled every nine and nine-tenths years?" The students concluded that the number of doublings was not integral but that the number of times the money doubled was between two and three. They only approximated a numerical solution. They also determined that the number of times the money doubled would be the solution to the equation $1800 = 400 \cdot 2^x$, where x was the number of times the money doubled. Students solved algebraically one step further to get

$$\frac{9}{2} = 2^x.$$

They did not know logarithms, however, so they did not have the algebra skills to solve an equation with the variable in the exponent. I told the students that they would need to use their graphing calculators. Before they picked up their calculators, they quickly made hand-sketched graphs of

$$y = \frac{9}{2}$$

and $y = 2^x$ (see fig. 5.2 for the graphs of these two equations). I asked, "If this is a picture on our graphing calculator, how is that picture going to help us solve

$$\frac{9}{2} = 2^x\text{?''}$$

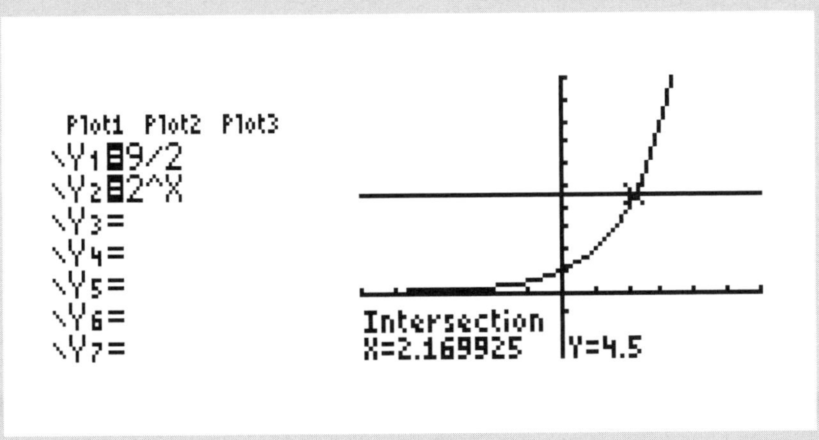

Fig. 5.2. Graphs of $y = \frac{9}{2}$ and $y = 2^x$

Twenty seconds later, one student suggested the point of intersection but was not able to say whether the solution to the equation was the point itself or one or both of the coordinates. Next, another student suggested that the *x*-coordinate of the intersection point was the solution. When I asked the rest of the class whether the *x*-value gave the solution to the equation, another ten seconds went by before someone responded. Two students proposed reasoning that was incorrect. For the first time in the lesson, I allowed students to graph the equation on their own calculators instead of viewing the image on the classroom overhead projector screen.

Even though we had not often used the graphing capabilities of the calculator in the course, I did not lead the students through exactly what to do to graph the equations, find an appropriate viewing window, and calculate the point of intersection. Instead of doing what I usually did and telling the students what the entries in the standard viewing menu meant, I asked them what they thought. For example, one student correctly guessed that the [XSCL] and [YSCL] were "how much each notch is." Unfortunately, at the moment, I believed that I had to give the students explicit instructions:

LLH: If that's the equation we want to solve, $\frac{9}{2} = 2^x$, then if we graph all the points where this [points to $y = \frac{9}{2}$] is true, and all the points where this [points to $y=2^x$] is true. If we want the right sides to be equal, then this point of intersection is the place where these two [equations] are true at the same time. They both equal nine-halves when x is 2.170.

[…]

LLH: Now let's go back and answer this question. How long will it take to have $1800? How many doubling periods? [Remember that] x represents the number of times [for the money] to double. Now looking at this solution, how many doubling periods will it take?"

And later:

LLH: So you can graph two curves and find the intersection point, but you have to do it for a reason. To come back here and answer these—How many doubling periods, and how many years?—talk at your tables. Show me what you get.

After three seemingly long minutes, some small groups generated answers to the questions in their groups. I told the rest of the small groups the correct answers I heard. Wow, I thought, either they were having a bad day or my assumption about them automatically making connections desperately needed to be challenged!

In previous years I just told the students how to calculate the point of intersection, use the x-value to get the number of doublings, multiply that number by nine and nine-tenths to get the number of years, and we were finished with the problem. This year, even with some careful changes, when I used a whole-class discussion and displayed the information to the students, they had not been able to articulate connections among the multiple representations. After viewing a recording of this class, I wrote in my notes:

> How to [structure] a discussion/activity for understanding a graphical solution to an algebraic problem? Next time set up an activity so that each kid and small group must consider how the graphical representation solves the algebraic problem. The structure should not be big group first, then short discussion. Make being able to articulate what is happening a bigger deal. (Journal Entry, 10/15/07)

I decided to shift from a large-group structure to smaller groups so that I could hear more students' thinking as they talked to one another. I could also ask individuals specific questions about the images on the graphing calculator as they occurred rather than make the entire class hear something they may not need to hear.

Second Classroom Example

During a subsequent opportunity to use calculators to make connections between algebraic and graphical representations, I decided to be more purposeful in ensuring that my students articulated the connections among multiple representations. I made sure that the activity had important mathematics in it, and I knew, specifically, what mathematical ideas in the activity I wanted students to be able to articulate. I asked students to use graphing calculators to graph six quadratic functions (e.g., $y = 5x^2 + 2x - 3$) and to pay attention to the number of x-intercepts. I also asked them to find the number of solutions to corresponding quadratic equations (e.g., $0 = 5x^2 + 2x - 3$). Students calculated the value of the discriminant, $b^2 - 4ac$ (i.e., the radicand in the quadratic formula), and noted whether the discriminant was positive, negative, or zero. I insisted that every student write a conjecture about the relationship between the discriminant and the real-number solutions of a quadratic equation.

As a result of reflecting on the previous lesson, I asked students to work individually or in small groups rather than have a discussion as a whole class. The students worked for ten minutes as I moved around the groups. I needed to say very little. Other than observe and listen for how well students seemed to understand what they were doing, I helped only two students who had crucial questions and attended to two students who were going to be absent. The next time I spoke, I said, "Keep going. You're working great. [The conjecture] is really the main point of it. You get to write a sentence, and I want to read the sentence."

After I read one student's conjecture, I said to him, "I am going to have you write that [conjecture] more mathematical. 'Twos?' What are 'twos' talking about? And what are 'positives' talking about?" My conversation with another pair of students went like this:

LLH: Carl, what did you write?

Carl: If the discriminant is two, there [is…]

LLH: [What] do you mean, "if the discriminant is two"?

Martin: If the answer is zero.

LLH: But what do you mean by "if the answer is zero"?

Martin: If b squared minus four ac is zero.

LLH: And what is that called?

Carl: The discriminant.

LLH: OK, if the discriminant is zero,...

Martin: ...then there is one x-intercept.

Carl: I got it.

[Ninety seconds later]

Carl: If the amount of solutions is two, there is a positive discriminant.

Once each student had written a conjecture, the whole class reconvened:

LLH: For the last couple minutes, let's say some things out loud that I know were going on at the tables. We noticed that when y equals zero, there's one solution to this equation [points to $0 = -4x^2 + 4x - 1$], and when we graph the parabola [points to $y = -4x^2 + 4x - 1$], there was one x-intercept. *How come those match up?*

Cindy: There is only one spot [on the graph] when y is zero.

LLH: When you saw one x-intercept [points to the graph] or you saw there was one solution [points to the equation], what was the discriminant like? The choices were positive, zero, or negative.

Jeffrey: The discriminant equaled zero.

LLH: *Why* does the discriminant of zero force there to be one solution? We can use this [points at the algebra written on the whiteboard by two students].

$$0 = -4x^2 + 4x - 1$$

$$x = \frac{-4 \pm \sqrt{16 - 4 \cdot -4 \cdot -1}}{2 \cdot -4}$$

$$x = \frac{-4 \pm \sqrt{0}}{-8}$$

$$x = \frac{1}{2} + 0 \quad x = \frac{1}{2} - 0$$

LLH: Why does a discriminant of zero mean only one solution?

Algebraically, what is the significance of zero under the square root?

Cindy: It takes away the plus or minus.

LLH: There is nothing to add or subtract from the line of symmetry to get to the x-intercepts. The vertex is the x-intercept. So now we have one like this. [A graph of $y = 2x^2 + x + 5$ is displayed on the overhead calculator.] Which is really the exciting part of the day! So, how many x-intercepts?

Multiple students: None. Zero.

LLH: All right, so then how many solutions would you expect to find if we let y equal zero?

[Students observed that $y = 2x^2 + x + 5$ had no x-intercepts because there were no places on the parabola where $y = 0$.]

LLH: So tell me about the discriminant in that case.

[Students calculated the discriminant to be negative.]

LLH: Why does it make sense that there is no solution [to $0 = 2x^2 + x + 5$, equation displayed on white board]?

$$0 = 2x^2 + x + 5$$

$$x = \frac{-b \pm \sqrt{b^2 - 4ac}}{2a}$$

$$x = \frac{-1 \pm \sqrt{1^2 - 4(2)(5)}}{2(2)}$$

$$x = \frac{-1 \pm \sqrt{-3}}{39}$$

Emily: Oh, because there is no negative square root.

LLH: In the real world there is no square root of a negative number. Why not? Why can't you take the square root of a negative number?

The students had no difficulty articulating why a number squared was always positive. Because we had pressed for an articulated understanding, the transition to complex numbers was more dramatic and fun—possibly even mind-blowing.

> ***LLH:*** You are right, we cannot take the square root of a negative number, not in the real world. So, close your eyes. Let's imagine that we can take the square root of a negative number. Now we can. In the real world, this is not possible, so it doesn't show up as an x-intercept. There are two solutions to this quadratic equation $[0 = 2x^2 + x + 5]$. We are going to imagine that we can take the square root of a negative number. So we come back tomorrow and we can.

I think that this activity allowed students to experience the wonder of mathematics much more than my saying something like, "By definition, $i = \sqrt{-1}$, and here is how the arithmetic goes with imaginary and complex numbers." When asked to consider what the most amazing thing they learned in the first semester was, many students responded similarly to this student: "Learning about and working with imaginary numbers. I love the algebra involved, and thought it was a cool way to solve an impossible problem."

Third Classroom Example

In April, the same students were asked to find four centers of triangles—the circumcenter, incenter, centroid, and orthocenter—by constructing the points of concurrency of perpendicular bisectors, angle bisectors, medians, and altitudes, respectively. Students made the segments by folding Patty Paper, which are squares of waxed paper that can be creased, written on, and traced on. First, students folded the perpendicular bisectors to locate the circumcenter. They used a compass to construct circles with the center at the circumcenter, one of which—the circumcircle—intersects the triangle at the vertices. Several students justified for their classmates why the circumcenter must be equidistant from the vertices. The exchange was terrific but not surprising. The students were successful in the construction and had become accustomed to justifying why things were true. Most were willing and many were eager to do so.

Students then folded the angle bisectors of their triangles to find that point of concurrence, the incenter. They did a nice job of reasoning why, unlike the circumcenter, the incenter would always be in the interior of the triangle. I told them that perpendiculars dropped from the incenter to each side of the triangle were congruent. Then I told them that they could make a circle that intersected each side exactly once.

Because it was hard to do so with a compass, these incircle constructions were not as precise as the circumcircles had been, and students were not very successful. To their credit, the students were not convinced by their constructions and were not willing to take my word about inscribing circles in triangles. I was very pleased that they had turned the expectation of justifying and providing reasons back on me. I was asking them to believe something that their own constructions did not allow them to inductively believe, and I did not ask them to make sense of it deductively, either.

The next day I opened the discussion as follows:

LLH: Here's the part I want to spend some time with today because you did such a great job of explaining things with the perpendicular bisectors. Then I made you kind of eyeball something, and it wasn't that convincing to you. So let's work this out. Angle bisectors were the second thing we did. We bisected the angles, and I think everyone got a point of concurrency, which is called what?

Several students: The incenter.

[I reviewed the process they went through the day before to inscribe the incircle within the triangle.]

LLH: So you didn't quite buy it, which I appreciate and don't blame you. Here's one sort of, not deductive proof, but it is a little more accurate than me saying, "Oh, try to figure out the shortest distance to a side and try that for [the radius of] a circle and see if it works."

[I constructed the incircle using Geometer's Sketchpad and projected it. (See fig. 5.3). It does work. [I change the triangle dynamically to demonstrate that the circle remains inscribed.]

LLH: Hopefully this is somewhat more convincing than otherwise. You can make a circle that is not big enough, and you can make a circle that is too big. I think that was easy to do yesterday. Now what I want you to do is see if you can figure out why [a circle inscribed in a triangle] works in the same way you did with the circumcenter before. Why are those three lengths [points to $\overline{AC}$, $\overline{AB}$, $\overline{AD}$] going to be the same?

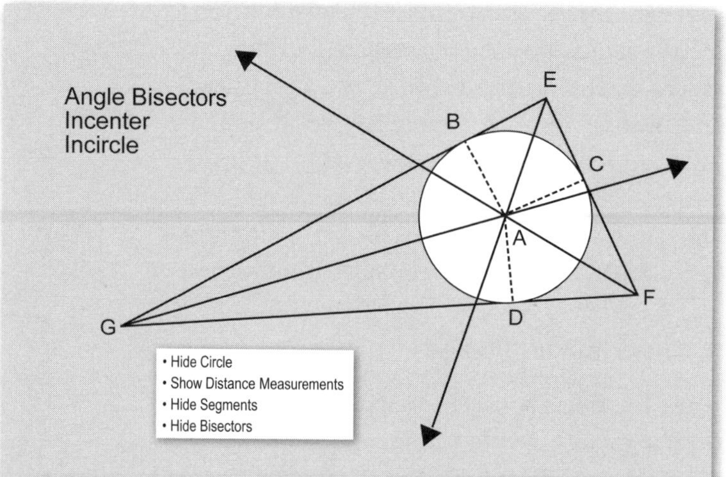

Fig. 5.3. Geometer's Sketchpad construction of the incenter

As students talked in groups of four, I said to some of the groups, "It's OK to know these [$\angle ABE$, $\angle ACF$, $\angle ADG$] are right angles. How come the red lengths [*AC*, *AB*, *AD*] have to be equal?"

To his tablemates, one student tried to justify $AC = AB = AD$ by saying that it was because "it's the radius of the circle and the incenter is the center of the circle and the radius is always the same." So I said, "What I am wanting you to justify is, Why would the circle be possible?" That table continued by stating a justification such as "because the distances are all the same like the radius of the circle is always the same."

The students at another table were standing up, leaning forward, and pointing toward the projected figure. One student was practically upside-down looking at the figure. Two-and-a-half minutes later, one student was out of his seat pointing directly at the figure:

Wee Tiong: I got it! And you know these two angles [$\angle DFA$, $\angle CFA$] are the same because it's an angle bisector, and I think these two angles [$\angle DAF$, $\angle CAF$] are the same because it is a bisector as well.

Joshua: And they have the same side [points to $\overline{AF}$].

Wee Tiong: They have the same side.

Joshua: That makes sense.

Wee Tiong: So ASA [angle-side-angle triangle congruence theorem].

Bettina: Oh, yeah.

Marcia: But they are different shapes.

Wee Tiong: No they are not. That's a whole kite right there [*ACFD*].

Marcia,

Joshua, Qing: Oh. Oh! I was looking at that wrong. OK. That makes sense.

Across the room another student justified her response to me:

Barbara: You can't know the other side. Right now you have the middle to itself [$\overline{AF}$] and you have ninety-degree angles [$\angle ADF$, $\angle ACF$]. You don't know one of the other sides is the same as the other.

LLH: So you got an angle and a side, you need either another side or angle. Keep looking.

Barbara found an additional pair of corresponding angles that were congruent, the pair formed by the angle bisector of $\angle DFG$. She concluded that $AC = AD$ because triangle *ADF* was congruent to triangle *ACF* by the angle-angle-side (AAS) triangle congruence theorem. The students' conversations moved to include students across the room rather than just at each table, so the whole class listened while Wee Tiong and Barbara repeated their justifications. Wee Tiong no longer believed he could justify $\angle DAF \cong \angle CAF$. When asked why $\angle DAF \cong \angle CAF$, Wee Tiong said, "That was my question. I don't know that's right now." He asked Barbara to clarify, "How do we know that those are ninety-degree angles?" A couple of students convinced him, and he responded, "Well then, we will just go with that."

LLH: I think Wee Tiong and Marcia are convinced. Anybody else?

Justin: That it's congruent?

LLH: Yeah. Can you describe it for the rest of us?

Justin: But they already did.

LLH: I know, but now somebody is willing to listen again. Can you do it with a different pair of triangles?

Justin: You could do it with *B*, *C* triangles—the ones in the upper-right corner. Up at the top where the angle is divided, that's a bisector. And the lines, where *A* to *B*, that angle had to be ninety degrees. That would be perpendicular. And the same with *A* to *C*. And they have the same side in common, so it would be just angle-angle-side.

Wee Tiong: I agree with that.

Qing: Exactly.

Seven minutes from when we started trying to solve this problem, students tried to justify, modified their thinking, and reiterated why a circle can always inscribe a triangle. I said, "I really appreciate you challenging me on that yesterday and not being so convinced with the 'kinda-sorta' eyeball-it way. That was fantastic." (Classroom videotape, 04/09/08)

Attending to Performance Gaps: Perceptions of Administrators and Students

The observations of the vice-principal of my school, who evaluated me during the school year, and my students have provided glimpses that the *performance gap* between what I profess to be closest to my heart and what actually happens in my classroom is closing. In my evaluation, the vice-principal noted:

> [Her] questioning techniques are thoughtful with great use of wait time after questions, student questions are given back to class for response; respect shown for individual students. Encourages and engages students in thinking, constantly monitors student learning. (Written Evaluation, 2/21/08)

These statements were a surprisingly positive, supportive experience for me for two reasons. First, the vice-principal noticed and commented on specific things that were happening in my classroom to which I had been paying attention, and she agreed that they were positive and important. Second, our discussion of the evaluation allowed her to learn about my participation in the Discourse Project, and she offered genuine interest in, and appreciation of, the depth of professional development work I was willing to do to help my students learn. That said, I certainly did not become involved in the project to look better in an administrator's eyes.

Understanding my students' perceptions is one of the tasks that seemed feasible but has taken much longer than I expected in the midst of actually teaching. Since I reviewed the first videorecording of a class period, my interest in students' perceptions can be seen throughout the entries in my journal. Noticing these reflections in my journal, I wondered whether I should design a survey, interview questions, or a questionnaire to get feedback. Most teachers in my department include a reflective question for the students to answer on the final examination. I included a question asking about the most interesting thing students learned during the semester and got responses different from what I was used to. To my great delight, many students responded with comments similar to these:

- [Proofs] are hard, and they challenge you to try to MAKE something be true, not just because you know they are. This also makes math SLIGHTLY fun!
- I used to just do math without thinking why or how. Proofs made me think deeper of why and how to solve problems, instead of just doing.
- Learning how to prove congruent triangles. I like it because it made me look at triangles and other shapes from a different way. Also proving things, not just shapes, but anything like an argument is important for other classes and life.
- Definitely proofs. When I paid attention, I got them. They're not that hard for me, and I think it's cool that instead of just accepting things in the mathematic world you can actually prove them! (Students' responses, emphases in originals, 5/20/08, 5/29/08)

I am delighted by these responses, but not because I want or really believe proofs to be the students' favorite part of mathematics. When they were asked to prove things, the students were absolutely unwilling to take a teacher's or a textbook's word for what they were learning. I take the feedback as evidence that they know that making sense of mathematics is expected of them and that they value the reasoning. Proofs became the place where students realized that mathematics was not going to be the same. Mathematics—not just proofs—involved thinking, understanding why, communicating, and justifying. No one said, "We went too slowly with all of the talking, and she kept making us say stuff we already knew. She is so patronizing."

My students also completed the Conceptions of Mathematics Inventory (Grouws 1994), which asks students to respond to a set of items using a six-point Likert scale (from strongly disagree [1] to strongly agree [6]). One of the items was, "When your method of solving a problem is different from your teacher's method, your method can be as correct as your teacher's." Everyone in my focus class agreed, and all but two responded with a five or six. This corresponded to the belief in my mapping that students are the drivers of their own mathematical busses. Almost all my students also strongly agreed with the survey item that said, "Knowing why an answer is correct in math is as important as getting a correct answer."

When asked to write about what they found most interesting in mathematics class, some students referred to things that intrigued them or expanded their minds:

- Space figures. Fun to learn and really stretched my mind.
- What a 4D cube looks like. I thought there is no way that guy [on a video we watched] can show us 4D. Then he explained it, and it made sense. That was cool.
- The videos we watched were cool b/c it really challenged the way I think.
- Space figures, flatland, and the 4th dimension. I could never imagine what a 4-d figure would look like. When I first heard about it, I tried to draw a 4-d cube but it didn't really work out. Then in the video it showed us what it looked like and it was really cool. (Students' reflections, 5/20/08 and 5/29/08)

In the past, students had rarely used the words *cool* or *fun* when referring to their mathematics class, but this year the students used them consistently to talk about some of the things they learned.

New Awareness and a Future Path on my Journey

Recently, I stumbled on something fascinating that I believe will help me learn even more about my students than the written reflections I shared above. In trying to confirm that each small group was connecting *x*-intercepts, solutions, and the discriminant in the quadratic activity I described previously, I unknowingly recorded how the individuals in *one* of the groups came to an understanding. Watching that videotape made me aware of the fact that closely observing students working in a small group could help me better understand how the students interact with one another. I watched with an interest in the roles within the group and who assumed those roles. Who said what kinds of things? All the group members spoke, but the student who was the lowest performer talked only about nonmathematical things. Why? Another student, who was struggling but motivated, asked others in his small group for help and clarification. Did he have enough confidence and mathematical power to participate even though doing so meant confessing understandings that might be perceived as inferior to those of his group members? One student talked very fast, as if she were just proclaiming her knowledge rather than sharing it to help others. The fourth student talked in support and confirmation at a tempo that made it easier to learn. This new awareness is important to pursue, yet I realize that it will be one of many paths I hope to continue on. For now, I celebrate the changes I have made and remain conscious of those areas in which more progress needs to be made.

I made strides by adding to each unit one technology-rich activity that has a clear mathematical goal. I am aware of hearing students' responses and being convinced by them, and I have overcome my fear of being patronizing. However, I am not yet where I want to be with my level of questioning, and simply making sure that small groups actually have something to do and indeed do it has been a big step for me. My own awareness of calculator-button-pushing language has changed what I do. I now make sure that students are engaging in conversations that focus on their conceptual understanding of the mathematics rather than on the use of the technology.

I am able to recognize and to grapple with multiple performance gaps! I have identified my beliefs, now hold them with conviction, and am able to observe what is happening without "coming undone." I can do something about my performance gaps. I have tools, vocabulary, support from research, and a desire to bridge the gap between my ideal and the actual. That has meant learning more about myself than I anticipated. I feel as though I am both continuing the same journey and starting another one. As willing as I have become to perceive as accurately as possible what is occurring in my classroom, I need to continue to know my students. The gap between the perceptions of my students and my own perception, rather than between my ideal and the actual, is my new performance gap to bridge.

Reflecting and Connecting with Practice

- When and how do you use technology in your classroom? What kinds of tasks do you use when you incorporate such technology as graphing calculators? How do you and your students talk around the technology? Are you using technology in a way that connects and extends concepts, or is most of the talk about which buttons to push? Consider ways in which you can use technology (graphing calculators, computer software, and so on) to help students make connections and extend concepts.
- What kinds of assumptions do you think you make about your students? For example, think about how you launch different activities or how you use technology. How do your assumptions and beliefs about your students affect what you do or do not do with them? Lana did not want to patronize her gifted students, and she realized that this desire was related to her assumptions about students' understandings. Do you take students' sense making for granted?

How could you determine whether students are making sense of concepts?

- Hopkins (2002) defined a "performance gap" as the gap that exists between what we *want* to happen in our classrooms and what *actually* happens (see chapter 1). What performance gaps do you think exist in your practice? Watch a videotape or listen to an audiorecording of your teaching to compare your teaching in practice with your beliefs mapping. What other gaps do you notice? Lana extended her performance gap to include such things as the gap between *her* perception of the classroom activity and *her students'* perceptions. Use some prompts the way Lana did, and ask your students to write about their classroom experiences. How do their perceptions differ from your own? What additional performance gaps do their responses highlight for you?
- Toward the end of the chapter, Lana made some powerful observations about her students as they worked in small groups. Pick one or two small groups in your classroom to observe carefully over a week. What do you notice? How are students interacting with one another and with the mathematics? What role does small-group interaction play in your instructional decision making? Do you hear similar or different things from what Lana observed? Make and implement a plan for helping *all* students contribute in mathematically and socially appropriate ways when they work in small groups.

Reference

Grouws, Douglas. *Conceptions of Mathematics Inventory.* Iowa City: University of Iowa, 1994.

Hopkins, David. *A Teacher's Guide to Classroom Research.* 3rd ed. New York: Open University Press and McGraw-Hill, 2002.

Thoughts to Remember

Courtney Cazden

This book is for both teachers and teacher educators, and could not be more timely for both. Widespread efforts are being made throughout the United States and in other countries to meet the economic challenges of globalization. The goal is to transform public education from a historically top-down transmission system for a stable economy to a more open classroom-communication system that values learners' engagement and learners' initiative in considering, even creating in imagination, alternatives to the status quo. I can personally attest to such efforts in Singapore despite its current high ranking in international achievement comparisons.

All such efforts require newly designed professional development. University researcher Beth's first chapter includes a brief description of the set of experiences that engaged the eight teacher-researcher authors over the project's first three years. The teacher-researchers' chapters, certainly those by Patty, Darin, and Lana to which I am responding, attest to the power of those experiences. And that affirmation, in turn, attests to the power of the professional development design. I could not tell from Beth's brief description how much the set of experiences enacted with the teacher-researchers and described here was completely preplanned, nor at what points the enactment was modified in response to Beth's reflection during the process or to suggestions from the teachers. From my overall sense of the importance of sensitive listening as one of the powerful messages of this book, my hunch is that the professional development, like the subsequent classroom teaching, was in some ways "co-designed." Here at the beginning, I highlight the importance of all the book's ideas for teacher educators.

The Power of Reflection

Patty tells us right at the beginning that hers is a "journey of reflection" and goes on to describe what that journey entailed. She lists three specific professional development experiences that became especially important: mapping her beliefs about mathematics teaching, the readings and group discussion of the readings, and being given the university researcher's analysis of her own baseline interaction with her students. The contrast between what she centrally believed—"Math is all about thinking."—and what she enacted—"all about right answers and learning procedures"—was particularly powerful. Patty describes the detailed changes that she planned for countering her IRE habits—changes in the questions she would ask and in the time she would wait after asking and after a student's response.

Learning in Small Groups

In contrast with Patty and Lana, Darin does not reproduce for us his mapping of "what is closest to my heart in teaching." Perhaps individual reflection, which so effectively contrasted for Patty with the realities of her baseline teaching, did not have the same effect for Darin. Instead he emphasizes what he gained from listening to his peers talk about their readings and about what was happening in their classrooms. When reading articles that contain ideas new to us, we are all too apt to adapt what we read to what we already know and believe. We are too apt to read, in other words, with our old mindset. So we benefit from talking over our interpretations with other readers who will offer different responses.

In the same way, when trying to make changes in our habitual ways of acting, we may have difficulty thinking beyond them and imagining anew. Again, Darin was helped to imagine how his classroom could become different by hearing about approaches that his peers were trying out. Because the group of all eight teacher-researchers and two university researchers adds to a seminar size of ten, I call it a small group, in which both listening and speaking are expected of all participants.

Even though we are not given descriptions of how these group discussions were conducted, their effectiveness reinforces for me the widespread recommendation that whenever possible, professional development should be planned to include such discussions and the mutual support they provide.

Issues about the Value of Academic Language

Both mathematics and discourse analysis have their own technical ways of naming and discussing ideas, and both teachers and teacher educators may wonder about their conceptual value. We read in chapter 2 that the teacher-researchers found some of these new ways of talking about discourse, such as *hedging,* amusing and had never felt the need to use that term themselves. But reading about *revoicing* clearly had a different afterlife within the project as a whole. "The idea of revoicing ... remains a significant idea that we have focused on in the group" and becomes a focus of several of the later teacher-researcher chapters.

As chapter 2 points out, learning new words is rarely just a matter of mere vocabulary; more important, the learning is conceptual as well. For students, learning the mathematical term *slope* serves the same valuable function as learning the term *revoicing* does for the teacher-researchers. In both instances, hearing and speaking the new word in a variety of contexts infuse it with an ever wider and richer set of meanings. Only the consistent use of the new term makes that accrual possible.

Between these extremes of dismissible hedges and widely adopted revoicing is a discourse event for which the teacher-researchers already have a colloquial name, "interruption." Why try to adopt the technical alternative, *overlapping speech?* Only if we have a valid pedagogical reason, and I suggest that we do. Naming an overlap by the pejorative term "interruption" assumes that the overlapper, by intent or effect, stops the first speaker in midthought. That outcome is often true when the teacher overlaps a student, simply by virtue of the teacher's authoritative position as leader of the discourse. But what if the overlappers are both, or all, students, erupting in too-eager engagement and without either the intent or the effect of silencing anyone. Do they always deserve the same negative judgment that the name "interruption" implies?

Valuable Benefits of Technology

Darin and Lana describe different benefits of various forms of technology. Almost in passing, Darin mentions the value of his school's new document projectors, especially for his students. "I think," he begins, with a modest hedge, "that this technology change allowed for students to take more ownership in the class and better represent their thinking because they could directly put their work up for all to see."

Lana started with an assumption of technology's conceptual benefits, and decided that her action research project would focus on how the students' talk around technology could be improved. A need for improvement became clear when watching videotapes of her teaching with graphing calculators showed that her assumption had been wrong. "Somehow in the act of *doing the procedure,* I assumed students would *understand the mathematical concept....* I believed that students automatically made sense of the mathematics, so it did not demand explanation, exploration, or communication" (emphasis in the original). Lana came to understand that technology can indeed enable richer conceptual understandings, but not by its use alone.

The Matter of Mathematics Equity

At the forefront in these three teacher-researcher reports is their understandable concern, first, for making changes in their teaching and their students' learning considering their students as a group. But at some point, teachers have to confront the fact of differentiated participation and learning among their students, even in the midst of "really good" discussions. They have to confront, in short, the problem of teaching for more equitable mathematics learning. Issues of equity pervade all subject areas. But they are especially acute in mathematics because of the crucial role of mathematics understanding and achievement in students' access to educational and employment opportunities.

Realizing that she could learn more about individual students by careful observation than through questionnaires, Lana videotaped her small problem-solving groups while engaged in solving quadratic problems. In one group, she listened carefully to how the different students interacted.

> All the group members spoke, but the student who was the lowest performer talked only about nonmathematical things. Why? Another student, who was struggling but motivated, asked others in his small group for help and clarification. Did he have enough confidence and mathematical power to participate even though doing so meant confessing understandings that might be perceived as inferior to those of his group members? One student talked very fast, as if she were just proclaiming her knowledge rather than sharing it to help others. The fourth student talked in support and confirmation at a tempo that made it easier to learn.

Lana gained this new awareness of individual differences near the end of her project, so it becomes "important to pursue." Yes, not easy but important—for university researchers and teacher educators as well, worthy itself of a focus for future projects. (See an article by Deborah Ball and colleagues [2005] about this issue, with an extended example of Cassandra, a third grader in the same class as Shea, the central student in the *Shea's Numbers* videorecording [Ball 1993] that all the teacher-researchers watched and discussed.)

In exploring ways to help students like that "lowest performer" in Lana's class, a suggestion of what *not* to do comes from a Singapore colleague. Ridzuan Bin Abdul Rahim has focused his research on mathematics teaching, especially as it may be differentiated for students in higher and lower achievement groups. In reading transcripts of tapes of classroom lessons, he noticed one striking instance in which two groups of students were studying the same mathematics concept, but only the higher-performing group was taught the appropriate technical terminology. Ridzuan, himself an experienced mathematics teacher, suggests that the confusions evident among students in the transcript of the lower-performing group were at least partly due to the absence of that discriminating term. Without it, both the teacher and the students had difficulty coordinating and focusing their attention on the mathematics phenomenon in question. So teachers are advised not to withhold technical terms in their efforts to help low-achieving students.

Changing Oneself Is Hard!

All three teacher-researchers understandably express feelings of discouragement and disappointment in themselves at some point during this project:

> My goal for next year is to begin the slow process of moving from a calculational approach to a conceptual approach to teaching. The article [by Thompson et al.] pointed out that making this shift is not only a challenge but can also be a bit scary.... I will always need to be on guard against falling back into the old habits. (Patty)

> I have an ongoing struggle in my head during the course of a discussion. At the end of a lesson I often feel worn out. I am mentally exhausted because of those internal battles.... I am continually listening to [students'] ideas and conducting my own conversation with myself. But ... the more I learned [from the discourse project], the more I realized that the changes were not as hard to make as I once thought. (Darin)

> This chapter is just a snapshot along a path of improvement that is longer and harder than I expected. I anticipated that changing my practice by examining and then improving the talk in my classroom would involve hard work. I did not anticipate that examining my practice in this way would require a deeper awareness of what happens in the process of learning, interacting, and knowing.... Increased awareness can be painful. (Lana)

The kind of support given to these volunteer teacher-researchers will become even more essential when teacher educators take on the harder, but eventually essential, job of working with teachers who have not volunteered.

References

Ball, Deborah L. *Shea's Numbers*. VHS. Ann Arbor: University of Michigan, 1993. Videorecording.

Ball, Deborah L., Imani M. Goffney, and Hyman Bass. "The Role of Mathematics Instruction in Building a Socially Just and Diverse Democracy." *Mathematics Educator* 15, no. 1 (2005): 2–6.

SECTION 3

Tensions, Dilemmas, and Questions in the Process of Changing Discourse Practices

CHAPTER 6

Students' Ownership and Relinquishing Control

Jeff Marks

My eighth-grade students come into the classroom on a day in November of 2005, some joking with one another or catching up on the latest gossip; others solemnly walk in a straight line to their desks, which in turn are arranged in straight lines. Animated conversation continues as the class bell rings, supposedly signifying the start of mathematics class, but the students' behavior does not change. Desktops are covered with notebooks that have not been opened. Students are turned around in their chairs, continuing their all-important talk.

A minute later, I, their mathematics teacher, walk to the overhead projector, engage in a little small talk with someone—although from the reactions of the students it is hard to ascertain exactly with whom I am speaking—and turn on the overhead projector, which contains a transparency that states today's date, the learning goal for the day, and the homework for that night.

JM: Thanks for showing up on this beautiful day. [One student says something inappropriate to another student.] Excuse me? That's kind of a harsh word. Were you just playing around?

Joe: It's raining out.

JM: From tornados on the weekend to snow supposedly later on. Not necessarily here, but it may to the north. Um, the assignment due today was nothing. We, uh, cross that off, because at the end of the period we just realized that it would probably be better to go with my longer plans and spend today working on it. Especially because we had a number of people absent yesterday, so it worked out better to keep it in terms with those same plans. The assignment tonight, you could cross out "tonight" and say "today in class" because that's what you're gonna be working on in class is, um, calculating area and perimeter, and the way I approach this is, starting off on Friday you folks were supposed to read about it on your own, because it's a review of sixth- and seventh-grade material. And then the focus today really is to try and call upon the knowledge that you already have and then to practice the form of it, how you write it out as much as anything else. Um, what's gonna serve as quote "the lesson of the day" is our warm-up. And really it should take about ten minutes just for me to finalize and make sure you know what you're supposed to do, and then you're off on your own the rest of the period. So if you have that down for your assignment, you can put [it] away. You hopefully have a calculator. You hopefully have your learning logs out. And I'll review this. If you weren't here yesterday, what we did is kind of finish up on those four-column notes that you worked on on Friday of last week.

And I continue as I reveal the warm-up problems for the class. The four warm-up problems are on perimeter and area of a parallelogram, triangle, and trapezoid and the area of a composite shape. As the students get started, I remind them of the three steps that the textbook suggested they take to solve the problems:

JM: What I would suggest to you is that you look at your notes from yesterday, if you were here, and especially look at those three steps, in general, that you're supposed to do. The first one is supposed to be, um, write down the formula. The second one is supposed to be substituting in the value of the variable. The third one, you were supposed to come up with your answer. And practice on the form, especially on these three. Because those are pretty clear-type formulas. And then number four, I think Andrew's quote "formula," or way of solving these, you have in your notes also, and try to, and go ahead and do these on your own

> the next couple of minutes. I'm just gonna walk around and pick people to write these up on the board. If you weren't here yesterday, try the best that you can based on what you read over the weekend. And you are about a day behind, but hopefully today you'll get caught up. Question? ...

As students begin to work on the problems at the board, the student I had had a conversation with in the hallway at the start of the class walks into the room and proceeds without a word to her desk in the back. Students quietly work on the problems as I drink water from my travel mug and then hand out papers by walking around to every student and placing a graded paper on his or her desk. More than six minutes have gone by, and I have not invited the students to join in any talk while I have spoken more than three hundred words.

The class continues with my picking certain students to go up to the board and write out their model answers—answers that I know will be correct because I had previously checked them while walking around as the students worked on them. After the students write out their answers, they turn around and walk back to their seats. *I* explain *their* solutions to the class. On the last problem, I reference another student's solution and how it provided an alternative way to solve a composite area problem. Students then proceed to work quietly on their assignment.

If an administrator had been doing an evaluation of this class period, a class period which, for me, could be referred to as fairly typical that year, she or he might have checked boxes that said things like "teacher exhibited control of the classroom" and "students were well-behaved." But as I grew aware of how I controlled aspects of my classroom I simultaneously grew more concerned about the effect that this control was having on the students' learning. In the following pages I provide background information, analyze several classroom exchanges to illustrate how I sometimes controlled students in ways that were surprising to me, and discuss how I am now giving up some of this control by structuring activities in ways that facilitate students' involvement and ownership. I conclude by pointing to where I hope to go from here.

Background

My teaching assignments over the past thirteen years have ranged from teaching first-year algebra to an accelerated group of sixth graders at a middle school to teaching geometry to ninth through twelfth graders this past year at the high school. The transcripts in this chapter are from an eighth-grade general mathematics class during the 2005–2006 school year and from a geometry class during the 2007–2008 school year.

The first few years of teaching middle school were an exhilarating experience for me. The unofficial mentors in my department formed the bedrock of the school district's mathematics teachers. With their support, I was able to carve out my own teaching identity. At the same time, however, I felt tense as I watched them teach in the same Initiate-Respond-Evaluate (IRE) format I had experienced as a student and that I ultimately implemented as a teacher. Although I expanded my knowledge about multiple intelligences, created lessons to appeal to different types of students, entertained (at least I thought I did) my students with monologues of jokes and witty references, and required my students to write in journals and do projects, I still assigned traditional homework and filled up entire class periods with my words and my actions.

Very few "whys" could be found in my questioning patterns (see chapter 3 for more on questioning patterns); instead, I threw out a question to my students and they responded with an answer. I typically then followed with another leading question that either dismissed or accepted their answer or even provided the students with the answer that I had wanted them to get. Although I could not articulate it at the time, I sensed that I was interfering with their learning, for, as Franke, Kazemi, and Battey (2007) said, "learning is not about receiving information; it is about engaging in sense making as we participate together" (pp. 228–29).

The feedback I was getting from administrators, both at the school level and at the district level, was still positive and complimentary, but what I was seeing in my classroom on a daily basis did not always merit praise. I knew things had to change—I even considered changing careers several times—and then went to a meeting about voluntary participation in a research project about "discourse" (whatever that meant!). A conversation with chocolate-croissant-armed Beth and Michelle and a reflective moment on my part about how I could use this opportunity as a vehicle to relieve the tension I was feeling in my teaching sealed my involvement with the project.

Although I am still uncertain about the exact reasons for the change—maybe a combination of frustration with changes in administration, changes in students' and parents' attitudes, and changes within myself—I finished teaching at the middle school during the 2005–2006 school year and then took an offer extended by a former colleague to join her at a high school in the same district. My classes at the high school level are much more racially diverse than those I taught at the middle school. More than 40 percent of the high school's population is eligible for free and reduced-price lunch, and many different languages are spoken in the hallways.

At about the same time as the school change occurred, I read an article by Robyn Zevenbergen (2001) titled "Mathematics, Social Class, and Linguistic Capital: An Analysis of Mathematics Classroom Interactions." A section that resonated with me was her summary of work done by Heath (1983) that said that students from "socially disadvantaged backgrounds are more likely to be exposed to declarative statements when expected to undertake tasks. In contrast, middle-class parents are more likely to pose a pseudoquestion when requesting that their children undertake tasks" (Zevenbergen 2001, p. 202). This quotation helped me understand that different students might come to school with different understandings and interpretations of the ways I was giving them directions and instructions. This realization made me leery about what I wanted to try in my much more racially and economically diverse high school classroom. The more diverse the students, the more potential that arose for misinterpretations of the ways in which I was trying to control—and now limit control of—students' social and mathematical behavior.

A Look at the Beginning Videotapes: Controlling the Classes

One of the first observations that was videotaped in September of 2005 made apparent the extent to which I controlled students—not only by the number of words I spoke but also by *how* I was speaking to students. The following transcript shows an interaction between myself and a student as I introduced the concept of slope by having students stack books, measure the height of the stack of books, record the height for each iteration, and make predictions based on the height and the resulting equation:

JM: Yeah, right. Now think, hold that thought, OK. Because you're not only just finding the thickness of twenty-five books, but you're also gonna put them on top of your desk. So what would you have to do after you found the thickness of twenty-five books?

Angie: You have to add forty-one and [inaudible].

JM: Does it sound plausible to you?

Angie: Yeah.

JM: OK, think about that, and work through that on number six, try [parts] A and B and then see if your answers to A and B are about the same as what those guys came up with. They're not gonna be exact, but they're gonna be close. And then go back and try number five. Wait a minute, now, this isn't quite—tell me what you did.

The exchange lasted only one minute, yet I essentially gave the student ten commands, ranging from *think* to *work* to *tell.* Again, not only did I utter a high number of teacher words compared with student words and not only is the IRE framework alive and well, but I also seem to exert a sense of control in the choice of words that I used: *think, work, see, wait,* and *tell.* I noticed that I did not use pronouns or students' names to refer to the people I was interacting with; rather, I used these words alone as depersonalized commands. In reading the transcript, I cringe as I think about the impersonal nature of these types of directions and wonder what kind of impact it had on the students. Were these commands the type of requests that this student was used to in her home life? Did the impersonal nature somehow make her feel disconnected and compel her to give up ownership of her learning in the classroom? Did my awareness of issues in her life outside school affect my word choice and tone? Did my perception of her socioeconomic status influence the manner in which I spoke to her, as Zevenbergen mentioned in her book chapter? Or did I bring some of my personal history to the classroom and direct her in a manner that I myself was directed as a student?

The following year, in my ninth-grade class at the new school, I experimented with suspending certain "normal" classroom talking rules, most notably the raising of hands before a student's contribution. I attempted to talk with the students about how they talked, and I encouraged the act of students' explaining to one another whenever questions arose. I feigned ignorance and adopted a shrug-of-the-shoulders approach in response to many questions. On many of the "good" days, students readily answered the questions that were raised by others, whether in their own small group or in other groups somewhere else in the room. On the equally many "bad" days, students seemed to be uneasy with my purposefully decreased use of commands and redirection of questions to class members.

The focus class for my action research project was a geometry class of twenty-three students, mainly ninth and tenth graders. Although I would like to think that no "typical" pattern of discussion was evident in my classroom, I noticed that, even after two years of reading articles about classroom discourse, the pendulum of change swung back hard to the days of teacher-dominated talk and students' passivity even when the activity was set up for students' discussion.

The transcript that follows is from a day in January of 2008. The students were arranged in small groups and given an assignment that involved reading and discussing a problem and then presenting a solution to the class. The following transcript begins about twenty minutes into the class period, when the students begin to present their work to the rest of the class:

> ***Julie:*** [standing at the front of the room] It says that a biconditional is a true statement about the conjunction of two conditionals. We said they are not false [inaudible few words], and then we said our example is, If it is freezing out if and only if it is cold and thirty-two degrees and then, then [student is staring at the transparency].
>
> ***JM:*** Where does it fit in the big picture of things?
>
> ***Julie:*** Oh yeah. We think it will deal with proofs and stuff like that, conditionals [inaudible].
>
> ***JM:*** Thank you. Does anyone have any questions or comments for Miss Julie? [Pause] How about do you have any [drawn out "e"], any concerns about her example? [Pause] How do you know it's a biconditional?
>
> ***Students:*** [overlapping, inaudible responses]
>
> ***JM:*** If and only if. What else? So it can work backwards. So if it is below thirty-two degrees, it's freezing then.... [Pause] Is it considered freezing? [Pause] I don't see anything wrong with it either. So, nice job. Thanks.

Although the student was in front of the room, I nonetheless stole the student's thinking during the whole-class presentation in this exchange. The format of the exchange fits the IRE format, too, even with the student in front of the room. The students in the classroom neither actively acknowledged nor questioned any part of Julie's presentation.

By the end of the period, I had spoken as many words as all the students combined.

When reflecting on what happened in the class period, I remember thinking that small-group work followed by the whole-class presentation was a success because even if students were not vocal during the whole-class portion, most of the students were engaged during the small-group portion. Still, I was not happy with my tendency to jump into the silence that overtook the room at times.

Several days after the class period just described, I made up a quick two-question survey that asked students to respond to the prompt "What do you expect when you come into the mathematics classroom?" Since I had begun watching some of the videotapes from various class periods and thinking about the parts of the class period that really irritated me—and the start of the class periods definitely did!—I wanted their perceptions on, and expectations for, how the class *ought* to start. Below are examples of responses that I received from the students:

- We come in the room to our desks, sit down, check homework, then work.
- Some students get in trouble.
- I think it's OK but we should play games once in a while.
- The teacher tells us what to do … and then beams when we get it right.
- Just about the same as what we did in other math classes.

Generally, their responses indicated that at least some of them understood that there was a routine in class, such as the student who wrote the first comment above or the students who said something about copying down the goal of the day and then attempting the warm-up problems. Some comments were difficult to understand. (One such was the "get in trouble" comment: I never really understood that one, although I do know that if you ask students to get out paper or to take their seats, some may interpret that instruction as "getting in trouble." I am not really sure why.) The types of students' comments that really struck me, however, were the ones that revealed that the students believed that they were receptors of information (such as the last two in the list) and that they were not really being active in the learning process.

From an informal survey that I did at the start of the school year, I remember typing up responses to the question "How do you best learn?"

The overwhelming majority of the students replied with comments that centered on the teacher's explaining concepts "good" or "completely." The tension that I felt during my earlier years of teaching came back with a greater force than I had experienced before. Here I was, four years after my initial realization and effort to change, and none of my students told me they learned best by being active contributors. Nearly all their responses focused on being observers and note takers and not doers and risk takers. Not only were the students' responses a source of tension for me, but tension also arose between the knowledge I had acquired from my participation in the project and my years of being a student and a teacher. Once again I felt the tension between trying to get students to take more ownership and what students expected of me.

Attempts to Resolve the Conflict and Tension

In April of 2008, Maurice sat in the front of the geometry classroom with the tablet PC. Students were sitting in straight rows—not by my choice but because of issues with sharing the room with another teacher. Maurice started class after I prompted him from the back of the room.

> *JM:* Now, Maurice, I apologize. I probably, I couldn't remember what problem I gave you exactly. So, um, hopefully while, I don't know if that's the exact same one I gave you or not, but hopefully it's close enough that you can figure… [student comment] OK, just wait for them to do it.

At the time, I thought that I would do Maurice a favor by saying something that could keep him from being embarrassed, since I had given him different problems to work on the day before in preparation for being the "student teacher of the day." However, I think I was trying to hear my voice and make my presence known—a sort of subtle way of trying to control some aspect of the class. The subtle control resurfaced throughout the next ten minutes as I supposedly "removed" myself from the warm-up problems.

> [Students are working on rational equation problems amidst a low-level buzz of conversation.]
>
> *Maurice:* Why doncha' raise ya'all's hands when you gets the answer?
>
> [A few hands go up, and students seemingly compare answers with a person near them. Maurice calls on Juan to explain the answer.]

Maurice: What's the first thing you do?

Juan: You, uh, do two...

Maurice: Two to the what?

Juan: x equals t over...

JM: [to Maurice] Um, you may have to click on the pen icon at the, above the '*D*.' There you go, yeah, now it's working.

Maurice: So x equals what?

Student: t plus two [inaudible].

Maurice: Mr. Marks, where can I write this?

JM: Um, you could do it to the left, and then you might have enough room on the right to substitute in or something. Unfortunately, with this program it's hard to erase some things.

The warm-up problems continued with Maurice trying to write on the PC tablet and with me interjecting comments every so often, sometimes about technology issues as shown above, sometimes not, as shown below:

[Another minute has passed—now 7.5 minutes into the class period.]

JM: Now the second problem, I did not give Maurice the second problem. But this, oh, this problem is from the test. The next problem is also from the test. These two were very frequently missed on the test. That's why I put them up here. Um, so, now go ahead and try this one. Maurice, you might want to work this one out on a scratch sheet of paper. You might just rely on the studio audience to help you out in a couple of minutes. Your choice, but that one in red is also frequently missed on the test.

Again, as at the beginning of the class period, I seemed to be providing a statement to keep Maurice from being embarrassed while at the same time justifying the choice of problems by mentioning that students missed them frequently on the test. In hindsight, if the problem was worthy of their attention, it should be able to stand on its own and not require my opinion. Instead, my comment seemed to be an instance of "marking importance" (Lemke 1990, p. 67), in which I, afraid of losing control of the class discussion, indicated that the topic at hand "was a matter of special importance." The irony in this situation is not lost on me: there I am trying to relinquish control and allow for student ownership, yet I act in a manner that is at odds with this goal.

What I notice from the videotape of this first day (in which I am attempting to minimize my footprint at the beginning of the period and give more students an opportunity to have a voice) is that, although I gave one student the opportunity to be in charge, I often felt the need to interject, either clearing up technology issues or giving the student in charge an excuse should he make a mistake. Whether I stepped in for control or whether I wanted to provide a "face-saving" (Bills 2000) measure in the event that Maurice stumbled is difficult for me to ascertain. Either way, I seemed to have difficulty allowing a mistake to occur—in much the same way that I controlled the answers in the transcript from November 2005 at the middle school.

On the positive side, I noticed that more students were contributing. The number of words spoken by the students grew compared with the word counts from the baseline data. Unfortunately, owing to the quality of the videorecording, I was not able to decipher many of the students' conversations.

Several days after the period in which Maurice was student teacher of the day, Alem agreed at the last second to lead the class. Although the students had readily agreed to take turns in leading the class, on some days I had neglected to clarify, in advance, who was going to be in charge of a particular class period. I knew Alem well, since he had been a student in my class the previous year, and I "volunteered" him to be in charge as he walked into the classroom.

As students came into the classroom, they were asked to put up solutions from their homework assignment to randomly chosen problems that focused on naming coordinates on rectangular prisms, finding midpoints, and finding distances. I did not think much at the time about calling students to the board without giving them prior warning, but several issues with this impromptu decision have stayed with me.

First, students were held accountable for their assignments, although they were not immediately put "on the spot" because the problems were solved ahead of time as homework. In fact, in the videotape, a couple of students are seen conferring with one another about their solution. From all the reflecting I have done regarding the choices I make in the classroom, I think that I am really aware of students' being uncomfortable in the mathematics classroom. Whether I have come to that feeling because of a number of students' comments over the years or because my wife never had a positive experience in mathematics class is unclear. I just know that I do have this feeling.

Second, in hindsight, I wonder what the impact would have been had I turned the task of assigning problems to students as they entered the classroom over to the student leader of the day. Envision Alem at the door informing the students of the problems they were expected to explain while in front of the room. This act would have minimized my presence at the start of the class even more and would have given the students more ownership of the beginning of the class.

Finally, going back to that day, I saw students in the videotape talking to one another, standing up at the board, and writing problems on the board before, during, and a bit after the bell rang. Alem readied himself in the front of the room with the teacher's edition of the textbook. Students finished recording the solutions on the board and moved to their seats. I moved to the back of the room, and Alem (who spent the first six years of his life in rural Sudan) started off:

[Miscellaneous chatter is occurring.]

Alem: Good mornin', class. How ya doin'?

[Several students comment, including a male student asking "Who are you?" Papers rustle, and low-level chatter continues.]

Alem: OK, I'm going to read off the questions.

[Alem reaches out to a student who was handing him Alem's own homework assignment.]

Alem: Is everyone ready to check?

JM: Maurice, turn around please. [I motion with a circular hand gesture to a student who is off-camera. The class be-comes quieter, but some quiet conversation is still apparent.]

Alem started reading the answers while one or two students who had yet to get out their assignments softly cried out, "Wait, wait." Alem continued to read answers to the questions that I had not asked students to put on the board. I had omitted these solutions because I assumed that no one would have difficulty with the first few homework problems.

Although Alem's reading of answers lasted a couple of minutes, I privately spoke to a student in the back to get him to pull his assignment out so that he could be ready if Alem needed him. When I compared this class beginning with the videotape from three years earlier, I saw that the students in the classroom were chattier, at least after the person "in charge" started the class, but some of that talk was because the class had started with students' putting problems on the board. The big change I saw was that several minutes after the bell had rung, I had spoken only four words in front of the class ("Maurice, turn around please").

The period continued with Alem reading the answers to the "easier" questions, and then opening the discussion:

Alem: Now we have number eleven. Whoever did number eleven, could you go up to the board now?

[Ned gets up and goes to the board.]

Ned: I got negative one, negative one, negative one [ordered triple (–1, –1, –1)] because, because that's what the answer is.

[Laughter by several students]

Peter: Could you explain the problem?

Ned: [interrupting Peter]: 'Cuz zero minus two divided by two, negative two, is negative one [Ned points to the other answers in the ordered triple]. And it's the same number.

Alem: Any questions for Ned?

[Some other indecipherable comments are made by other students. Most are asking one another what Ned said because he was relatively soft-spoken. A few students chuckle.]

Safet: Over here. Yeah, I have a question. How did I get negative two, negative two, negative two [ordered triple (–2, –2, –2)]?

Tom: 'Cuz you added wrong.

Safet: Are you serious?

Peter: You add the integers.

Ellen: I don't think you, did you not square-root it?

Safet: I don't know.

[A chorus of students say, "What!?" which makes Ellen's question hard to hear. Safet's response occurred at the same time. Ellen laughs and says, "Wait, that's wrong too!"]

Now the class was in collective disarray. Several students were laughing. A couple of other students told Ellen, "No, you square-root the distance formula." Peter also attempted to explain the problem to Ellen, and one male student was now checking his cell phone. Alem, who was still sitting at the front of the class, said something to the class. I intervened to get the class to focus on the problem:

JM: Hey, hey. Ned, can you show your work on this? So, yeah. Tom, can you loan your book to Ned so he can see the problem?

I continued to walk around the classroom with my grade book in hand as the students showed me their homework assignments. Since moving to the high school, I had adopted the practice of other mathematics teachers in the department of giving "credit" for completion of the assignment. Although I am walking around the room, my contact with the students was fairly brief and did not seem very controlling or authoritative. In the class that day, the students were exhibiting a lot more ownership of both how the class was running and the grades they were receiving on their assignments. I am not quite sure now, however, how much more beneficial this outcome was to the students' learning. In fact, much of the students' sharing focused on the procedures and steps students took rather than why the answers made sense (for more about this aspect, see chapter 3). Progress was evident, however, in students' ownership of the activities taking place.

Ned continued writing the problem on the board with Peter's help. Some discussion occurred about the difference between subtracting positive numbers and adding negative numbers. I refocused the class again because it seemed that about half the students were watching Ned and half were not.

JM: So, in general, Ned, how do you find the midpoint?

[Class is now totally silent.]

Ned: You take, um, x one, x one minus x two.

JM: Careful.

Peter: Plus *x* two.

Ned: Plus *x* two.

Peter: Which happens to be negative.

Ned: So when you add, it's like subtracting.

Alem: Any questions?

A number of other students chimed in, either to their neighbors or to Ned, who was standing at the board. Judging from the videotape, fourteen of the eighteen students who were present that day appeared to have interacted either with the whole class or with a person sitting near them.

A couple of other random comments and questions were made. Alem then thanked Ned, who returned to his seat. Alem returned to reading homework answers. I continued to walk around the room to record assignments. DeJone walked to the side blackboard, seemingly getting ready to explain his problem, then sat down as Alem went on. Alem backtracked, and DeJone wrote his work out on the board, with his back to the class, then quietly read his answers. Again, he was thanked, a few students clapped lightly, and more answers were read by Alem.

As Alem read the answers to the part of the assignment involving calculating distances, Julian asked if someone could explain. I told him that, on the next one, someone would explain up at the board, and he replied with an "OK."

Tricia: [as she approached her solution on the board]: OK, so the origin is just zero, zero, zero [(0, 0, 0)]. So you just take two minus zero, which is two. Then you square it, and you get four. And since all of these are the same, you do four plus four plus four, which is twelve, and then you have to take the square root of twelve, which is this [pointed to her answer].

A smattering of applause occurred as she walked back to her seat, and Alem went back to reading the answers. Nine minutes into the class now, and I thought that my presence at the start was minimal. The conventions and routines of the classroom worked on that day. As with other successful moments in my classrooms, I think that several small components worked together. The consistent reinforcement of classroom expectations for behavior, the daily greeting of students as they walked into my classroom, the routines of the class, the choice of the student to lead the class, and the topic being studied each played a role in why the class functioned well that day. Students worked together to go over homework problems, talked to one another, moved around the room, shared solutions, and so on. Furthermore, I relinquished much of my control over the beginning of the class period.

A Glimpse into the Future

Students come into my classroom on a day in 2012. The students' conversation does not subside. Rather, it changes its focus from being social to being about derivatives of functions. After a quick check-in with the teacher, the students are soon at their desks, arranged in groups of three or four, and continue with an exploration of the rate of change of cooling liquids. The classroom procedures have already been discussed and rehearsed so that off-task behaviors are minimized and learning opportunities are maximized.

All students are expected to be able to report their findings to the whole class at some point. Working on ensuring the accuracy of their findings, some students are seen moving quietly from group to group and occasionally going to the whiteboard, where they have more space to write out ideas and discuss a solution in front of a larger group of students. I am not seen as the primary source of knowledge. Rather, I remain out of the spotlight and mingle with the groups of students to monitor their progress on the task at hand. I am not the final judge of right and wrong answers, nor do I need to control all the interactions.

To get to this stage, I need to have many more conversations with my students and make explicit the behaviors I want to see. Something I recently tried to do is occasionally make more personal connections with students so as to create a safe environment for them to work. In my own experiences as a student, I know I was not willing to take risks socially or mathematically until I felt safe and felt a connection, and this reservoir of experiences is a driving force for many of the things I do as a teacher. Although very few students have commented to me about how I sometimes start the class period with a quote of the day, a comic strip or poem related to mathematics, or even a few lines from a song that I think might connect with students' experiences, I envision that, as I try to turn over the start of the class to the students, they will be compelled to share lines from their own favorite songs or poetry or quotes. I hope that this kind of sharing can be an entrée into creating an environment in which students will feel safe taking mathematical risks. I just need to remind myself to set the boundaries and let the students engage in making sense of mathematics together. I continue to work toward more careful decisions about when and how I intervene and control. This process will evolve every year, and I hope to continue to relinquish control so that students feel safe to share ideas and to challenge one another in mathematically productive ways.

Reflecting and Connecting with Practice

- Administer a short survey to, or have a brief discussion with, your students about what they expect in your classroom in terms of participating and actively engaging with mathematics. What expectations and assumptions do your students have about mathematics or mathematics class?
- Consider suspending some of your "normal" classroom talking rules, such as raising hands before student contributions. What might be some benefits of this change? For two weeks, tell students that they do not have to raise their hands to contribute to the discussion. How does this change seem to influence the ways in which students participate?
- Select an activity structure from your own classroom that you think you would like to change, and try some of Jeff's suggestions for turning over more ownership to students. What are some of the challenges? What are some of the payoffs? Do you invite your students to participate in mathematics every day? If so, how? If not, what might you do to extend this invitation?
- Jeff considered both social and mathematical aspects of his control in the classroom. When and how do you see yourself intervening socially? When and how do you see yourself controlling the mathematics? What are your reasons for controlling each of these aspects of the classroom? What may you be losing by controlling each of them? What may your students be losing because of your control in these situations?
- Jeff ended his chapter with a description of a hypothetical scenario from his classroom in the future. Reflect on what your "ideal" classroom discourse would be, and write about your future classroom. What goals do you have for your discourse? For your students? What kinds of tasks are they engaged in? Who is facilitating the discussion?

References

Bills, Liz. "Politeness in Teacher-Student Dialogue in Mathematics: A Sociolinguistic Analysis." *For the Learning of Mathematics* 20 (2000): 40–47.

Franke, Megan, Elham Kazemi, and Daniel Battey. "Understanding Teaching and Classroom Practice in Mathematics." In *Second Handbook of Research on Mathematics Teaching and Learning*, edited by Frank Lester, pp. 225–56. Charlotte, N.C.: Information Age Publishing and National Council of Teachers of Mathematics, 2007.

Heath, Shirley B. *Ways with Words: Language, Life, and Work in Communities and Classrooms.* New York: Cambridge University Press, 1983.

Lemke, Jay. *Talking Science: Language, Learning, and Values.* Norwood, N.J: Ablex Publishing Corporation, 1990.

Zevenbergen, Robyn. "Mathematics, Social Class, and Linguistic Capital: An Analysis of Mathematics Classroom Interactions." In *Sociocultural Research on Mathematics Education,* edited by Bill Atweh, Helen J. Forgasz, and Ben Nebres, pp. 201–16. Mahwah, N.J.: Lawrence Erlbaum Associates, 2001.

CHAPTER 7

Revoicing: The Good, the Bad, and the Questions

Jean Krusi

I HAVE always been interested in how students think about mathematics. I was also interested in starting more meaningful conversations in my classroom. I wanted students to take more ownership of the mathematical discourse in the classroom. I joined the Discourse Project with this goal in mind. When I looked at the analysis of my baseline discourse data, however, and saw how much I was talking (lots!) compared with how much my students were talking (brief turns), I was horrified. How could this discrepancy be occurring? I asked a lot of questions. I probed for student thinking. I certainly asked, "How did you get that?" and "Can you explain your thinking?" *a lot.* What other habits did I need to pay attention to, habits that might have counteracted my probing of students' thinking? In this chapter, I describe some of the language choices I have made and the issues, tensions, and questions I have grappled with as a result of those choices.

Looking at My Classroom Discourse

Looking at the videotapes of my classroom practice, and especially at the transcripts of those lessons, I realized that I asked the kinds of questions that probe students' thinking, but I was not as good at really listening and following up with additional questions. My classroom also rarely had student-to-student interactions rather than student-to-teacher interactions. Where were the conversations I thought would help my students understand and learn mathematics?

As we read and discussed the literature about discourse and analyzed and discussed our classroom practice, I worked to improve my teaching

Some of the ideas we read about and talked about resonated with me, and I tried to incorporate them into my teaching. Some strategies, such as "wait time" *after asking a question* (Rowe 1986), were familiar although not always implemented well. Wait time *after a student's response* was a new idea to me. In fact, not only did I not give wait time after a response, I sometimes began revoicing while the student was still speaking. This habit of overlapping the speech of my students appalled me. I realized that if I wanted students to react to the comments of other students, I needed to give them time to think about and frame a response, and I also needed to give them the opportunity to formulate a response. So I decided to work on wait time, pacing, and revoicing.

Looking at Revoicing

I found the idea of *revoicing* (O'Connor and Michaels 1993, 1996) particularly interesting. I use the term *revoicing* to mean any form of restating an idea presented by another. Revoicing may be a simple parroting back of what was previously said, or it may be a restatement that reshapes the original in some way, perhaps with clearer language or with the addition of mathematical vocabulary. *Revoicing* was a move that I already used. I started to pay attention to how I used it. The more I looked at revoicing in my classroom, the more questions I had, such as, What was the role of revoicing in my classroom? How does revoicing support or undermine students' thinking? When I revoiced, did the student still "own" the idea? At what point am I clarifying or promoting the student's idea, and at what point may I somehow take it over? Did revoicing focus students' attention, or did students get the idea that they did not actually need to listen to one another, because I would revoice important ideas and questions? How does revoicing encourage students to react to an idea? In what ways did my revoicing control the conversation? How could I get the students to revoice instead of doing it myself?

I found that revoicing filled a number of different functions in my classroom. Here is a short transcript from my classroom at the beginning of the Discourse Project.

JK: OK, let's think about this for a second. Here's my [equilateral] triangle; here's
my [regular] hexagon [pointing to a diagram on the board]. The perimeter is the
same for both of them, so what do I know about the sides of the hexagon compared

04 to the sides of the triangle?

05 *MS:* They're half as long.

06 *JK:* They're half as long. How do you know they're half as long?

07 *MS:* 'Cuz there's twice as many.

08 *JK:* There's twice as many equaling the same total, right? Does that make sense?

(Classroom Transcript, 12/31/05)

At the beginning of the Discourse Project, my revoicing often seemed to be a connector, affirming and amplifying what the student said and connecting what the student said with what I said next. The first sentence in line 06 is an example. This type of revoicing move, in which I repeated what the student said, was pervasive in my classroom discourse. I think the affirmation of the student's comment can be helpful, but I do not think my revoicing in line 06 adds anything mathematical to the conversation. However, it did make my voice much more dominant. One of my goals is to increase students' involvement and participation, and this type of revoicing may, in fact, do the opposite. It may increase my voice and decrease the opportunity for, or at least the impact of, the students' voices.

Another function of revoicing is to help clarify a student's statement. The revoicing in line 08 is an example in which I added some information to clarify the student's statement and make it more precise, asking for his confirmation that this extra information fit his statement by adding the query "right?" However, pausing at that juncture would be important to allow him time to agree or disagree, and I am not sure that I did so. The second question shifted the question to the class. The underlying assumption was that we both, as well as the rest of the class, understood that we were talking about twice as many *sides*. My revoicing could have made this assumption explicit. As I read this transcript now, I ask myself whether this revoicing was helpful to my students. Could I have asked another student to do this revoicing? Would that approach have been more productive?

Revoicing can also layer mathematical vocabulary onto a statement (see chapter 9 for more about this topic). In another example from the first year, we were reviewing linear equations in slope-intercept form. My statement served to layer two mathematical terms (*vertical component* and *y-intercept*), reinforcing mathematical vocabulary.

JK: Okay, Kevin, what do I need to know?

Kevin: Um, the vertical component.

JK: Okay, can I say the *y*-intercept?

Kevin: Yes.

Another function was to revoice back to a student to determine whether the restatement would trigger reevaluation of the original statement. I found that the inflection I used in revoicing differed when I was revoicing an incorrect statement as compared with a correct one. When revoicing an incorrect statement, I tended to lift my voice at the end, making it a question, thus cuing that I was questioning the student's idea. I revoiced correct contributions with statements, which seemed to confirm the student's contribution. In these situations, revoicing served an evaluative role. After realizing this effect, I tried not to indicate whether the statement was correct or incorrect in my revoicing. Rather, I encouraged students to react to the original statement, allowing the students to offer changes to the original.

An obvious function of revoicing is to give students voice. Rebroadcasting a student's statement helps ensure that the statement is heard. The most common use of revoicing for me was to rebroadcast a statement to the whole class, usually with an explicit or implied message to react. I assumed that this rebroadcasting function was important, so I repeated many student statements.

Investigating Revoicing in My Classroom

As I examined my practice, I began to wonder whether what I was doing enabled students to opt out of listening to one another. After all, if I was going to restate what the student said, louder and maybe more clearly, why should my students put forth the effort to listen to one another? If students were not listening to one another, they certainly would not be responding directly to one another either. This kind of revoicing might have been undermining one of my goals. I wanted to determine whether I could stop being the intermediary in the conversations. I also worried that the students might think that an idea counted only when the teacher said it. If that was true, who owned the idea—the originator or the teacher? The questions I have been raising so far nagged at me more and more.

I began to pay more attention to how and when I was revoicing. What would happen if I revoiced less? What would happen if I used revoicing differently? I decided to try several things. I would attempt to get students to revoice more often. I would try to revoice only when I thought revoicing was important, which meant breaking the pattern I often used of repeating students' contributions. I paid attention to the role of revoicing in my classroom as I made these changes to better understand the way the functions of revoicing changed. I would also pay attention to the nature of the classroom discourse itself; that is, I would attend to whether students seemed to listen to one another more and whether and how they might start to respond to one another's ideas.

As I thought about how I wanted to change the discourse patterns in my classroom, I decided I wanted to involve my students in the process. I started by asking them what made a good classroom discussion. The students seemed to be importing ideas about class discussion from their other classes, possibly indicating that they did not think of mathematics classes as places for rich discussion. We used the ideas of what makes a good discussion, more generally, to produce the following set of discussion norms for our classroom:

- Everyone is listening. Everyone is involved. Everyone puts out ideas. No one is left out.
- No one is talking while someone else is. Take turns.
- Questions are asked. Make your point clearly and quickly. Have facts to back up your point. It is safe to be wrong.
- No rude comments or put-downs. All ideas and opinions are respected. Different points of view are valued. "Out of the box" thinking can be helpful.
- Everyone is understanding—if not at the beginning, then by the end.

Most of these norms are social norms. Some, such as "have facts to back up your point" and "everyone is understanding," do have the potential to suggest mathematical norms. During our discussions, I found that I needed to bring up mathematical norms, such as what counts as evidence in mathematics or the idea of generalizing statements. In the future, I would like to try having a discussion about elements particular to mathematical discourse as a class, with the idea of generating mathematical norms as well as social norms.

Occasionally I asked students to comment on their own participation in our whole-class discussions, sometimes in writing and sometimes orally. Spending time evaluating and discussing participation helps students understand some of the ways they might contribute or participate and also reinforces the expectation that they do participate.

I used the think-pair-share technique quite frequently. When posing a question for whole-class discussion, I asked my students to think about the question individually first, then share their ideas with a partner. This strategy allowed students time to think about their answers and to test them before sharing with the whole group. It also increased the number of students who had a voice and a stake in the discussion. It allowed me to eavesdrop and get an idea of the different approaches students took and the difficulties they were having. I could use this information to sequence responses in the whole-class discussion.

Changes in Revoicing

The following transcript is from September of 2007. Students were given a problem that showed two lines on a grid and were asked to find the point of intersection, which occurred off the grid they were given. The first student made a table of x- and y-values for both lines and found where both lines had the same coordinates.

JK: OK, and how did you decide what to put in the chart? Your chart had what?

Caitlin: x and y.

JK: x and y. So coordinates of points.

Revoicing can function to help make connections between ideas explicit. Here I repeated Caitlin's response and also clarified what x and y referred to, helping her and also her classmates connect the numbers in her chart with the coordinates of the points on the graph. Was my comment helpful for the students? Did I help Caitlin present her idea? Was this connection something I should have asked the class to make, or was saying it myself more efficient and appropriate?

Another student then presented a different strategy for solving the problem:

Robert: [Pointing to an overhead of the graph] Well, these two lines are three squares away, and so it's one, two, three, four, five, six, up. And put the next one where it's only one square away. And then, since at six, right there, it'd have to be, you'd have to go six more to get one square closer; so it'd be twelve.

JK: Okay, what's twelve? The *x*-coordinate or the *y*-coordinate?

Robert: Uh, the *y*-coordinate.

JK: Okay, so you're saying they meet at something, twelve? [writes (__, 12) on the board.] Did you figure out what the *x*-coordinate was?

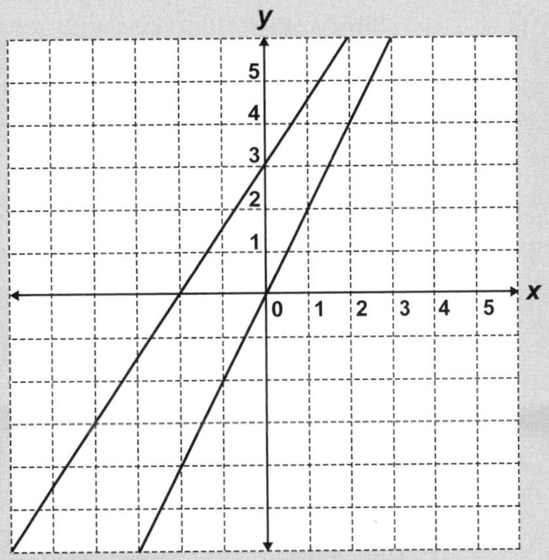

Fig. 7.1. Students were shown this grid and asked to find the point of intersection of the two lines.

Robert: Six.

JK: OK, all right. So who can summarize, don't go away Robert, because you might have to answer questions. Who can summarize what Robert says, do you think?

[A few seconds later]

Lauren: Uh, where he drew the line here earlier, there is [sic] two squares in between the points. And the next two points, that they got closer together, they got six up, one apart. And so if he thought, if he went up another six they would meet.

JK: Okay. Did she summarize accurately?

Robert: Yep.

JK: Is there anything you'd like to add to that?

Robert: Nope.

Here the goal of the revoicing was to help clarify Robert's somewhat unclear explanation of how he found the point of intersection on the basis of the pattern of what happened each time the lines were (horizontally) one unit closer together. Robert used patterns in the geometry of the lines relative to the grid. I wanted other students to understand how to visualize the relationship between the lines in different ways. I wanted the students to see and understand Robert's strategy, since most of them used other methods. I was not sure, however, whether most of Robert's classmates understood his explanation. Revoicing occurred twice here; once by me and once by a classmate. When Robert affirmed that the y-coordinate was 12, I rephrased the answer to indicate several things, both to Robert and to the class. By my saying, "OK, so you're saying they meet at something, twelve?" I reinforced his claim that the y-coordinate was 12, but I also indicated that we were looking at a point, and that we didn't yet know what the x-coordinate was. I also revoiced this idea using written text, recording on the board the point (__ , 12). I was making a shift and a transition from a number to the point, although the shift was not explicit. I followed up by asking about the x-coordinate.

My goal for the second revoicing was to have another student summarize Robert's method. I chose to ask another student, both to increase student participation and to give students the voice and the responsibility for listening, thinking, and summarizing. Asking students to revoice removed me as the significant participant in the conversation. My intention now was to help students take this role. Lauren's ability to revoice accurately, to Robert's satisfaction, indicated that she understood his strategy for solving the problem well enough to say it in her own words. Her explanation was clearer, and was accompanied by nods from her classmates, seemingly indicating that they understood and agreed.

The transcript of this lesson showed a change in some of the discourse patterns from the earlier transcripts. I tried to avoid just repeating what was said and to revoice only when I believed that my revoicing made an important contribution to the discourse. I think that the students more clearly retained their voice and ownership of their ideas. Students were listening to one another, students' turns were longer, and more mathematical thinking and communication were expected. By stepping out of the conversation somewhat, I allowed the students opportunities to step in.

The following is a transcript in which the students were discussing the day's mental-mathematics opener: What is 100 times nine-tenths?

JK: How about 100 times nine-tenths? You might think of it in terms of a decimal. You might think of it as a fraction. OK, tell me how I would do that?

William: Well, it's just like nine-tenths, and then you know that's, ah, a whole, it's ten-tenths is a whole, and so you take off a ten, or one tenth, and basically, it's, like, a tenth could also be, like, ten hundredths. So then you could just then take ten from it.

JK: OK, I think I understood what you are saying. I think....

William: I can't explain.

JK: I think I can sum up what you said, William. You have nine-tenths of 100, and so one-tenth of 100 is ten, so you take that away and you have nine-tenths [of 100]?

William: Yeah.

As I watched this videotape, I found this exchange somewhat problematic. William explained his thinking the first time. Why did he think that he could not do it again? Did my statement "I think I understand" (instead of "I understand") signal to him that his explanation was unclear, and, thinking that he had already done the best he could, he could not respond further? Why did I let him abdicate here and then do the explanation for him? Students had several different strategies for solving this problem. Many students have difficulty with fraction operations, so I wanted all the strategies that students generated to be heard and understood. This mental-mathematics opener was supposed to go relatively quickly, so time was an issue for me. Would asking a student to revoice here have taken much more time? Did my robbing William of his ownership and explanation lead to any larger benefit?

In the following transcript from April 2008, I used revoicing more sparingly. Although I still served as the intermediary and directed a lot of the conversation, my role was more often manager rather than participant. Students were responding directly to one another more often, sometimes to the point that several students were reacting at once.

The textbook provided an arithmetic sequence, starting with two, and increasing by seven each time. The first four terms appeared in a number strip. I wrote this information on the board. We noted the constant increase of seven, and I showed an arrow with plus seven from one term of the sequence to the next. Students needed to decide whether the number 100 would be one of the numbers on the strip.

JK: Think first. [Pause] When you can answer, raise your hand. Do not shout anything out. So the question is, Is 100 on this strip? [Pause] So if I keep listing the numbers, will 100 be one of the numbers I write, or not? So I need a yes or a no from you, and a why.

[Long pause. A number of students have raised their hands.]

JK: Anna, do you think it will be or won't be?

Anna: Will be.

JK: OK. How do you know?

Anna: Uhh …

Ethan: Did she say will or won't?

JK: She said will.

Here, I spoke for Anna. I wish Ethan had asked Anna directly. Should I have directed Ethan's question to Anna to answer? After all, it was her claim! Perhaps my answering the question prevented Ethan's interruption from distracting Anna from framing her explanation.

Anna: If you minus two from a hundred, it's ninety-eight, and it goes into that fourteen times.

JK: Seven times fourteen is ninety-eight? [Pause] Does that convince you the number will be on the strip?

[Several students murmur their assent.]

Here I revoiced to rebroadcast. Anna participated in discussion reluctantly, and I was glad that she was willing to volunteer. She spoke very quietly. This revoicing was to be sure that she was heard.

Ethan: What if you did it, like, a different way?

JK: OK, what did you think about to answer the question, Ethan? Did you agree with Anna or disagree?

Ethan: I concur.

JK: OK. Why do you think it is on the strip?

Ethan: Because if you add seven to twenty-three, it's thirty. There's seventy left, and obviously seven goes into seventy.

JK: OK. That's an interesting strategy. Did you understand what he said?

[Several students agree.]

JK: Okay. [I write it on board.]

Recording Ethan's contribution on the board served as a written revoicing that provided a more permanent record of what Ethan said.

JK: OK, anybody have a different way to think about this one? [Pause] Are some of you not convinced yet?

Luke: [Vehemently] That's not right! [Incredulous tone] That's right?

JK: Well, what do you think?

Luke: No!

JK: No. Why not?

My short revoicing of Luke's turn was used mainly to focus the conversation and to be sure his reasoning was heard. I also deliberately revoiced the "no" as a statement and not as a question. I was trying to remain neutral and not give the students a clue as to whether Luke's claim was valid.

Luke: Because it starts at two.

JK: Yes.

Luke: So, it wouldn't be right, because, um, two isn't, like, a multiple of seven and I don't believe a hundred is, either.

Ben: It's not.

Luke: It's not.

JK: Are any of the numbers on here, on the list, a multiple of seven?

Luke: No. But they aren't a multiple of two.

JK: OK, so Luke needs to be convinced by either Anna or Ethan that 100 is on the strip. Or by someone else.

At this point, I could have restated Luke's argument before inviting students to respond. By not doing so, I was giving the students the message that I thought that they heard and understood what he said and that they were able to respond. At this point, the conversation in the classroom became more animated and more students got involved. Students were also responding directly to one another, with minimal intervention from me. Occasionally several students were speaking at the same time, some in small groups, so sometimes individual comments were hard to hear. Luke continued to maintain that 100 was not on the list.

Luke: No, it's not, though.

Andy: It's right.

LaNiece: I said no at first. I said no.

JK: Ben?

Ben: OK, uh, the way I thought of it was, you subtract seven from a hundred, and it will be ninety-three and then you divide seven by ninety-three and it's not an even number.

Minh: What are you talking about?

[Unidentified student, to Ben]: You mean a whole number?

Ben: Yeah.

Winston: [Talking over Ben] Ben, that makes no sense.

JK: Amy is looking with a very puzzled expression. Do you have a question for Ben? [Pause] It doesn't make sense to you?

Here was a little different spin on a revoicing move. Rather than say something that Amy said, I interpreted Amy's facial expression verbally for the class, many of whom could not see her face. I was giving voice to the confusion many students appeared to experience in the wake of Ben's statement. Ben's statement was an instance of a student's agreement with the correct conclusion based on erroneous reasoning. Ben's reasoning would not have been visible without this type of conversation.

LaNiece: I'm so confused!

Ben: You have a hundred. Subtract seven from it, and it equals ninety-three. And you take ninety-three divided by seven, and it should give you how many ... things.

Ben was now revoicing himself. He restated his previous contribution, using more mathematical language and correcting the division error. He also spoke more slowly, more distinctly, and a little louder. It seemed to me that he was emulating a typical move that teachers use when students do not understand. Students continued to respond to his statement.

Winston: Why would you take away seven?

Amy: Yeah.

[Several students talking at once]

Minh: Well, because you are adding seven, but I don't think it's right.

[Several students talking]

Sarah: Is he talking about it is one hundred or it's not a hundred?

JK: Ask him!

[Several students talking]

Andy: How 'bout you just let me add seven, like, a whole bunch of times.

JK: OK.

Luke: Yeah, just add seven up the thing [the strip the numbers were written on]. That's not the point, though.

JK: Andy, do you think, you are thinking what? If you do what, it'll work?

Andy: Just take the long route and just add seven to, like, each one.

Winston: No, use a calculator.

JK: What are we going to start with when we start adding seven?

Andy: Two. We're gonna start at two.

JK: OK. So grab a calculator, and do that and see if it gets you to a hundred.

Ben: Also, you could divide, a hundred divided by seven, and if doesn't come out as a whole number, then it's not on the list.

[There was overlapping conversation going on at this point. I wanted to refocus the group.]

JK: Winston has a comment to make, 'kay? Winston?

Winston: Ninety-eight is a multiple of seven. And when you start at two, that's adding two. So it's basically, it's like a hundred equals ninety-eight plus two. [Pause] Uh, it equals seven times fourteen plus two.

JK: OK. Is this true?

Andy: I think it's true!

JK: Is one hundred equal to seven times fourteen plus two?

Many students: Sure. Yes.

At this point, I turned Winston's claim into a question. I wanted students to verify this statement after hearing Ben's arithmetic. Then I asked the more important question:

JK: Does this statement mean one hundred is on the list?

Many students: Yes.

Some students: Uhh.

Deepti: Yes, it is.

JK: OK, why, Andy?

Andy: Because, like, that would mean ninety-eight. ... Wait, hold on.

Luke: It's on the list.

JK: Let Andy think for a second.

Andy: Yeah, I just know it is.

JK: I'm not convinced by "Yeah, I know it is."

Although not revoicing, I was trying to allow time for Andy to think and state his reasoning. I also indicated that some statements did not count as mathematical evidence of a claim. In this example, I was working to establish mathematical norms for what was expected, or at least what was not acceptable, in a mathematical argument.

Deepti: Because, uh, I wrote down the formula for this and then I multiplied seven by fourteen. I got ninety-eight. And then I added two.

JK: OK. [Several students are talking at once.] You are interrupting. So what I am hearing you say is sort of like Winston said, seven times fourteen plus two is one hundred.

I chose to revoice Deepti's contribution because she was soft-spoken and some students were still arguing with one another in the background. I was fairly certain that many students had not heard her. I could have asked her to repeat what she said after calling everyone to attention, but I thought that request would impose a burden on her. In addition, I linked her response with Winston's. A better choice might have been to ask the students to notice whose responses were similar to Deepti's.

Several students: It's right!

JK: So the question is, If I do this, does that give me a number on the list?

Deepti: Yes.

JK: Convince me that that gets me a number on the list.

Here I injected myself unnecessarily into the center of the argument. Why did they need to convince *me*? Presumably I already knew whether 100 was on the strip and why. The students needed to convince their classmates, not me.

LaNiece: That doesn't tell you that a hundred will be on it. It tells you that ninety-eight'll be on it.

JK: Deepti?

Deepti explained how to use the dot patterns we used previously to represent the numbers in the pattern and showed that each number on the strip could be represented by groups of seven plus two more, which made 7 times 14 plus 2 a number on the strip. I drew the dot patterns on the board over the numbers in the sequence as she explained. (Not all parts of her turn are audible on the tape.) After Deepti's contribution, LaNiece indicated that she understood. Luke informed us that 100 was on the list, and proceeded to give an explanation similar to Anna's and Winston's.

I think that by choosing to revoice less, I actually facilitated more student conversation. My role was to keep the conversation moving, to provide some focus through questions, and to try to make sure many voices were heard. As I look at the transcript of this lesson, I wonder whether I could have removed myself even more from the conversation and still had it progress in a way that helped all the students in the class understand. By allowing time for this conversation, I let students spend time really thinking about and analyzing the sequence and better understand the structure of an arithmetic sequence. Taking the time to talk about different strategies for solving the problem made the mathematics underlying the pattern much more visible and enabled more students to understand it.

Final Thoughts and Questions

As I limited my revoicing and increased my pauses, I found that students seemed to step in to share their ideas and reasoning more often. The length of my speaking turns decreased, and my students' turn lengths, involvement, and participation increased. The students attempted to explain so that others could understand, and they seemed to listen to one another more. The mathematical content of the students' turns also seemed to be deeper, showing how the students thought about mathematical ideas. When the mathematical thinking was made visible through the students' sharing, their misconceptions were easier to address. This type of discourse also allowed all students access to different ways of thinking about mathematical topics. Students modeled their thinking for one another, so students learned from one another.

As I revoiced less, I needed to remember that my revoicing did have a potentially important role. In particular, my revoicing could model mathematical language and arguments. I could insert mathematical vocabulary and help move the students to more "official mathematical language" (Herbel-Eisenmann 2002). (See chapter 8 for more about supporting the development of mathematical language.) I needed to pay careful attention to times when my revoicing could help students develop mathematically and times when refraining from revoicing would empower my students to take greater ownership of the mathematical conversation and give them more opportunities for their own learning.

At the end of the year, I asked students whether they thought classroom discussions were different now than at the beginning of the year. Several students said that they were participating more and that discussions were more fun. When I talked to a student who did not often participate, but made very insightful and helpful contributions when she did, about what helped her feel comfortable and willing to participate, she commented that she particularly liked the think-pair-share technique, which she felt gave her a chance to try out her ideas before sharing in front of everyone.

I was often surprised by how differently the classroom discourse would unfold in different class periods, even though it was based on the same problems. I am sure that I refined what I did with practice and experience each day, but I also think that the nature of the discourse can depend a great deal on the particular students who participate. Classroom discourse is somewhat like a dance, in which the moves vary depending on the partners. I would like to think about how and why certain students take on certain roles and how I can encourage and build on the strengths of all the participants in each class. Perhaps classroom discourse should be more like a puzzle, in which everyone's piece is needed to make a coherent whole.

Changing my discourse patterns is an ongoing process—a process I believe I have just begun. Change is not easy. I have taught for sixteen years, so many patterns in my teaching are well-practiced and deeply ingrained. I find that I need to remind myself frequently to think about how to frame the problems I pose and the questions I ask so as to elicit students' thinking and to bite my tongue and pause to give students enough wait time to think and respond to me and to one another. Planning ahead for these modifications in my lessons has been helpful. I continue to struggle, however, and work to break my old habits. My transcripts show that I have made some changes but also indicate many opportunities for improvement.

Reflecting and Connecting with Practice

- Jean asked her students what makes a "good discussion." Ask your students what they think a good discussion entails. How does your students' list compare with Jean's? Did your students include both social and mathematical aspects of discussion? If students listed only the social aspects of discussion, what might you do to help refine the list, for instance, to include the ways that mathematical argumentation and justification may be different from arguing and justifying outside the mathematics classroom (e.g., in English classes or in life outside school)? Because Jean's students included mainly social aspects of a good discussion, Jean explicitly discussed with them the kinds of sociomathematical norms that she wanted to use in her classroom. Do you engage in similar discussions with your students? What kinds of standards and norms are you explicit about? What do you think you should be more explicit about to help all students participate in mathematically powerful ways?
- Jean was surprised when she received the data that compared the length of her talk-turns with her students'. What is the nature of your students' turns? Are they short, like some of Jean's students' earlier turns? Are they longer, like some of Jean's students' later turns? What factors seem to prompt either brief or long student-turns?
- Consider a time when you sense that you took ownership of an idea away from a student. What led you to do so? How can you avoid this outcome in the future? What are some strategies for increasing students' sense of ownership?
- Revoicing consists primarily of two parts: (1) a restatement or reformulation of a student's words and (2) a question back to the student to determine whether she or he agrees with the teacher's words. Listen to a segment of your recorded lesson. Note instances of revoicing, and consider the nature of your revoicing. Jean's reflection on revoicing included some instances in which she only restated or reformulated a student's contribution and other instances in which she used both moves. She also wrote about revoicing that signaled that she was evaluating contributions by the rising intonation in her voice. Which of these language moves do you tend to use in your teaching, and when and how do you use them? Which students do you tend to revoice, and how do you revoice them? What are some reasons you use revoicing? If you think you revoice too

frequently, try some of Jean's strategies for being more selective about your revoicing. How does this change seem to influence students' contributions?

- In addition to revoicing, Jean discussed two other aspects of her classroom discourse: overlapping speech and pauses. How do you use these aspects of language? While watching yourself on videotape, keep track of how and when you interrupt or pause. What seem to be your criteria for interrupting and pausing? What is the relationship between control and the ways you see yourself interrupting?

References

Herbel-Eisenmann, Beth. "Using Student Contributions and Multiple Representations to Develop Mathematical Language." *Mathematics Teaching in the Middle School* 8 (October 2002): 100–105.

O'Connor, M. Catherine, and Sarah Michaels. "Aligning Academic Task and Participation Status through Revoicing: Analysis of a Classroom Discourse Strategy." *Anthropology and Education Quarterly* 24 (December 1993): 318–35.

———. "Shifting Participant Frameworks: Orchestrating Thinking Practices in Group Discussion." In *Discourse, Learning, and Schooling*, edited by Deborah Hicks. New York: Cambridge University Press, 1996.

Rowe, Mary B. "Wait Time: Slowing Down May Be a Way of Speeding Up." *Journal of Teacher Education* 37, no. 1 (January–February 1986): 43–50.

Opening Up the Public Speech Channel

David Pimm

In the previous two chapters, we read about the efforts and explorations of two teacher-researchers, Jeff Marks and Jean Krusi, as they seek to change the ways in which they are vocally present in the classroom, more specifically the forms of discourse they use in whole-class discussions. In so doing, they consider the connections among their desired goals as pedagogic agents, their use of different linguistic practices, and the empirical effects they observe.

A commonplace saying is that change is never easy, particularly in a classroom setting. One reason for this systemic difficulty arises from the fact that entrenching practices and making them routine are ways to free conscious attention for other, more important considerations. A classroom teacher, like anyone else, has only a certain amount of attention to give, to show, to pay. During the early years of a teacher's professional life, much time is spent developing a relatively stable and reliable practice of his or her own. Consequently, attempting to change a consistent practice involves going against a well-established grain.

Second, and possibly even more important, the teacher is not alone in the classroom. The students themselves have strong views about how things *should* go in the familiar, if sometimes dull or silencing, realm of the mathematics class, in whose waters they have been made to bathe since kindergarten. Trying to change this balance can involve pushing against a strong tide and almost always creates turbulence. Students do not immediately take to being made to do more or work in different ways. As we read more fully in Joseph Obrycki's chapter in a later section, which is entirely based on interviews of students, they often resist change in the familiar routines, because with those routines they at least know what is expected. To a certain extent, they are themselves codependent with the teacher in preserving a certain status quo.

In the chapters by Jeff and Jean, we read of thoughtful teachers at work on themselves and their chosen classroom site of exploration, genuinely questing and questioning (not least as a result of being exposed to the work of certain discourse-oriented mathematics educators, as well as the regular discussion, commentary, and critique of other teachers and researchers in the project). Both teachers use strong words to describe their perceived failings or inability to achieve their newly conceived ends. Jeff tells of how he sensed that he "stole the students' thinking," and Jean worries, "Did my robbing William of his ownership and explanation lead to any larger benefit?"

I want to start by lauding these authors for their openness and willingness to write publicly about their difficulties and challenges as they engaged in trying to change an established, familiar practice. Both teachers offer us revelations they received in the process of exploring elements of their own practice: "I seemed to have difficulty allowing a mistake to occur," says Jeff. It is never easy to struggle, supported or not, let alone struggle in the public gaze. My experience has been that many teachers attempting such a task are very hard on themselves, unnecessarily hard in my view. Yet I also recall from a long time ago an expert teacher with an extraordinary practice to my eye (and ear) commenting, "I am nowhere near where I want to be," echoing Browning's poetic observation in "Andrea del Sarto": "Ah, but a man's reach should exceed his grasp, /Or what's a heaven for?" This dissatisfied striving for something perceived as better is, for me, a major sign of a thinking, challenging teacher hard at work. And Browning's use of *should* is very strong to my ear, asserting that this is the proper state of things.

In what follows, I take the two chapters in turn and make some specific comments, picking out certain features of each chapter that struck me in some way or reminded me of other work on mathematics classroom discourse. Then, near the end of this short response, I look across both contributions and discuss some things that I see them as having in common.

Who Is Controlling What to What Effect?

Jeff Marks is working hard at finding new ways of lessening his perceived grip on classroom language in whole-class settings. He questions his control, especially over the public speech channel in his geometry classroom, and explores what happens if he begins to rescind some of that control and speech dominance. Jeff honestly reports the unease of his students as he decreases his use of imperatives (instruction based on instructions) and redirects questions to which he would "normally" have responded toward other members of the class.

When the teacher steps away from the public speech channel in such ways, refusing to fill it, at first a certain vacuum is often created. The classroom does not immediately function in the relatively seamless way it used to. Turbulence is created, and students do not generally like turbulence. Attempting to change a familiar and established routine has consequent costs. And strong, if tacit, pressures may be exerted by the students (as well as by the teacher) to return to the known (or as Paul Simon puts it in his song "Still Crazy after All These Years," "I seem to lean on old familiar ways"). Jeff tells how he "jumped into the silence that overtook the room at times." Such is a common and very understandable response. A necessary and important codependence is generated between teacher and students, and yet, like many such links, each party can serve as a brake on the other's attempts to change or do something different. The tension Jeff writes of, "between trying to get students to take more ownership and what students expected of me," spoke to me very strongly.

The "student teacher of the day" technique brought some of these issues to a head. When placed in an unfamiliar role, students are going to retreat to the known. So, for instance, in the transcript, when Maurice is acting as teacher, he is focused on *what* to do, on the procedures that form much of the surface of "doing mathematics" in a public arena such as a secondary school classroom. In addition, on what language models are students who are thrust into the limelight going to draw so as to "sound like the teacher," if not the ones with which they are most familiar? And does the teacher still assert the right to metacomment on the students' utterances or respond when the student out front asks the teacher a direct question, thus thrusting the teacher back into the familiar role of authority? If so, despite doing his or her best, the student is not really "being the teacher." If nothing else, in such moments students reveal their internalized normative images of how a teacher of mathematics should speak and behave.

Jeff's recounting reminded me of when student teachers are invited to "be the teacher" in their own university classrooms. This practice has certain problematic elements, especially when the actual teacher is reluctant to cede the role completely. As we hear from Jeff, this relinquishing, too, has its challenges for him, not least because the actual teacher rightly has specifically mathematical pedagogic intentions for his or her class, something that student teachers do not have, thus influencing both what the teacher selects to say and how it is said.

Also, in the light of certain reform practices, having a student report back has become an increasingly common situation in the mathematics classroom (see Pimm [1992]). A number of significant linguistic challenges arise for anyone placed in such a position. Who is the audience for the student's comments? Does the student "out in front" talk to them, address them directly, or is the "real" teacher still the focus for comments, so that the other students once more are cast in the role of "overhearers"?

The ancient Pythagoreans distinguished between students who could be directly involved in being part of the teaching (the *mathematici*) and students who were solely listeners (the *acoustici*), who were permitted only to overhear the proceedings. I am led to wonder to what extent this distinction continues to be made, whether explicitly or tacitly, in mathematics classrooms.

Voice and Revoice

In her chapter, Jean Krusi explores the existing practice of revoicing by linking its purposes and effects, as well as exploring whether the teacher needs to be the revoicer or whether other students, including the initial "voicer," might be encouraged to take it on themselves. Her desire, not necessarily that of her students, was that they "take more ownership of the mathematical discourse in the classroom."

With Jean's primary focus on revoicing, her explorations show a shift away from revoicing as an explicit practice while not giving up on metacommenting (Stubbs 1975; Pimm 1994), that is, making comments about the utterances or the speech situation as the sole content of a speaker's contribution. I believe metacommenting to be one of the hallmarks of teaching, one of the core ways in which teachers' talk differentiates itself from students' talk. And in relation to my previous comments on students "doing being the teacher," the presence or absence of students' metacomments can clearly indicate the extent to which they, tacitly at least, notice this difference between the ways the teacher and students talk.

Jean seems to be exploring classroom conversation more deeply. At the outset, she tells us that she was already asking "the kinds of questions that probe students' thinking," but her attention then went to the way she was working with the responses, with what came back. Related to the depth of possible moves in her conversations, her actions seemed like those of a chess player trying to look further ahead in the game. Elsewhere (Pimm 1987), I have talked about teaching "gambits," another chess notion—moves or sequences of moves that involve a short-term sacrifice in return for a hoped-for long-term gain. To me, Jean's revoicing seemed like an established practice whose power and limits she was now subjecting to close scrutiny as she became more aware of some of the sacrifices involved.

In identifying a difference in her intonation when revoicing a correct versus an incorrect statement, Jean picked up on a subtle cue (a "tell," in gambling terminology) that she was providing about her stance on what she was saying, turning a potentially neutral conversational move into an evaluative one. The omnipresence of the IRE interactional structure (discussed by Herbel-Eisenmann in chapters 1 and 2) challenges teachers to counteract the impression that anything that follows a student's response to a teacher's question can be interpreted as an evaluation.

Jean also makes some interesting observations about overlapping speech, both with regard to her revoicing before the student had finished speaking and the general concern with overlapping speech. One of the things that most classroom transcripts mask (simply as an artifact of the "normal" form—although see Jefferson [2004] for an alternative) is that overlapping speech is the norm in normal conversation. So a tension or dilemma arises between, on the one hand, wanting student conversations to be more direct, addressed to one another rather than to the teacher acting as the conversational hub, and, on the other hand, in the interests of communicating clearly and showing respect, wanting students to speak without overlapping. Jean herself notes, "Occasionally several students were speaking at the same time, some in small groups, so sometimes individual comments were hard to hear." (A similar result is seen in the work of filmmaker Robert Altman, who consistently uses overlapping speech in his films, reducing audience comprehensibility while mirroring "real" dialogue more faithfully.)

I appreciated Jean's plentiful transcribed examples as well as the nuances she finds in ways to revoice herself less while having other students or the original speaker provide the revoicing. To have students monitor the quality of the communication in an ongoing conversation and be willing to remark on it are goals not easily won. But I was interested to note that, even in the later examples, Jean still made important metacomments (e.g., "Winston has a comment to make" or "Amy is looking with a very puzzled expression") and redirected questions, as when she responded to Sarah with, "Ask him!"

But my last observation is that she was still ready and willing to take a turn, as when she said, "I'm not convinced by 'Yeah, I know it is.'" Too often when teachers explore an apparent exhortation to say less, they actually drop too far back, being reluctant to play any mathematical part at all in the proceedings. Needless to say, I think that this going too far disempowers the teacher's own voice (see also Chazan and Ball [1999]).

"Control," "Ownership," and "Norms"

Two words that often appear in the literature of mathematics education occurred in both chapters: *ownership* and *norm.* Despite what some people say and write these days, control is not necessarily a bad thing, depending on how it is achieved and maintained and the ends to which it is used. Sometimes ownership may have to be thrust onto the rightful owner, who may not want it.

Both teachers also asked their students about classroom discourse structures, making those structures an explicit part of the classroom agenda. In so doing, they were attempting to draw their students' attention to discourse structures. David Wagner (2006), for his doctoral dissertation, spent a semester coteaching in another teacher's eleventh-grade class, and attempted to draw students' attention explicitly to some of the discourse features of the class and their textbook. As Jeff did, Wagner found this work challenging, but on a number of occasions he succeeded in making the students more aware of the power of language in shaping and structuring their learning environment (see also Wagner and Herbel-Eisenmann [2008]).

For me, this idea came to a head in the notion of conversational "norms" in the classroom, also discussed in both chapters. The word *norm* itself seems to be used in two rather different ways in mathematics education: as a description of what is often true (what is empirically "normal") and as a hoped-for future state (what is empirically *not* the norm at the moment but is desired, usually by the teacher or some outside group, to become the norm in the future). The installation of new norms, so that they become genuinely normal (and hence unremarked, even if objectively remarkable), seems to me to be the focal aim of both teachers whose work we read about here.

References

Chazan, Daniel, and Deborah Ball. "Beyond Being Told Not to Tell." *For the Learning of Mathematics* 19 (January 1999): 2–10.

Jefferson, Gail. "Glossary of Transcript Symbols with an Introduction." In *Conversation Analysis: Studies from the First Generation*, edited by Gene Lerner, pp. 13–31. Philadelphia, Pa.: John Benjamin, 2004.

Pimm, David. *Speaking Mathematically: Communication in Mathematics Classrooms.* London: Routledge & Kegan Paul, 1987.

———. "*Why Are We Doing This?* Reporting Back on Investigations." In *Communication in the Mathematics Classroom,* Mathematics Council of the Alberta Teachers Association monograph, edited by Daiyo Sawada, pp. 43–56. Edmonton, Alberta: Alberta Teachers Association, 1992.

———. "Spoken Mathematical Classroom Culture: Artifice and Artificiality." In *Cultural Perspectives on the Mathematics Classroom,* edited by Stephen Lerman, pp. 133–47. Boston, Mass.: Kluwer Academic Publishers, 1994.

Stubbs, Michael. *Organizing Classroom Talk.* Occasional paper 19. Edinburgh, Scotland: Centre for Research in the Educational Sciences, University of Edinburgh, 1975.

Wagner, David. "Silence and Voice in the Secondary Mathematics Classroom." Unpublished doctoral dissertation, University of Alberta, 2006.

Wagner, David, and Beth Herbel-Eisenmann. "'Just Don't': The Suppression and Invitation of Dialogue in Mathematics Classrooms." *Educational Studies in Mathematics* 67 (February 2008): 143–57.

SECTION 4

Images of Productive Discourse Practices

CHAPTER 8

"It," "That," and "What"? Vagueness and the Development of Mathematical Vocabulary

Tammie Cass

I AM AN elementary school certified teacher who teaches fifth- and sixth-grade mathematics, and I am the only mathematics teacher at those levels in our small, rural district. I would not say that I have the mathematics content knowledge that many secondary school mathematics teachers have, but I think that I understand the content for the grades that I teach. I have a long and broad teaching background (i.e., elementary and middle school, language arts, and special education classes), which I try to pair with a desire to continually learn and grow in my profession.

I use the *Connected Mathematics Project* (Lappan et al. 2006) curriculum materials, and I have excellent support in this endeavor. Throughout the Discourse Project, the fact that I had both great materials to work with and the support that I needed significantly enhanced the work I was trying to do. Having a curriculum based on conceptual understanding meant that I could work on other areas of my teaching without having to search for conceptual problems.

During the past four years, we project participants have written in our journals about topics in the readings and discussion points that resonated with us. I have always strongly believed that students should be able to communicate about their mathematical thinking, reasoning, and processing through both oral and written communication. My early journal entries were about mathematical vocabulary and vague referencing. In July and October of 2006, I wrote that I was concerned about the students' ability to use mathematical vocabulary in meaningful ways. I wanted them to be able to use the correct terms and to be specific about their thinking, reasoning, and processing of mathematical content. I knew that, in the long run, this ability would be important if they were to be successful in mathematics.

Focusing on Vague References and Mathematical Vocabulary

As I worked through the process of action research, the issues that became important to me were students' use of vague references and nonmathematical vocabulary when communicating both verbally and in written form their mathematical thinking and learning. By "vague references" I mean that I wanted to pay attention to when my students and I used such words as *it, that,* and *this* to stand for the names of mathematical objects and processes (see, e.g., Rowland [1999]). I came to realize that students' use of specific mathematical words was important for many reasons, which I share below. My focus questions were, How do I get students to use specific words instead of vague references? How do I get students to use mathematical vocabulary in meaningful ways in both their oral and written communication about mathematics?

I began the action research process by watching a videotape of myself teaching. In several places I noticed that although I used mathematical vocabulary, my students did not use it meaningfully. The students were sometimes able to spout definitions, but they seemed to have little conceptual understanding of the words. An example occurred when we were talking about improper fractions in November of 2005. The students were looking for decimal benchmarks by using fraction benchmarks (e.g., 1/4 = .25, so 1/8 is 1/2 of .25, or .125). We had progressed to the point of discussing improper fractions. Improper fractions had been taught in a way that focused on conceptual understanding, and students had practiced converting improper fractions to mixed numbers, so this idea should not have been new to the students.

> ***TC:*** Think about six-fifths. What type of fraction is that? Alice?
>
> ***Alice:*** Improper.
>
> ***TC:*** Improper, which means?
>
> ***Alice:*** You can't do it.

On other occasions, Alice had been able to recognize that the numerator was larger than the denominator, but here she seemed to have no idea that the fraction was greater than 1. Her response pointed out to me that even though Alice seemed to know a definition for improper fraction and could even identify an improper fraction, she had little understanding of the concept behind the term *improper fraction*. She thought that the fraction was wrong and that "you can't do it." This response also pointed out to me that she might not know that fractions can be larger than 1. She seemed to have acquired the vocabulary, but she did not necessarily understand the concept attached to the vocabulary.

The same idea appeared in a videotape of a lesson in January of 2006. That lesson, which came from *Data about Us* (Lappan et al. 1998), involved identifying the number of letters in a set of students' names, then using those data to look at the median length of the names. My sixth-grade students were using index cards, each of which showed a name and the number of letters in the name. The cards were arranged in a line with the name and the number of letters in the name facing the students. We were manipulating the median by adding and subtracting cards with names of different lengths. The students were discovering what happened to the median when they added or removed two cards from either end or added or removed one card from each end. (I use bold and underlined text to draw attention to some of the vague references that I discuss after the example.)

01 TC: It [adding cards] pulled the median up to here, which is twelve, right? Right? **It** went

02 to twelve, and when we pulled **it** this way, when we added two cards this way, what's my

03 median now?

04 *Kristie:* Eleven.

05 *TC:* Eleven. How much difference between eleven

06 and five-tenths and twelve, and eleven and five-tenths and eleven? How much difference is there between these values?

07 *Mark:* Point five.

08 *TC:* Five-tenths, a half, right? Five-tenths, not very much, that median didn't fluctuate

09 very much, did **it**? What do you think is going to happen if I add one card that has sixteen

10 letters on it? OK, if I add a card over here that has sixteen letters, right here, what happens

11 to my median?

12 *Lauren:* **It** goes down to eleven point five.

13 *TC:* OK, one, two, three, four, five [counting the cards from one end]. Now one, two,

three, four, five [counting the cards from the other end]. My median is right here on this card, which is twelve. So when I added a card that had sixteen letters, my median went to twelve. What if I add a card that had one thousand nineteen letters? It's that girl's name, Rosheshannahsas, that long name, whatever her name was. What's going to happen to my median when I'm adding all those letters?

Julia: Twelve and a half?

TC: You think **it's** going to be twelve and a half? How many think **it's** going to shoot way up? Raise your hand if you think that the median is going to go way up? [A few students raise their hands.] How many think **it's** going to go way down? [A few students raise their hands.] Okay, how many think **it's** going to go up but maybe just by a little bit? [Many students raise their hands.] Anybody think **it's** just going to go down by a little bit?

Katie: I think **it's** going to go to twelve.

TC: You think **it's** going to go to twelve? So where is our median now? One, two, three, four, five,... one, two, three, four, five, **it's** on twelve. When I added a card that had one thousand nineteen letters on it, my median went to twelve. Why didn't my median go up a whole bunch?

Jimmy: We added one card only with a lot of letters.

TC: OK, Jimmy, you are hitting the point. Let's see if we can help him rephrase that. He said we didn't add a bunch of cards, we just added one card with a lot of letters on it. Is the median the middle of the number of letters, or is **it** the middle of the number of cards?

Kevin: Middle of the number of cards.

TC: Middle of the cards, so median is the middle of the data, not the values that the data equals. **It's** the middle of the data points, the midpoint. So no matter whether we add or remove cards at one end of the data, it pulls the median but it doesn't pull **it** very much. If we wanted that median to go up a whole bunch, we'd have to add a whole bunch of cards over here, wouldn't we? On this end? And that would pull the median higher? Or if we wanted to decrease **it,** we'd have to add a bunch to the lower end and that would pull **it** that way, and the same way when we remove. When we remove, it's the opposite, when

42 we remove from the low end, the median got bigger, didn't **it**? And when we removed
43 from the big end, the median got smaller. So that median is our middle point, **it's** our
44 middle spot of the data. That's why I say "median" like this, right? Median—middle, middle point.

When I first read this transcript, I noticed how much I was talking and how little students were talking. How could I expect students to use mathematical vocabulary with meaning if I was not giving them an opportunity to talk? What kind of sense was I getting of their meanings if they were not talking to me? Toward the end of this transcript, the students were able to repeat that the median of a set of data was the middle. Yet, without my "funneling" (Wood 1998; Herbel-Eisenmann and Breyfogle 2005) them down to this answer, they seemed unable to identify the median as the middle value in the ordered set of data, not the average of the values of the data.

In my daily reflections on the lesson described above, I wrote that the students were getting the concepts and that it was a fairly good day; the lesson showed evidence of good teaching and good interaction between me and the students. Now as I reflect back, I think that my students were probably repeating vocabulary without understanding the concepts. As I look more carefully at the words that were being used for the main mathematical idea (i.e., *median*), I notice more things. I notice that I often used vague references to refer to median, especially the word *it*. In fact, when I looked at the word *it* in this transcript, I saw that I used *it* twenty-six times. Eighteen of these *it*s (the ones in boldface) refer to the *median*, whereas the other eight (the ones that are underlined) refer to something completely different. For example, in the first line of the transcript, I begin with the word *it* to refer to the process of adding cards to the set of data, then thirteen words later, I use *it* to refer to median. If students stopped paying attention for a moment, would they know what *it* referred to? This kind of change of reference also happened in lines 9–10, 26–28, and 32–33 and a few times in lines 36–43. In lines 36–43, I used *it* to refer to the median (boldface text), to the process of adding and removing cards (e.g., in line 37), and to something else (in line 41) that is not clear to me even now. Did students know that I meant different things when I used the word *it?*

I also noticed that, even though I used the word *median* more than twenty times, my students did not use it once. In fact, the only reference that students made to the idea of *median* was in line 12, and the student chose to use the word *it* instead of *median*. I wondered whether, if I had asked Lauren what she meant by *it*, she would have been able to tell me not only what *it* referred to but also how what she was saying related to the idea of *median*. I realized that if I wanted students to use mathematical vocabulary in meaningful ways, I needed not only to provide more opportunity for them to do so but also to do something to help them use the desired language. I decided to focus on vague references and teaching vocabulary more explicitly in the context of actually using that vocabulary.

The discourse analysis of my baseline data further supported my need to focus on issues of vague references and mathematical vocabulary. One point of the analysis of my baseline data stated, "When going over group work, mathematical terms were not used very often." Also, a section that referred to vague references pointed out that I used vague references fifty times during one activity structure, and, of those references, I used the word *it* thirty-five times. The section went on to state that when I used *it*, I had used the subject or antecedent in the previous sentence, so the listener could probably follow my statements and figure out what *it* referred to. Although as a teacher I realize the need for the subject or antecedent to precede the pronoun, many of my students might not identify this need when speaking and writing. How could I expect my students to improve in these areas when I was not modeling the desired language practices? I realized that I needed to make some changes in my communication with students if I wanted them to be able to make the changes I wanted.

Taking a Look at the Literature

At this point we began to read the discourse literature. Through these readings, I learned more about mathematical vocabulary and vague referencing. In an article by Thompson and Rubenstein (2000), "Learning Mathematics Vocabulary: Potential Pitfalls and Instructional Strategies," the authors stated that "fluent use of terminology is a necessary, albeit not sufficient, condition for overall mathematics achievement" (p. 568). They further stated that "the vocabulary issues we have discussed are the 'surface structures' used to transmit ideas as we engage students in discussions that lead to the 'deep structures' of mathematical concepts" (p. 568). In other words, without the correct mathematical vocabulary, students have difficulty engaging in meaningful discussions, then learning the mathematical concepts that lead to overall mathematics understanding.

From Chapin, O'Connor, and Anderson's (2003) book I learned—

> If students are to become competent mathematical thinkers, able to work with and communicate about mathematical ideas, they must become familiar with mathematical words. [...] Simply providing students with definitions for mathematical terms doesn't result in students gaining a deep understanding of those terms. Understanding a term entails understanding the concept or action that the term refers to, and the relationships that exist between that concept and related concepts and ideas. (p. 87)

The connections between concepts and terms and between terms and related concepts was just what I was not seeing in my classroom. The students did not seem to understand the mathematical terms they were using, and because they did not understand the terms, they were less able to communicate effectively.

I continued reading about classroom talk and how to facilitate richer classroom discourse. A chapter by Barnett-Clarke and Ramirez (2004) titled "Language Pitfalls and Pathways to Mathematics" gave me a start. The authors highlighted the fact that students need to express themselves verbally because doing so helps them clarify and organize their thoughts. Students need to be taught to be active listeners and encouraged both to be critical listeners and to exhibit verbal fluency in their explanations. I needed to shift away from teacher's exposition in the mathematical activities I chose, and I needed to give students opportunities to use technical vocabulary.

Moving toward More Productive Discourse Practices

So where did I go next? Obviously I needed to make some changes. I decided to make some broader general changes and to start using specific strategies to teach students how to speak and write using more mathematical language. This section is an attempt to capture some of the changes I made in both these areas.

Making Opportunities for Students to Use Vocabulary

My next task was to begin implementing general changes that would support an environment in which students felt they could participate and use the mathematical language that I wanted them to use. I began by making physical changes to the room setup (see chapter 4 for more on room arrangement). I arranged the tables to be more like the spokes of a wheel, with a small table in the middle for my materials. In essence, I was teaching in the round. In reviewing a videotape from before this change, I could see that my classroom definitely had a "front" and a "back." I was standing at the front by the instructional white board, and the students were sitting in a semicircle facing me. I had another white board on the opposite side of the room but used it only for posters and daily assignments. My changes included using both boards for work and not having a "front" to the classroom.

I also started moving around the room and not standing in one place. When students were talking, I made sure that I was out of the picture by standing behind them or away from them. The students then had to communicate with the class and not just with me. I also directly prompted my students to talk to the class, not to me. I worked on aspects of my classroom discourse that supported them in being active listeners. I would ask the same student or another student to repeat the comment if I thought someone was not listening carefully. I asked the students to think about a question or a response by deciding whether they agreed or disagreed, and about the point with which they agreed or disagreed. I also asked whether they had something they could add to the response or whether they had questions. This change opened up the conversation immensely. Students now had a place to start. I began hearing such comments as "I agree, but I want to add on…" or "I disagree because …." Students were also questioning one another about their responses, for example, "I understand this point, but then I get lost." The student-to-student discourse began to evolve because I was standing back and expecting them to do the talking. I was focusing not only on the vague references and mathematical vocabulary but on the student-to-student discourse as well.

We also began a "no-hands" policy (Lee 2006), in which raising one's hand meant that one had a question, not a response or an answer. This approach was much more difficult than I thought it would be, both for the students and for me. The students had been trained to raise their hands, and I was accustomed to calling on a person with his or her hand up. The students had difficulty not raising their hands, I had difficulty not calling on individuals with raised hands. The old habit was very easy to fall into. We definitely did not master the no-hands policy during the year, and I plan to continue to work on the new approach over time.

Teaching Vocabulary More Explicitly in Relationship to Concepts

Teaching vocabulary now meant that I had to encourage students to talk mathematically in small groups as well as in whole-class activities. To help with the small-group processing, I began using more cooperative learning strategies. The students were asked to think-pair-share and to jigsaw their conclusions. (The jigsaw technique is a cooperative learning strategy in which each student is responsible for part of the solution, then shares her or his findings with group members so that they can arrive at their solution or conclusion.) I made the expectations clear to my students: they would be called on in class and had to be prepared to share, using mathematical words whenever possible. Many times I would ask students to rehearse their responses at their tables first, then be ready to share with the whole class. This setting allowed students to practice their mathematical words with a small audience before having to share them in front of the whole class. In fact, just as the writing process involves several drafts, this process of rehearsing responses allowed students to move from less formal, more tentative "exploratory talk" to "final draft talk" (Barnes 1976) that was more mathematically precise.

As a class, we developed a set of expectations for small-group discussion and taped them to the tables. The students used these guidelines to help lead their small-group discussions. Students who were less vocal were allowed to share with me before they shared with the class. I purposely worked to make sure that every student responded at some time during the class, and I supported and encouraged them to use mathematical words as well as to explain how the words related to the concepts we were studying.

To support students' use of mathematical vocabulary in whole-class discussions, I began to use revoicing (Chapin, O'Connor, and Anderson 2003) in more careful ways (see chapters 7 and 9 for more on revoicing). I revoiced what the students said in mathematically precise ways, and many times I asked students to revoice one another, requesting that they try to restate using precise language for mathematical ideas. Asking students to revoice one another not only encouraged the students to listen carefully and to process what the speaker said but also gave them an opportunity to use mathematical words. An example of my own revoicing occurs in the following discussion:

> ***TC:*** Talk to me about some of the special words in that paragraph that says *regular polygon*. What does the word *regular* tell you about each of the angles?
>
> ***Mark:*** All the angles are equal.
>
> ***TC:*** If the shape is a regular polygon, then all the sides and all

the angles are congruent. So we can divide the angle sum by the number of angles.

By revoicing Mark's response, I was able to get the idea in front of all the students and also emphasize that in a regular polygon all the sides and the angles are congruent. I purposely used the mathematical terms *regular polygon, sides, congruent,* and *angles.* I wanted my students to hear the words used correctly in a sentence and to be able to associate them with the mathematical objects we were examining.

I began a mathematics vocabulary board to keep mathematical terms readily available to the students, and I had them keep a mathematics vocabulary journal. We developed definitions for words as a class, and the students wrote them in their journals for future reference. I reinforced the use of what I called "strong math vocabulary" by making such statements as "I like the way Chris used strong math words in his explanation." I continually reinforced the words and the definitions in relation to the mathematical objects we were studying so that students learned when and how to use the mathematical words. When students found a word they did not know, I encouraged them to think about a resource that might help them. I made mathematics reference books readily available and provided notes that could help students when they did homework.

In looking at my own prompting of students, I see that the format I use has changed. Instead of funneling their talk, I am trying to encourage them to formulate their own ideas and concepts. We look for ways that problems are similar and ways they are different. We talk about the major concepts or big ideas that a lesson conveys. I am also trying to ask more open-ended questions instead of questions that have one-word responses (see chapter 3 for more on questioning patterns).

Comparing different strategies and applying new strategies are also important components of my teaching. I continued to videotape and watch my lessons during the action research phase of the project to evaluate how the new strategies were working. In the transcript that follows, students were finding the angle sum of polygons by dividing the polygons into triangles. Zane created his triangles by going from one vertex of the polygon to the opposite vertices. Davis divided the polygon into triangles from a center point (see fig. 8.1).

TC: Look at the two problems that Zane and Davis did. What is alike about their solutions?

Greg: They used triangles in both of them.

TC: What is different in the two? What did Zane have to do that Davis didn't have to do?

Greg: Well, Zane had to take off three-hundred-sixty degrees because of the center angles.

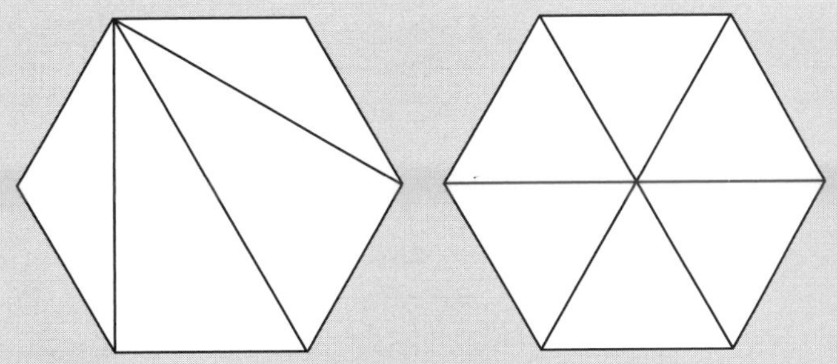

Fig. 8.1. Using triangles to determine polygon angle sums

First of all, I was pleased that both Zane and Davis were able to use a strategy to find the angle sizes of their polygons. Greg compared and contrasted their solutions with the polygon-angle-sum problem and noticed that the two students divided the shape into triangles (compare), and that one student then had to subtract 360 degrees for the center circle (contrast). I was also pleased that the class was able to see the similarity and difference between the two solutions and was able to explain, using several mathematical terms, why one student had to subtract 360 degrees.

Another example from the same videotape shows the strong use of mathematical vocabulary and an understanding of the concepts. The students used angle sums of polygons to determine the size of the missing angle.

Matthew: Basically, you take the shape's angle sum, which in a triangle's case is one hundred eighty, and you want to add up every angle to get a hundred eighty. So ninety plus thirty is one hundred twenty. So one hundred twenty plus sixty is a hundred eighty, therefore that [angle] is sixty degrees.

Julia: I added forty-five and forty-five. That's ninety. Since the triangle's angle sum is a hundred eighty, then I knew the other angle was ninety degrees.

Katie: A quadrilateral equals three hundred sixty degrees altogether. So I just added sixty plus sixty which is a hundred and twenty degrees.

TC: So now what?

Katie: So then I thought that three hundred sixty degrees minus one hundred twenty, that equaled two hundred forty degrees. There's two of the *x's* [unknown angles], so I did two hundred forty. Half of two hundred forty is one hundred twenty degrees.

I was impressed with Matthew's response because he often struggled to stay on task and to verbalize his thoughts and processes. The students' use of the words *angle sum, triangle,* and *quadrilateral,* and the ideas they seemed to attach to those terms, was a step in the right direction.

My students also do a great deal of writing as part of their mathematics education. They write responses to declarative, procedural, and critical questions, and they write about their thought processes. An emphasis on strong use of mathematical vocabulary and avoidance of vague references helps clarify the meaning of their work. To help students develop mathematical language, I use the strategy of having them explain how they solved problems by writing about their thinking in their journals. After students have done this writing on their own, I often ask someone to volunteer his or her response, and I then pose the following question to the class: "What can you add to the solution to strengthen the math concepts or math vocabulary in order to make the meaning clearer?" We also do something similar when students give verbal responses in class. For example, one day I asked students to mentally compute 17 × 50. One student offered the following explanation, which I recorded on the board:

> First, I took 20 times 50 and got 1000. And I knew it was 3 times 50 more than 17 times 50. So, I timesed 3 times 50 and took away 150 minus 1000 and got 850. That's the answer.

When I asked the class how we could make changes to use "strong math words" and concepts, we worked on the explanation and changed it to read as follows:

> First, I multiplied 20 times 50 to get a product of 1000. And I knew this product was 3 times 50 (or 150) more than the product of 17 times 50, since I multiplied 50 by 20 instead of 17. This gave me 3 more groups of 50 than I really needed. So I multiplied 3 times 50 to get 150 and then subtracted 150 from 1000. This gave me an answer of 850.

This version of the solution, although quite a bit longer, is more mathematically precise and clearer than the previous version. I reminded students of the importance of understanding and using mathematical terms, because doing so exhibits that they are part of the mathematical community that knows and understands those ideas. My hope is that the process of working together on their writing and speaking helps students realize that different versions of an explanation are acceptable. I also hope that this process provides a structure for them to think about how they can improve their own speaking and writing to incorporate more mathematical vocabulary.

Progress Made

So what has happened? I have seen a number of improvements. Below is the example of an interaction I had with a group of students in which they used strong mathematical vocabulary:

TC: Talk to the people at your table about the angles of a parallelogram.

Kevin: The angles are congruent.

TC: All four angles are congruent? All four angles are congruent on a parallelogram.

Davis: If they are all congruent, then they wouldn't be parallelograms. If all the angles are congruent, they have to be ninety degrees.

TC: So explain more? What is congruent?

Davis: I just think it isn't because if they are congruent, then, yes, they would be.

TC: You changed your mind, why?

Davis: If a parallelogram is all congruent, they would have to equal three hundred sixty degrees angle sum.

TC: They would have to have three hundred sixty because the angles of a quadrilateral equal three hundred sixty degrees.

Davis: They would have to equal three hundred sixty degrees.

TC: Can someone rephrase what Davis said?

Stephanie: Well, I know that for parallelograms basically if all sides are congruent, that would make it a square and not a parallelogram—that parallelograms have opposite angles that are the same.

TC: We have some more good things coming out with what Stephanie said. Can someone expand on what Stephanie said?

John: On a parallelogram two sides have to be equal to each other, not crossing or going in a way that they could cross. And there's four parts right here and all four of them are parallel with the other sides. So, they would have to be, yeah.

TC: What would have to be yeah?

John: Congruent. The angles are congruent.

TC: We have had some interesting things come out. One is that if all the angles of a parallelogram are congruent, then Davis said that since it is a quadrilateral, it has an angle sum of three hundred sixty degrees. So he divided three hundred sixty degrees by four angles. So, do the angles have to be congruent? The only time the angles are congruent is when the polygon is a rectangle. So the difference between a parallelogram and a rectangle is the ninety-degree angles. Do you see that?

[Looking at a Venn diagram of quadrilaterals.]

TC: Remember everything inside this outer shape is a parallelogram. So rectangles are parallelograms. But rectangles have ninety-degree angles. Do all parallelograms have to have ninety-degree angles?

Students: No.

TC: No, we have some special ones that do, but they do not all have to have ninety-degree angles. So what does that mean for parallelograms? What angles are congruent?

Caitlin: On a rhombus, for example, the angle in the bottom-right corner would be congruent with the one in the upper-left corner. And the one in the bottom-left corner would be congruent with the one in the upper-right corner.

TC: So we are saying its opposite angles are congruent. The same is true for a parallelogram.

Throughout this class videotape, several things became apparent to me. Students were using precise mathematical vocabulary and were working toward understanding the concepts underneath the vocabulary by talking about the ideas. They were adding onto, and responding to, one another's ideas and grappling with the mathematical concepts. Many students were engaged in the task, and all students were talking at their tables about the task and concepts. This involvement was evident from the number of students participating in the conversation.

In January of 2008, we were adding and subtracting fractions and mixed numbers. In this example, students were using mathematics words to express their answers.

TC: What about Jamar's strategy? Seven-twelfths plus five-eighths equals fourteen twenty-fourths plus fifteen twenty-fourths. [Points to 7/12 + 5/8 = 14/24 + 15/24, which is written on the board.] What do you think about his strategy? Do you agree? Disagree? Where can we go with it?

Stephanie: I agree with him because seven-twelfths takes each of them times two.

TC: Each of what times two?

Stephanie: The numerator and denominator times two for seven-twelfths. So, he took seven times two and got fourteen and twelve times two and got twenty-four. And then on five-eighths, he took the numerator and the denominator times three. Five times three equals fifteen, and eight times three equals twenty-four.

TC: Now what?

Stephanie: Then you add, you don't add the denominator, so you add fourteen plus fifteen. So twenty-nine twenty-fourths.

TC: Think about that fraction.

Greg: Isn't it an improper fraction? It's over a whole. It's over a whole, so it will equal one and five twenty-fourths.

In this instance Stephanie commented about multiplying the "numerator" and "denominator" by two instead of the "top number" and the "bottom number." Greg used the term "improper fraction" and explained that the fraction is greater than one. They were also able to convert the improper fraction to the mixed number. Another improvement occurred in the verbal communication about the mathematics.

The students used specific mathematical terms and avoided the use of vague references, especially the word *it*.

Although these indicators are all small steps, they represent a great deal of work that I hope will lead to students' better understanding and achievement in the long run. I now feel confident and able to find new ways of improving mathematical discourse in my classroom. After all, my instructional goal is to support mathematical thinking and learning. My action research focus was to improve the use of mathematics vocabulary and avoid vague references, and I think I have begun that task.

Goals for the Future

As long as I am in this profession, I believe I must continue to push myself to improve in my teaching practice. I want to continue incorporating changes in the classroom and will continue to focus on vague references, mathematical vocabulary, the no-hands policy, and student-to-student discourse. I also want to focus on my questioning techniques. I want to ask more open-ended questions and think about the focusing and funneling of my interactions with students. Needless to say, my work is never done!

Reflecting and Connecting with Practice

- Consider the ways in which you can facilitate your students' use of mathematical language. Do you mainly use vocabulary lists and definitions, or do you have other strategies? What are some other ways that you can get your students to use mathematical language meaningfully in your classroom?
- Refer back to your videotape or audiotape, and as you watch or listen, keep track of the vague pronouns you use. In each instance that you use *it, that,* or *this*, are you referring to the same thing? How often do you use gestures to help students know what you are referring to? Do you always make clear what these pronouns and gestures refer to? In what ways might the use of these words hinder your students' understanding? What could you do to change this effect?
- When and how often do you use mathematically precise language? When do you tend to use vague references? When would the precise language provide a better learning opportunity for students, and when might less precise language, such as the pronouns *it* or *that,* be more appropriate?

- When and how do your students use mathematically precise language? When do they use vague references? Try to pay attention to when and how your students use vague language. In some of these instances, ask them to clarify their meanings when their explanations include such pronouns as *it, this,* and *that.* What do these clarifications offer in terms of formative assessment?
- Tammie mentioned that she purposely made sure that every student responded at some time during the class. In other chapters, the teacher-researchers also wrote about not wanting to embarrass their shy students by calling on them in front of everyone. In what ways can you balance a desire to have everyone participate and your concern for students' comfort levels? Try Tammie's strategy of letting the shy students practice their talk in small groups before having them present their "final draft" to the class. Check in with these students afterward to learn whether this scaffolding helped them feel comfortable about engaging in discussion.
- In what ways do you incorporate writing in your classroom to help students learn to communicate mathematically? Can you find more ways to incorporate writing? Which aspects of Tammie's description might help you implement this strategy better? What learning opportunities might writing provide that speaking does not?

Reference

Barnes, Douglas. "Language in the Secondary Classroom." In *Language, the Learner and the School.* Baltimore, Md: Penguin Books, 1969.

Barnett-Clarke, Carne, and Alma Ramirez. "Language Pitfalls and Pathways to Mathematics." In *Perspectives on the Teaching of Mathematic:* Sixty-sixth Yearbook of the National Council of Teachers of Mathematics (NCTM), edited by Rheta N. Rubenstein and George W. Bright, pp. 56–66. Reston, Va.: NCTM, 2004.

Chapin, Suzanne H., M. Catherine O'Connor, and Nancy C. Anderson. *Classroom Discussions: Using Math Talk to Help Students Learn.* Sausalito, Calif.: Math Solutions Publications, 2003.

Herbel-Eisenmann, Beth A., and M. Lynn Breyfogle. "Questioning Our Patterns of Questions." In *Mathematics Teaching in the Middle School* 10 (May 2005): 484–89.

Lappan, Glenda, James Fey, William Fitzgerald, Susan Friel, and Elizabeth Phillips. *Data about Us.* Menlo Park, Calif.: Dale Seymour Publishers, 1998.

———.*The Connected Mathematics Project 2.* Needham, Mass.: Pearson Prentice Hall, 2006.

Lee, Clare. *Language for Learning Mathematics: Assessment for Learning in Practice.* New York: Open University Press, 2006.

Rowland, Tim. "Pronouns in Mathematical Talk: Power, Vagueness, and Generalisation." *For the Learning of Mathematics* 19 (July 1999): 19–26.

Thompson, Denisse R., and Rheta N. Rubenstein. "Learning Mathematics Vocabulary: Potential Pitfalls and Instructional Strategies." *Mathematics Teacher* 93, no. 7 (October 2000): 568–74.

Wood, Terry. "Alternative Patterns of Communication in Mathematics Classes: Funneling or Focusing?" In *Language and Communication in the Mathematics Classroom,* edited by Heinz Steinbring, Maria G. Bartolini Bussi, and Anna Sierpinska, pp. 167–78. Reston, Va.: National Council of Teachers of Mathematics, 1998.

CHAPTER 9

Maintaining Mathematical Momentum through "Talk Moves"

Angie Shindelar

FOR THE past twelve years I have been teaching seventh- and eighth-grade mathematics. Before that, I taught third grade. The first several years of my mathematics instruction, my approach consisted of teaching the procedures and algorithms, then expecting students to practice those procedures and algorithms repeatedly. I had learned mathematics in that way as a student, and I did not think about other possibilities. A change in my thinking about mathematics teaching was prompted by reading *Curriculum and Evaluation Standards for School Mathematics* (National Council of Teachers of Mathematics [NCTM] 1989). By reading the literature of mathematics education and reflecting on my own teaching, I began to see the possibilities for mathematics to be more meaningful, and I discovered ways to help more students be successful. I decided that my teaching had to improve, and I began working to incorporate productive practices that have had a significant impact on my teaching and my own understanding of mathematics.

The efforts to improve my mathematics teaching were significantly reinforced when I began a master's degree program in mathematics for the middle grades. The program supported NCTM's vision, helped me deepen my content knowledge, and prepared me to make changes in my teaching. The next phase of my journey was beginning to use the *Connected Mathematics Project* (CMP) (Lappan et al. 1998, 2006a, 2006b), a curriculum program funded by the National Science Foundation (NSF) and based on the NCTM *Standards.* These teaching materials support my philosophy that students need to learn mathematics conceptually with a focus on understanding big mathematical ideas. The most recent phase of my continuing push toward improvement has been my participation in the Discourse Project. The project has given me the opportunity to reflect on my work as a mathematics teacher, discuss instructional issues with other concerned teachers, and focus on an area of my teaching that I want to improve.

Using the CMP Materials

The lessons in the CMP materials are structured to engage students in tasks that involve inquiry. These tasks are designed for work in a small group followed by a whole-class discussion to summarize the learning. After I launch the task, I monitor the small-group work by listening, asking questions, clarifying, and getting a general sense of how students are doing. I am there for support, but students have to listen to one another's ideas, read the text thoroughly, and work through questions and uncertainty together. I try to be continually ready to provide a scaffold and support students' learning when necessary. In the whole-class discussions that follow the task, I facilitate by having students share their strategies and discuss different representations and ways of thinking about the task. I try to pose questions that will help students pull their work and ideas together to form connections and generalizations. I have thought a lot about these activities over the past five years or so, and I have worked hard to try to do them well.

Establishing social norms (see Yackel and Cobb [1996] for more about social norms) is an important part of teaching with the CMP materials because of their emphasis on inquiry and group work. At the beginning of the year, we spend time discussing how our learning environment will look and sound. I provide the students with examples and nonexamples of appropriate communication, appropriate collaboration, and appropriate times to seek support from me. Students are usually able to identify various aspects of "good" discussions. For example, my students generated these characteristics:

- Several people are involved.
- Everyone is listening to what is being discussed.
- People do not talk over others.
- There is focus on the speaker.

As the groups are working, I do a lot of social coaching, such as encouraging students and dealing with problems as they arise. For instance, when members of a group are arguing or acting disrespectful toward one another, I will join the group and ask each student to explain the issue. After we listen to one another, I ask them to tell me what they need to do differently to work productively. I then monitor them closely and look for improvements so that I can give them positive feedback. I also periodically point out the successes that the groups in general are having with the social norms, or I bring attention to things that they need to work on. These social norms are different from those in the students' other classes, so they need time to adjust to and understand the expectations (see chapter 7 for more about social and mathematical norms).

As my comfort with the middle-grades curriculum and the CMP materials grew, I began to think more deeply about the summary part of the lesson, when most of the whole-class discussions occurred. I knew that developing an environment in which students shared their thinking and reasoning was essential to their understanding. I wanted my students to understand that their ideas and strategies were important, and I wanted them to be willing to share and take part in discussions. For example, in September of 2005, students were asked to find the product of 3/4 and 21. After students worked on this problem in small groups, I called on students to present their solution strategies and explain their thinking. I called on Gavin to share his solution first:

AS: So Gavin, did you do the pictures?

Gavin: Yes.

AS: All right. So, just keep talking while I'm drawing, OK?

Gavin: Um, I did a little three-fourths, twenty-one, but then I realized that two boxes equaled one-half, so I kept adding, every two boxes, one-half.

AS: So I'm gonna stop drawing for a minute, and I'm gonna go back to what you just said. You said that every two boxes is a half. Will you explain that to us?

Gavin: It equals one and one-half.

AS: One and one-half? OK. Will you explain that to me, how you know that?

Gavin: Um, three-fourths plus three-fourths is, like, seventy-five plus seventy-five, which equals one-fifty, and then you just take one off of the three-fourths and add in the other three-fourths, and it equals one, and you only have two boxes left (see fig. 9.1).

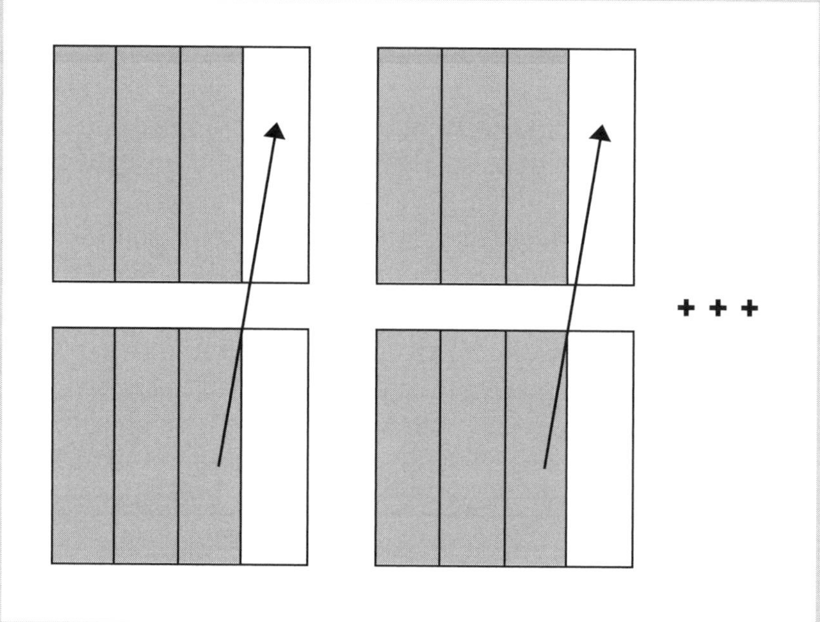

Fig. 9.1. Depiction of Gavin's method of grouping by one and one-half

AS: OK, so you kinda had two ways, and your two ways were kinda reassuring yourself that you had it right. You changed it to percentages—one hundred fifty percent is one and a half—but then going back and pulling that one-fourth up to fill in the box takes away this one, and he sees the one and a half. OK, I like the way that you said two ways to kinda verify your thinking, that's awesome. So let's go back to your initial statement. You said every time you had two of these [points to the shaded part], you had one and a half, right? So I'm gonna go up here [on the board] and I'm gonna write that down. Now where did you go from there?

Gavin: Um, then I just kept that in mind [inaudible].

AS: OK, so you quickly saw that there would be a way to make this go a little quicker. OK, so right here then, and right here, and you kept going. How many one-and-a-halves did you end up with?

Gavin: I ended up with sixteen and a half.

AS: OK, I'm gonna say that one more time because I think we're saying two different things. How many groups of one and a half … [Gavin seems to start to draw rectangles on his sheet of paper] … did you end up with first? That's OK. I'm drawing, too, take your time. Two, four, six, eight, ten, twelve, fourteen, sixteen, eighteen, that's why I'm not coming up with ten, because I'm not quite done here. There's twenty and there's twenty-one. OK. [Looks at the class] Do you guys see his groups? I kinda quit drawing them like they were three-fourths, is everyone following what I'm doing? Okay, so he continues to have one-and-a-half all the way down [points to the board]. And so how did you handle all your one-and-a-halves, Gavin?

Gavin: Uh, I never seen them as one and a half thing until I got them all drawn, and then, I did one and a half and one and a half. I did three.

AS: Oh, so I get to pull these up even more than one and one half? Now these [points to two sets of one and one half] equal three?

Gavin: I added, um, another one that equals three.

[Students count the groups of three, and Gavin finds his counting mistake. I then summarize the two ways Gavin counted and ask the other students why Gavin did what he did.]

When I read this example, I see that I asked Gavin to explain his thinking. In fact, I asked him several times to explain what he did. I made explicit that he used ideas about both fractions and percentages in his thinking, a connection that is important for students to make. I referred back to the picture to help Gavin see his counting mistake. I ended this portion of the whole-class discussion by summarizing Gavin's strategy, making it clear and succinct for all the students to hear again. I asked other students to explain why Gavin's method of counting worked and then called on two other students to share their solutions, and similar interactions took place. In fact, we were able to take strategies like Gavin's and connect them with other strategies that students were using that did not require a picture to solve the problem. Doing so eventually helped students see that the algorithm made sense because they could connect it with what was happening in the picture.

When I began to reflect on whole-class discussions like this one, however, I sensed that too many of the students were sitting there passively observing (and were possibly not even paying attention!). I noticed that many of my interactions consisted of my going back and forth with a single student as she or he described the reasoning and justified the thinking behind the solution. And I noticed that this "ping-pong" game I was having with a single student who was explaining his or her thinking also happened with other students on other days. Although I believed that I had made a lot of progress from my early years of teaching procedures and having students practice them, I thought that the discussions needed to consist of more interactions among the students instead of interactions primarily between a student and me.

The summary portion of a CMP lesson was intended to help students make connections and generalizations about the concepts, but too few students were involved in the discussion, and I was doing most of the talking about the connections and generalizations. Although leading discussions and directing students toward big mathematical ideas are certainly appropriate and necessary on the part of a teacher, I realized that I was not building from the energy of the small-group work. In small groups, most students were highly engaged and talking to one another, but after coming back together as a whole group, most seemed to sit and listen while a few students shared their thinking with me.

Continued Improvement of Whole-Class Discussions

The process of trying to figure out how to improve the whole-class discussions involved a tremendous amount of reading about questioning, classroom discussions, and other topics on mathematical discourse. The readings had me in a constant state of reflection about my teaching. One book that helped me visualize how to frame whole-class discussions was *Classroom Discussions: Using Math Talk to Help Students Learn* (Chapin, O'Connor, and Anderson 2003). I became particularly interested in the authors' descriptions of productive "talk moves" to use during whole-class discussions. I realized that when I asked students to share their thinking and their strategies for solving problems, I did not get a lot of reactions or comments from students because I had not structured the discussion in a way that invited interaction. I needed to use strategies that would invite students to enter the discussion. Because the purpose of a summary is to help students make connections and generalizations about mathematical concepts, increasing their participation in the summary discussion could push their thinking to a higher level and help deepen their conceptual understanding.

I focused my work on one of my eighth-grade classes. I began the year by talking about whole-class discussions and why I thought we needed to improve them. Because I had taught most of the students the previous year, in seventh grade, I explained that I would continue to expect them to share reasoning and include mathematical explanations of how their reasoning made sense. However, I was also going to encourage them to respond and interact directly with one another regarding their reasoning and explanations. I proposed that they could actually improve their mathematical reasoning and conceptual understanding if they would more often engage with one another's thinking. I reminded them that they were already having important mathematical discussions in their small groups as they grappled with the tasks, so that increasing the level of interaction in the large-group discussions should be feasible and could help them better understand the concepts. I described the biggest difference they would notice when someone shared a strategy or reasoning: I would now expect comments or questions from them about what was shared. I needed them to decide whether they agreed with what was shared or whether they had questions. I would support the conversation and help keep it moving, but I was going to expect them to listen, respond, and help one another make sense of the mathematics. I knew that the students would not fully realize this description of my expectations until we actually started the whole-class discussions. They were probably going to feel somewhat unsure and reluctant at first, but I was confident that they had had enough experience talking about their strategies and their reasoning to make such collaboration work.

The rest of this chapter centers on one example of a whole-class discussion. I present the episode in pieces so as to better explain the three talk moves that I found especially helpful: (1) prompting students for further participation, (2) asking students to apply their own reasoning to someone else's reasoning, and (3) revoicing (Chapin, O'Connor, and Anderson 2003). These talk moves are described in more detail and illustrated in the next section.

An Analysis of a Whole-Class Discussion

The whole-class discussion that follows is from an introductory problem for a unit on similarity of figures called "Stretching and Shrinking" (Lappan et al. 2006b). Using a double rubber-band stretcher and a drawing that was based on a right triangle (see fig. 9.2), students created a similar right triangle whose base and height were twice the original triangle's base and height. Because this activity was students' initial experience with the concept of similarity, they were not aware of the characteristics or relationships of similar shapes. After using the rubber-band stretcher to draw the image, students worked in small groups to determine what, if any, changes occurred in the shape, side lengths, angle measures, perimeter, and area of the new triangle. The following excerpts are from the summary discussion in which the students compared the area of the original triangle with the area of the enlarged triangle.

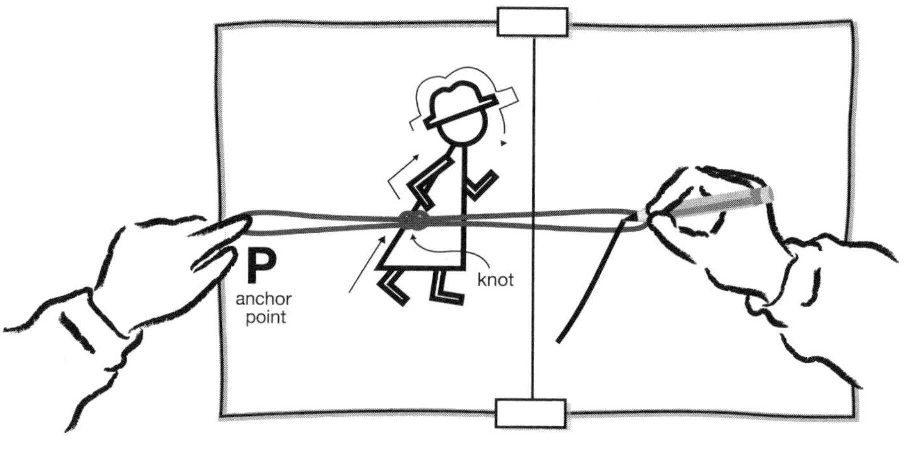

Fig. 9.2. Using rubber bands to draw similar figures

Karen: The area is two times bigger.

AS: Do you have a way that you can back this up or a way that you can have us think about it?

Karen: Not really. It just looks like it.

AS: So, *does anyone want to add on or question?*

Lane: I want to add on. If the perimeter was twice as big, then the area would have to be

07 twice as big, because if you stretch it out, there still has to be something in there.

08 *AS:* So you're saying the area can't be the same, it has to be bigger?

09 *Lane:* Yes.

10 *AS:* So do you have a reason why it has to be *two* times bigger?

11 Lane: Because the first triangle is not as much as the second, but there's a strip that looks

12 about the same size.

13 *AS:* Can you go up [to the board] and show us what you mean?

14 *Lane:* I used my hands like this. That strip [height of original triangle] looks about the same

15 size as this. [Lane shows that he can fit two of the original triangles into the new triangle by

16 placing one triangle in the lower-left corner next to the ninety-degree angle and another on

17 top of it.]

18 *AS:* So you're saying you think that this one here will fit along the base and another will fit

19 along the height?

20 *Lane:* Yes.

21 *AS: Does anyone want to add on, go a different direction, ask a question?*

The first talk move that I used was *prompting students for further participation.* In lines 1 and 4, Karen began the discussion by suggesting that the area of the larger triangle was twice the area of the original triangle. She did not give any explanation for her reasoning, so her thinking just sat there for others to consider. It appeared to me that she had guessed and did not want to explain further, so I prompted the rest of the class to continue from Karen's comment. Following a lengthy explanation by Lane, this segment concluded with my prompting the students to respond to his reasoning.

This talk move can help students understand that they are expected to make sense of the problem and work together. My expectation that students participate further by commenting on other students' comments helps them realize that I will not be evaluating their contributions for correctness. Instead, they are responsible for making sense of one another's reasoning and reaching conclusions together. I have a higher expectation for whole-class discussion than I did during my earlier teaching: now I expect the students to listen closely and decide whether what they are hearing makes sense and whether it is mathematically correct. I hope that this expectation will push students to think critically about what they are hearing and try to understand.

The classroom discussion continued as follows and contains examples of the second talk move, which I explain after the transcript.

Grant: We thought the area was the same, 'cause pretty much all the angles are the same.

AS: So you're thinking that if the angles stay the same [points to corresponding angles], then the amount of space inside it should stay the same as well?

Grant: Yes.

AS: OK, *so you have Lane's explanation and Grant's. Can anyone explain why they agree or disagree with either of these?*

Craig: You can't rely on the angles to figure out the area, because a ninety-degree angle will always stay ninety degrees no matter how big it is and stuff, so the area should be bigger.

AS: So you're disagreeing with the idea of using the angles to decide?

Craig: Yeah.

AS: Let's get more of you to join in. Craig isn't agreeing with Grant's reasoning about the angles. *Can anyone describe if you agree or disagree with anything you have heard so far?* [Long pause] *Maybe you don't agree with Craig—maybe you want to back up Grant and his group. You might say something like, "Yes I think the angles would stay the same because. . . ."*

Sydney: I disagree, I don't think you should go with the angles just because the angles are the same. The lengths are different, and the lengths being different makes the whole shape bigger.

AS: If I pick this length right here, the height of the triangle, and I pick the height of the other triangle—that's a length, right?—and I put that together with the base that formed the ninety-degree angle, right? So what I heard you say is just because those two angles are the same, the actual lengths changed, which makes the space inside the original triangle smaller than the space inside the new one. *So you are saying you don't agree that the areas being the same, but do you agree that it is two times bigger?*

Sydney: Yes.

A talk move that I used here was *asking students to apply their own reasoning to someone else's reasoning*. In line 23, Grant reported that his group thought the areas of the two triangles were the same. The students had also already heard Lane (in lines 14–17) describe why he thought the area of the larger triangle was twice as big. I chose to prompt students to agree or disagree (e.g., in lines 27–28) with the two opposing explanations, knowing that neither was correct. I wanted everyone to grapple with the reasoning. With two different explanations available, students had to determine whether either seemed reasonable.

Asking a student to apply his or her own reasoning to what someone else says extends the first talk move—it promotes participation by specifically prompting student-to-student interaction. The hope is that students will realize that they have the responsibility of making sense of the concepts that their fellow classmates are grappling with, and that they should respond to one another in the discussion. These discourse strategies raised the level of interaction during the whole-class discussions, extending the critical thinking that occurred in the small groups and keeping more students engaged.

The third talk move being used is *revoicing*, in which "the teacher essentially tries to repeat some or all of what the student has said" (Chapin, O'Connor, and Anderson 2003, p. 12). Revoicing can be used to help the class make sense of what another student is trying to say. At times a student's reasoning can be difficult to follow from his or her explanation. Thus the whole-class discussion can become confusing rather quickly. In lines 6–7, Lane described how the larger triangle was stretched from the original. I thought that his utterance "there still has to be something in there" was vague, so I chose to revoice. In the subsequent turn, I said, "So you're saying the area can't be the same, it has to be bigger?" I thought that this question would make Lane's reasoning more apparent to the rest of the class, and I was able simultaneously to translate the notion of "something in there" to the more mathematical term *area*. Also, in lines 23–34, Grant's and Craig's comments about angles were brief and not very detailed. Although each was explaining his thinking, neither stated a conclusion. I thought that I should revoice to make sure everyone understood: "So you're thinking that if the angles stay the same [points to corresponding angles], then the amount of space inside it should stay the same as well?" With this utterance (lines 24–25) I formed their fragmented reasoning into a conditional statement with which they could agree or disagree. Also, in line 32, I took

Craig's comment "You can't rely on the angles to figure out the area" and revoiced it as "disagreeing with the idea of using angles to decide" because I wanted to continue to promote the interaction of students' ideas.

Sometimes the class benefits from hearing a student's thinking repeated through my revoicing. This revoicing also provides more time to absorb what is being said. For example, let us revisit lines 39 through 47:

Sydney: I disagree, I don't think you should go with the angles just because the angles are the same. The lengths are different, and the lengths being different makes the whole shape bigger.

AS: If I pick this length right here, the height of the triangle, and I pick the height of the other triangle—that's a length, right?–and I put that together with the base that formed the ninety-degree angle, right? *So what I heard you say is just because those two angles are the same, the actual lengths changed, which makes the space inside the original triangle smaller than the space inside the new one. So you are saying you don't agree that the areas being the same, but do you agree that it is two times bigger?*

Revoicing what a student has said requires a teacher to consider carefully what the student is trying to say. The temptation to add something substantial in revoicing is difficult to ignore. I do not want to take away the student's voice, but I want to make sure that the rest of the class can follow and participate in the discussion. When I reflect on the instance of revoicing in the last turn, I sense that I could have given Sydney the opportunity to elaborate on and clarify her thinking if I had asked her some clarifying questions. Instead, I chose to revoice her comments and added my interpretation of what I thought she said.

Even as I write these reflections, I do not always feel sure about when to revoice, and I am aware that when I try to revoice, I sometimes add something that the student did not intend (for more about tensions and questions that arise in considering revoicing, see chapter 7). The talk move of revoicing facilitates whole-class discussions, but I find it the most difficult one to use in the act of teaching. If I do not use revoicing carefully, I can find myself talking too much during the discussions and undermining the students' voices. I will continue to work on revoicing, and I anticipate that my skills in using this talk move purposefully will improve over time.

Conclusion

I am committed to continuing to work on improving the discourse in my classes' summary discussions. I have already noticed that using the talk moves I discuss above is changing the dynamics of my summary discussions: students now listen to one another and reflect on what is being said. With more practice, I hope that my comfort level will increase.

In analyzing my use of the three talk moves described, I have observed instances in which the moves were not as effective as I would have liked. I realize that this process of improvement will take time and that, as the students become more accustomed to the expectations, we will all improve together. As I continue this work, I am interested in looking more closely at how using these talk moves during summary discussions affects students' performance. I also plan to incorporate written prompts for students before and after summary discussions to determine whether the discussions are helping them improve their mathematical reasoning and strengthen their understanding of concepts. I am optimistic about what I will find.

Reflecting and Connecting with Practice

- Create a list of important social and mathematical norms. Which of these norms have you negotiated successfully with your students, and how did you do so? For example, do students address one another respectfully? Do students know that they need to provide mathematical reasons for their solutions? How might you establish additional norms? What techniques could you use to engage students in explicit discussions about social and mathematical norms for your class?
- All Angie's examples show some interesting discussions happening during "whole-class discussions." What important things do you see in each example? Which of these aspects of classroom interation are you already using? Which ones could you try to determine whether they benefit students in your class?
- If you have a "summary" part of your lesson, as Angie does, who does the summarizing? What techniques could you use to involve more

students in summarizing essential mathematical ideas? What might be some reasons for doing so?

- Part of Angie's focus in the "summary" part of her lesson is to have students share their different strategies for solving problems. When and how do you have students share multiple strategies? Videotape yourself during a time when you ask students to share multiple strategies. How did you decide which solutions to have students share? What role did you play in facilitating the sharing? In what ways did you use the multiple solutions to help students see connections among various representations or make mathematical generalizations?
- Angie is working on three talk moves in particular, because she believes they will help her classroom discourse be more mathematically productive. Do you use these talk moves in your classroom interactions? How do you think the talk moves might be beneficial in your classroom? How can you use these talk moves to give students more ownership of ideas? Try out the three talk moves. How did they affect students' participation?

References

Chapin, Suzanne H., M. Catherine O'Connor, and Nancy C. Anderson. *Classroom Discussions: Using Math Talk to Help Students Learn.* Sausalito, Calif.: Math Solutions Publications, 2003.

Lappan, Glenda, James Fey, William Fitzgerald, Susan Friel, and Elizabeth Phillips. *The Connected Mathematics Project.* Palo Alto, Calif.: Dale Seymour Publications, 1998.

———. *The Connected Mathematics Project 2.* Needham, Mass.: Pearson Prentice Hall, 2006a.

———. *Stretching and Shrinking (Connected Mathematics Project 2).* Needham, Mass.: Pearson Prentice Hall, 2006b.

National Council of Teachers of Mathematics (NCTM). *Curriculum and Evaluation Standards for School Mathematics.* Reston, Va.: NCTM, 1989.

Yackel, Erna, and Paul Cobb. "Sociomathematical Norms, Argumentation, and Autonomy in Mathematics." *Journal for Research in Mathematics Education* 27 (July 1996): 458–77.

Reflecting on and Adjusting One's Own Talk

Catherine O'Connor

THE work of teaching mathematics is undeniably complex. The teacher is called on to coordinate many dimensions of the subject's contents: mathematical concepts, entities, and procedures; graphic, linguistic, and numerical representations of those elements; and the everyday objects and experiences that the curriculum employs to make all the content comprehensible to students. The teacher is also called on to coordinate many dimensions not related to the contents: the tendency of twenty-five students to pay attention to different things, including one another; the ways that social relationships can filter into academic settings; and the joint management of time and content and activity.

Teaching mathematics becomes even more complex (although often more rewarding and productive) when one decides to use classroom talk strategically and intensively, as the teachers in this group have done. The teacher must still, of course, create and deliver a coherent lesson, using prescribed activities and materials, and he or she must still strive to engage students at each point along the way. Behavior and attention must still be managed. But in addition, for talk to be used effectively, a classroom culture of respect must be in place, and the teacher must ensure that all students can participate in the discourse, not just those who are most willing or able to jump into the talk. Most daunting is the fact that when teachers open the lesson up to participatory talk by all students, they have no way of knowing what ideas will emerge. Wrong ideas, insightful but unexpected ideas, earnest but unintelligible contributions—all these emerge when classroom talk is used extensively.

From this perspective, we can easily understand why many teachers shrink from using classroom discourse in their mathematics teaching as extensively as the authors of these chapters. And when we consider the pressures on these authors (and all teachers) to meet the demands of ever-expanding "accountability" testing, we get a glimpse of how significant their achievements really are. Each author demonstrates impressive insight into teaching, and equally impressive commitment to examining her own teaching. These teachers have intelligently explored the ideas in the research the group read—and many of those ideas are not easy to apply to the complexities of one's own teaching. (Nor are they all clearly laid out in the literature; see reference to the work of O'Connor and Michaels, and that of Chapin, O'Connor, and Anderson, below.) The degree to which each teacher has successfully engaged in the difficult tasks of reflecting on, analyzing, and then attempting to change her own use of talk is quite amazing.

Tammie Cass, in her chapter titled "'It,' 'That,' and 'What'? Vagueness and the Development of Mathematical Vocabulary," explores a difficult topic—how we use language in moment-to-moment interactions in ways that make sense to the speaker but not always to listeners. For many years, linguists have tried to characterize the many ways that humans refer to objects, individuals, and events using elliptical expressions that do not convey all the necessary information, yet are somehow understood. When someone says, "I'm parked out back," the hearer does not usually say, "But how can that be? You're standing here talking to me!" When a waiter says, "The ham sandwich left without paying," no one runs to the door looking for a fleeing sandwich. And listeners often have no problem understanding the referent of the very uninformative third-person singular neuter pronoun *it.*

In describing an activity designed to give students a robust sense of the concept of *median,* Cass gives us the following sequence of utterances. I have added numbers to each instance of *it* for easier reference:

> [W]e just added one card with a lot of letters on *it* (1) . ... So no matter whether we add or remove cards at one end of the data, *it* (2) pulls the median but *it* (3) doesn't pull **it** (4) very much. ...When we remove [cards], *it's* (5) the opposite, when we remove from the low end, the median got bigger, didn't **it**? (6)

The referents are easy for us, adult readers, to decipher: (1) is a card; (2) and (3) refer to the action of adding cards at the high or low end; (4) is a reference to the median itself. The fifth *it* refers to the outcome of that action, and (6) is another reference to the median. The preceding is normal human discourse, no more vague or communicatively inadequate than most conversations. As long as we know what is being talked about, we can follow the conversation.

As Cass insightfully notes, however, correct interpretation of this stream of "its" *depends on the focused attention of the listener.* If one is thinking about something else, one may come back to attention to hear someone using the word *it* and not be able to figure out what "it" refers to. And focused attention is sometimes in short supply in the complexity of the middle school classroom. In fact, focused attention is just one of the dimensions that a teacher must coordinate along with everything else.

So what is a teacher to do about the vagueness of pronouns? Cass takes the approach that I think is the most likely to succeed: she tries to raise the level of attention of *all classroom participants.* By using such talk moves as repetition by students, revoicing by the teacher, and queries about reasons for agreeing and disagreeing, Cass institutes a classroom culture that is itself the only reliable corrective for the indeterminacy that is rampant in human communication.

Early in the chapter, Cass herself provides us with an ideal example of the unavoidable difficulty that teachers encounter when the topic of conversation is a complex amalgam of concepts, words, procedures, visual and verbal representations, events, and actions.

TC: Think about six-fifths. What type of fraction is that? Alice?

Alice: Improper.

TC: Improper, which means?

Alice: You can't do it.

Cass assumes that Alice means "You can't do the fraction," and is concerned that Alice's previous understanding about fractions whose numerators are larger than their denominators has vanished. I think that another interpretation is possible: Alice may have thought she was answering the question "What does *improper* mean?" Her answer "you can't do it" may thus be a definitional statement: to say that something is improper means that it is off limits.

Both speakers are intelligent and trying hard to communicate, but this example reminds us that classrooms are places in which words, concepts, objects, and symbolic and graphic representations all coexist as entities that may be mentioned in the discourse, giving rise to endless instances of confusion. If this point were not clear enough, one has only to read Angie Shindelar's analysis of her student Gavin's solution path for the problem 3/4 × 21. Her understanding of students' mathematical reasoning (and possibly some psychic abilities) are revealed in her adept responses. Here, readers are at a disadvantage: what exactly is Gavin trying to say? Because we are not there, with the board and the representations in front of us, his meaning is almost impossible to understand.

Angie Shindelar succeeds in taking us the next step in her journey, pointing to yet another coordination challenge: she may succeed at drawing out Gavin's complex meaning, and those of other students, one by one, but this process leads to other students' tuning out, or at least sitting silently, possibly unengaged. Her realization that the first stage of using discourse more intensively to understand students' reasoning can result in a "ping-pong game" is a brilliant insight. The system of talk and action that one is trying to put into place is a complex and interconnected structure—a push here produces a pull there. A choice of one interaction precludes another. Shindelar decides to restructure the way her classroom works, strategically introducing discourse moves to change the balance of participation, particularly in whole-class discussion. She had already succeeded in eliciting productive discussion in small-group work, and she wanted to leverage this level of discussion in whole-group discussions.

Shindelar provides excellent examples of her students' initial responses to her use of three moves: (1) prompting students for further participation, (2) asking students to apply their own reasoning to someone else's reasoning, and (3) revoicing. I focus here on her last example. Shindelar skillfully uses revoicing to make sure that all students can hear and understand another student's contribution. (This "rebroadcasting" function is fully appreciated by these teacher-researchers, given their familiarity with the noise and confusion of the classroom. Many university researchers overlook this fundamental function.) But, like Jean Krusi in chapter 7, Shindelar worries that sometimes she adds too much of her own thinking to the student's utterance, going beyond what that student intended. Krusi even worries that her revoicing actually forecloses her students' opportunities to reason about their own or other students' contributions. I have encountered other teachers who have the same feeling, and these wonderful chapters have prompted me to take this opportunity to issue a word of encouragement and reassurance.

I have learned from skillful teachers that the essential ingredient in making sure that your revoicing results in more participation by students rather than less lies in the *second* part of the move, after whatever reformulation you utter. After you repeat or rephrase what the student has said, always go back to the originator of the idea and offer an explicit opportunity for a response. The easiest way to do so, we have learned from watching, is to ask, "Is that what you said?" or "Is that what you meant?" or even just to finish your reformulation with a rising intonation, as Krusi does in this example: "OK, so you're saying they meet at something, twelve?" (The importance of this second part of the revoicing move was not clear in O'Connor and Michaels [1996] but is made explicit in Chapin, O'Connor, and Anderson [2003].)

Krusi notices her own patterns in this kind of discourse:

> When revoicing an incorrect statement, I tended to lift my voice at the end, making it a question, thus cuing that I was questioning the student's idea. I revoiced correct contributions with statements, which seemed to confirm the student's contribution. In these cases, the revoicing served an evaluative role.

We have found that when this checking back or questioning is used only with incorrect statements, the revoicing move has less power to elicit participation. In contrast, when every revoicing ends with this checking back, asking the student for verification or clarification, the discussion really opens up. Students quickly overcome any hesitation they may have about correcting the teacher's interpretation of their utterance. They start to take ownership of the formulations that teachers offer, even when the teachers use terms or phrases that the students are not yet ready to use on their own. In my experience, checking back can actually accelerate students' willingness to use mathematical terminology and more academic language. The ability of these teacher-researchers to observe and analyze the fine-grained details of their own classroom discourse will no doubt ensure their success in making this small adjustment.

Careful readers will be struck by the beauty of these teachers' respect for their students' ideas and their commitment to each student's right to have his or her ideas discussed intact. The fact that these worries about revoicing emerged in their action research reflects their deep commitment to fostering the intellectual growth of each individual learner on his or her own terms. Yet my experience tells me that they need not worry too much. The intellectual environment they have provided for their students, as evidenced in these transcripts, is supportive, participatory, and everything the NCTM Standards writers could have hoped for. By bringing the tools of action research to bear on their classrooms, they have offered those of us who are not in the classroom a set of cogent pointers to the real complexity of the work we write about, and the realistic paths to making that complex reality work for all students.

References

Chapin, Suzanne H., Catherine O'Connor, and Nancy Canavan Anderson. *Classroom Discussions: Using Math Talk to Help Students Learn.* Sausalito, Calif.: Math Solutions Publications, 2003.

O'Connor, M. Catherine, and Sarah Michaels. "Shifting Participant Frameworks: Orchestrating Thinking Practices in Group Discussion." In *Discourse, Learning, and Schooling,* edited by Deborah Hicks, pp. 63–103. New York: Cambridge University Press, 1996.

SECTION 5

Selective Listening: Ignoring and Hearing Students' Voices

CHAPTER 10

Listening to My Students' Thoughts on Mathematics Education

Joseph Obrycki

> That they do it—that they have to spend some time sorting things out by themselves—this doesn't touch anybody? It doesn't make you wonder—how do they work, these children? How do they use their minds?
>
> —*Caleb Gattegno*

> Now I can look at a theorem and wonder how it works or why it works and then I can work it through myself. And understand.
>
> —*Kevin, tenth-grade geometry student*

Who knows what is best for students? Who determines what mathematical topics are covered or not covered, what questions are asked, answered, or unanswered? Who asks the questions, and who answers the questions? Who decides what textbooks are used, what formulas are memorized, and what is understood by the students? Who knows what mathematics they will need to be successful in life? Who defines what it means to be mathematically successful?

I believe that teachers and students are in the best position to judge and shape the mathematics classroom, and therefore mathematics education. In classrooms all across America, teachers and students are the people who constitute what mathematics education actually is. Many mathematics educators spend time in classrooms, studying and writing about what mathematics education is, or what it should be. Many mathematicians spend time looking at textbooks, thinking about the curricula, and making comments or suggestions. Many administrators spend time in classrooms doing observations and then writing evaluations criticizing or praising the teacher. Many parents spend time looking at their child's mathematics homework, talking about the class, and voicing their opinions. I do not want to imply that these parties are unimportant or without merit. Clearly, they each bring an informative perspective to mathematics teaching and learning. But the people with a primary interest in teaching and learning mathematics are those who engage with it daily, year in and year out—the students and their teachers. In my opinion, precisely these two voices are the ones that need to be heard; yet these voices are in danger of being drowned out by the previously mentioned parties.

Other chapters in this book show that teachers are informed, poised, knowledgeable, and thoughtful. I hope the previous chapters will convince readers that teachers should form one of the authoritative voices in mathematics education. I would therefore like to spend a little time listening to another authoritative voice in mathematics education—the students. I hope to give my students some time and space to share their thoughts about our classroom, about other mathematics classrooms, and about mathematics teaching and learning. By listening to our students, we can gain a better understanding of mathematics education from the people who, it seems to me, are really the ones most influenced by it.

As teachers, we have the professional responsibility to guide our students and help them become better citizens who are knowledgeable about mathematics. This statement does not suggest that we should respond to all their demands in the affirmative. Rather, I am suggesting that we listen, in a serious and thoughtful manner, to what they have to say about mathematics education. We should not dismiss everything our students have to say about mathematics teaching off-hand simply because they are our students and we consider ourselves to be in authority over them. Similarly, we should not elevate the students' perspective to that of total policy control. Indeed, every story of mathematical education has two sides: the teacher's and the students'.

Background

The material in this chapter is based on my teaching of geometry and precalculus to high school students in a suburban school district. Rather than have my students follow formulas and procedures, I believed (and still believe) that students should understand the mathematics they are learning. My philosophy of teaching mathematics can be summed up in two statements:

1. Mathematics makes sense.
2. Our students can, and should, make sense of mathematics.

The first statement is about the nature of mathematics and mathematical thought. Mathematics is not a random collection of rules and procedures, disconnected and decreed from on high. It is a set of human inventions and conventions abstracted from daily life and focused on truth. The quadratic formula (the quintessential example) did not fall out of the sky and hit mathematicians on the head. It was arrived at through a consistent thought process that ultimately made sense.

The second statement is about the teaching and learning of mathematics. Not only does mathematics make sense, but our students also must make sense of the mathematics we are teaching. Students can understand where the quadratic formula comes from, why the Pythagorean theorem is true, and why $\sin^2\theta + \cos^2\theta = 1$. This statement goes one step beyond the *possibility* of students' making sense of mathematics and says that making sense of mathematics is an important outcome for students. However, some teachers believe that although students are able to make sense of mathematics, to teach toward that outcome would take too long and not as much material would be covered. Others believe that if we teach the procedures now, students will come to understand the concepts later. I firmly believe that teaching students *why* the formulas work the way they do and that they can make sense of mathematics is important for their mathematical and intellectual development.

My philosophical justification for this position is that we are teaching humans, not machines. If we teach only formulas and procedures, then we are teaching only things that we could program a machine or computer to do. We are then programming students to act in certain ways when confronted with certain situations, treating them only as intellectual animals. If we want to program machines, we should become computer scientists. We chose to become teachers so that we could teach humans. Only humans can understand *why* a certain procedure makes sense. Only humans can generate mathematical knowledge. A computer cannot create a formula, reason a new way to solve a problem, or connect pieces of mathematical knowledge into a coherent whole. Only humans can do so, and since we teach humans, we should treat them as such.

This, then, is my philosophy about, and approach to, teaching mathematics. I continually try to ask students to understand the mathematics they are learning, to explain why a mathematical concept makes sense, or to justify a formula. I see all mathematical knowledge as being connected, and I believe that students can and should learn the concepts of mathematics. I believe that concepts guide procedures, not the other way around.

I anticipate that not much of this thinking is new to the readers of this piece. The National Council of Teachers of Mathematics (1989, 1991, 2000) has been saying similar things—although perhaps not as bluntly—for many years now. But this type of shift in instructional focus is not without repercussions, which I have felt in the form of frustration expressed by my students throughout my participation in the Discourse Project. This very participation, however, has acted to counterweight the voices telling me that what I was doing was not effective, was noninstructional, and was not best practice. My participation in the project gave me a place and a time to interact with people who were like-minded about mathematics teaching, were interested in becoming better teachers, and were attempting to make the same types of changes in their classroom discourse as I was. The indirect support I received from the people involved in the project kept me from shutting off the part of my teaching brain that told me to teach for understanding and to teach concepts as well as procedures. A much easier course of action for me would have been to go back to a more conventional method and resort to standing up in front of the classroom, writing formulas and examples on the board. But this type of move would have been intellectually dishonest (see Ball [1993] for a discussion of being "intellectually honest" in her teaching)—not only to the mathematics but to myself, and perhaps most important, to my students.

Listening to My Students

I believe that we teachers need to be concerned with the students' perspective. What will help them understand mathematics now? What will help them learn and remember mathematics for the future? What will help them on the standardized tests that they will need to move into college? What will get them ready for the mathematical and intellectual demands of college? Through my attempt to answer these questions, I forced myself to look at classroom discourse, or more specifically, the *lack of* students' contributions in my classroom. My students are the ones who need to learn mathematics, not I. To learn mathematics means to speak it, write it, and participate in mathematical thought and conversation on a daily basis. "Teaching is mostly listening, learning is mostly telling" is a tenet easy enough to understand in theory but difficult to put into practice. The opportunity to see veteran teachers whom I knew and respected trying the same sorts of changes gave me great courage and the stamina to see these changes through an entire school year.

As large as the shift from teacher-centered to student-centered or group-centered discourse may seem to teachers, it must seem even greater to our students—especially to secondary school students. After years of education during which their role has been to sit quietly at their desks, face forward, raise their hands when they want to talk, and generally turn off the cognitive processing part of their brains, shifting to a classroom where they are asked to talk, wonder, apply, and actively think about mathematics represents a colossal change. Mathematicians, parents, administrators, and certainly mathematics educators have had their own opportunities to speak about the impact of this shift, but the students, for the most part, have not. I hope to contribute to this conversation an opportunity for others to listen to what my students have said about mathematics teaching and learning.

Student Interviews

At the end of my fourth year of teaching, I selected six students to interview. Because many students at my school switch teachers at the semester break because of scheduling, I selected three sets of students, each consisting of one boy and one girl whom I had taught only first semester, only second semester, or both semesters. I chose students who had done equally well in my class and previous mathematics classes. I did so to minimize the effect that a higher or lower grade might have on their responses. I deliberately did not select students who I knew or sensed had a particular bias, either positive or negative, toward me and my class. Clearly, the students selected were not without opinions, as the interviews show; but I tried to select students who I thought could not immediately be dismissed as clearly either "pro-Obrycki" or "anti-Obrycki."

The students were individually interviewed by Michelle Cirillo, not by me, so that my presence would not affect the students' responses. Michelle was already familiar with both the content of geometry and my classroom environment, so she was an obvious choice to conduct the interviews. I wrote several drafts of questions, and after she and I discussed them, I revised them. I was not present during any of the interviews, and Michelle was free to amend or add questions as she saw fit.

Before the interview, I told the students that they were going to be asked questions about mathematics teaching and asked to compare my class with other mathematics classes. The students were told that although the interviews were being recorded, I would not have access to them until the weekend after school ended. Therefore, I would not be listening to the interviews until the participants were no longer my students. In the sections that follow, I describe some of the important themes that I heard in the interviews.

Differences in Teaching Styles

One of the first things that I noticed was the students' consistent descriptions of other mathematics classes and of my classes, and their perceived differences between them. All the students described their previous mathematics classes as consisting of memorization and applications of formulas without any real understanding of why the formulas made sense. In contrast, they described my mathematics class using such words as *figure out, explain, think, why,* and *understand.* Furthermore, all the students used these words from the beginning, and implicitly contrasted using the formulas mechanically (typical of previous or other mathematics classes) with understanding the concepts and why the formulas work (typical of my mathematics class). They talked about this aspect within the first few minutes of the interview, before they were asked about the balance between concepts and procedures in a mathematics class. To these students, the difference between my mathematics class and their previous mathematics classes was immediately and clearly obvious. In her interview, for example, Chloe volunteered to explain the differences that she noted even before Michelle asked her about them.

MC: Okay, so first, how would you describe math classes you have had in the past before you had Mr. Obrycki this year? What does math class typically look like?

Chloe: Um, I don't know. It seems like a lot of times they give us the formulas, we go through it, so, you know, we know how to get through it without messing up, and then we get homework on it, and then we have to memorize the formulas and stuff, usually.

MC: OK.

Chloe: And then, like, do you want me to compare it to what [Mr. Obrycki] does?

MC: Yes, that's my next question. And so then describe what math class has been like this semester for you.

Chloe: Now it's more of, like, we have to figure out *why* it works that way, and it's not, like, he doesn't just give us formulas, we have to kind of figure out the formulas, and, like, figure out why those formulas would work.

Chloe's description of her previous mathematics class is consistent with typical descriptions of conventional mathematics classes in the United States (e.g., Schoenfeld [1988]; Stigler and Hiebert, [1999]). Her previous mathematics classes had emphasized getting the correct answer "without messing up" and memorizing formulas. In contrast, Chloe said that my mathematics class placed more emphasis on students' understanding rather than on just memorizing the formulas. In addition, she pointed out that the students were responsible for creating the understanding of the formulas ("we have to kind of figure out the formulas"). These ideas also appeared in other students' interviews, for example, the interview with Kevin and the one with Leah:

Kevin: Obrycki likes to explain theorems to us and try to make us figure them out so we can understand them, not just having them but understanding *why* they work in the first place.

Leah: You get to see, like, a lot more of *why*. It's not just "This is the formula, do it." It's "This is the formula, this is what it involves," and you had to find it out for yourself. So it's more of a challenge.

My students said that although *their previous mathematics classes had focused on formulas and memorization,* my classroom instruction departed from this norm because *I also expected them to understand the formulas.* Furthermore, I expected them to *actively generate these understandings* for themselves rather than passively receive them from me. Each of these three themes was discussed in detail throughout the interviews.

In the sections that follow, I use the interview data to illustrate the ways that students talked about several topics: the fact that most of their previous experiences told them that learning mathematics is about following step-by-step procedures; the ways that my class asked them to think; and how, through that thinking, they grew to understand that they could generate mathematical understandings themselves.

Following Step-by-Step Procedures

A potential consequence of learning that mathematics is primarily about memorizing procedures to get the right answer is that it fosters a belief that mathematics, as a body of knowledge, consists of lists of steps to be taken or procedures to be followed when confronted with certain problems. Learning mathematics, then, is only a process of memorizing those steps, then reproducing them on cue. Since my class did not emphasize this methodology, I was curious about what my students would say when asked whether learning mathematics is mostly learning what steps to follow. The following excerpt from one of the interviews provides an example:

> ***MC:*** If somebody said to you, "Well, learning mathematics is mostly learning what steps to follow," do you agree with that, disagree with that?
>
> ***Jonathan:*** Um, I think I disagree with that because it's not learning what steps to follow.... I think it's being able to lead yourself through steps. 'Cause when you say "follow," I think of what you had said earlier about explaining something, just like repeating what someone told you. But you kind of have to find your own path through the problem, I guess. So I wouldn't say it's following steps, necessarily.
>
> ***MC:*** Do you think last semester you might have agreed with that statement?
>
> ***Jonathan:*** I would have thought differently about that statement last semester. I would have said the exact opposite.

Here Jonathan pointed out a subtle distinction between following and using steps: just because mathematical problems are solved using steps does not mean that those steps are the solution to the mathematical problem. Students should not be asked to follow already constructed procedures to solve problems; instead, as Jonathan said, students need to "find [their] own path through the problem." Clearly this path will consist of steps, but this statement in no way implies or mandates that those steps be spelled out by the teacher. The transcripts from Chloe's and Leah's interviews seem to show that my students understood that learning mathematics involves more than just learning what steps to follow, even though at times the steps are emphasized.

Chloe: Um, I think [following steps is] what's taught sometimes, but that's not necessarily what it is. Like, you have to understand why something is what it is and how it affects other stuff … and how that makes you get your answer.

Leah: Um, I agree that you have to learn the steps to follow, but I don't think that's all of it. I think it's also learning what's behind the steps that you are following.

Both Chloe and Leah indicated that mathematics also consists of learning concepts "behind" the procedures and understanding how these concepts interact. Their perception shows that they had developed a more sophisticated view of mathematics, which included both concepts and procedures.

Thinking

A focus on procedural learning emphasizes mathematical behaviors: do this, then this, then arrive at the answer. A shift to include mathematical concepts entails an emphasis on the processes of mathematical thinking. Several students mentioned thinking as an important element of my class, which I anticipated as a possible departure from their previous experiences in mathematics classes. I had not anticipated that the notion of thinking in school might represent a departure from their entire educational experience, as described by Ruth in the following passage:

Ruth: The first semester, it was more of … he would give us a problem, and then tell us to apply it. And I was not used to that at all. I was not used to—*in any class*—being given a basic problem and then this, like, crazy, elaborate problem and saying, "You can use this equation to solve this problem." And I was, like, "I have no idea how to do that. You're giving me this huge problem and a teeny piece of it, and you want me to, like …"

MC: Think?

Ruth: Yeah, I don't know. Yeah, *it is more of thinking than any other class* just because usually, it's, like [in other classes], this is a problem in the book, you get the same problem on your test with different numbers. But then [in this class] we're given more elaborate problems to solve, and none of us are used to that.

Although in this exchange Michelle supplied the significant word for Ruth, several other students used the word *think* to describe my class without Michelle's prompting. For example, Jonathan, Chloe, and Kevin all talked about how they have to think more in my class:

Jonathan: I was used to being lazy the last few years 'cause you just knew the formula and you could just go through and do your homework real fast, but now *you actually have to think* through things more, I guess.

Chloe: I think [Mr. Obrycki's approach is] good 'cause … before it just seems like there's a lot of memorizing or you just write it down on your paper and then just go through the steps. And now it's … more … *you actually have to think,* I guess.

Kevin: Here, *he makes us think about it,* and more get into depth of it.

In these examples, my students explicitly contrast using formulas and following steps with thinking. Their comments make clear that they do not believe that using a prescribed procedure to get an answer constitutes thinking. Both Jonathan and Chloe used almost identical phrases to describe using formulas ("just go through and do your homework real fast" and "just write it down on your paper and then just go through the steps") and to articulate what was asked of them during my class ("you actually have to think"). Kevin pointed out that merely learning procedures represents shallow learning, whereas understanding concepts represents "depth" of mathematical knowledge. I am encouraged by the fact that, when given the opportunity to describe their experiences, these students were able to differentiate between what I would call surface learning and deep learning.

Generating Mathematical Knowledge

Simply giving students a command to think, however, is not all that helpful. All thinking is intentional; that is, *thinking* requires *thinking about* something. Rather than give students formulas and procedures to memorize and copy, I prefer to ask students to think about and generate their own mathematical knowledge. After they had spent time in my class, I wanted to know whether students believed that they could do so. Although many students asked Michelle to clarify the question before answering, all six interviewed students said that it was possible for students to generate mathematical knowledge. In the first example that follows, Michelle presented her typical clarification of the question when asked by the students.

> ***MC:*** So do you think it's possible for students to generate mathematical knowledge?
>
> ***Leah:*** To start being able to think mathematically?
>
> ***MC:*** To generate mathematical knowledge—that you would, um, the bell rings and you start math class, and there's something that you didn't know, and by the end of math class there's something that you now know because you generated it yourself without having someone tell you.
>
> ***Leah:*** Yeah, I think that's a good way to learn, actually. I think that's my favorite way to pick up on things.... As long as you stay on task, I think everyone generates ideas in math class.

Here Leah not only agreed that students can generate mathematical knowledge but also stated that everyone does so provided that they stay on task. For Leah, generating mathematical knowledge was not just a possibility but her preferred learning method and something that every student does automatically just by paying attention. Other students were not necessarily as strong in their agreement, but they all did agree with the basic premise that students can generate their own mathematical knowledge. For example:

> ***Ruth:*** I definitely think that with enough time and some Obrycki direction, we can figure stuff out. I don't think there's anything keeping us from doing so, and I think this class has helped us be able to do so.

My students' acknowledgment of this idea is significant, because a teacher cannot successfully use the techniques that NCTM describes unless students change their perspective on where knowledge originates. If students believe that all knowledge must come from the teacher or textbook, they are more likely to resist attempts to move away from a teacher-centered discourse. If, in contrast, students believe that they can create their own mathematical knowledge, and if they are comfortable with this method of *learning*, the teacher's task changes dramatically. For teachers, this shift in students' perspectives can increase the ease with which we can change our classroom discourse; we can become the proverbial "guide on the side" rather than the "sage on the stage."

Sorting Things Out by Themselves

How does the change to "guide on the side" play out in the classroom? What are teachers to do if not share our knowledge with our students? If we do not show students how to solve problems, how will they learn the skills to be successful? Rather than rehash other views on these questions or insert my own thoughts, I will again yield the floor to my students.

> ***MC:*** So what is it that [Mr. Obrycki] does?
>
> ***Jonathan:*** I don't know. I guess he knows how to approach something in a way we're familiar with so we can decipher it for ourselves, I guess.
>
> ***MC:*** So does he ask questions, does he give you hints, like what kind of …
>
> ***Jonathan:*** He asks a lot of questions, like "Why would this work?" or sometimes he'll give us small hints, but he never comes straight out and says, "This is how you do it" until we're done with it and we figure it out for ourselves.

As Jonathan said, having the students "figure it out for [them]selves" is, of course, the entire point. Students' ownership of the mathematics is a crucial piece of teaching that I believe conventional pedagogy lacks. Jonathan explained this outcome later in the interview:

> ***Jonathan:*** And [Obrycki]'ll make us work through it, and while we're thinking, he'll sit in his chair up there and we'll just be sitting there for sometimes, like, five minutes at a time, just trying to figure out what to do next. And he doesn't give us the answers, he just makes us think through it and he kind of guides us.

Students need to believe that they can make sense of the mathematics they are studying. *Giving* students the reasons that formulas work but continuing to own those reasons as the teacher just pushes the problem of conventional pedagogy back one step. Alternatively, setting up situations in which students generate concepts and understandings *for themselves* is, in my opinion, a necessary and crucial piece of students' full participation in mathematics. Other students also noticed this emphasis on students' ownership of the mathematics and the mathematical understanding, as exemplified in the following transcripts from the interviews with Leah, Kevin, and Ruth:

> **Leah:** I would say [the biggest difference between Mr. Obrycki's class and other mathematics classes is] the way Mr. Obrycki went about teaching. ... He had you more understand it yourself, where other teachers just explain it all to you right up front. ... They just explain it all to you. But he forced you to look at it yourself and explain—almost like force yourself to explain why the different formulas are how they are.
>
> **Kevin:** He makes us do a lot of the work, like explaining things. He'll give a theorem up on the board, but we have to walk through it with him, he doesn't just give it to us. And I think that comes hard for a lot of people, because in the past we've just been given theorems and given the actual problems. And here he makes us think about it and more get into depth of it.
>
> **Ruth:** [The activities we do in class] it basically just ... tells you to do step by step and then, at the end *you've* reached the formula. *You* figure out the formula and then it says, it'll be, like, now you have the formula. You'll figure it out, but you didn't realize this whole time that you were building the formula.

The quotations above draw out the main shift in pedagogy that I was trying to make—the change from a discourse centered on, and owned by, the teacher to a discourse centered on, and owned by, the students. I want my students to be the ones who think, discuss, and justify mathematical ideas, because ultimately they are the ones who need to learn the mathematics.

Conclusion

So what does this all mean? To me, it moves the aspect of teaching that I really care about to the forefront: the students. The students are the ones who need to learn mathematics, not the teacher; therefore the students need to be talking, conjecturing, experimenting, thinking, generating, and participating in mathematical discourse. If as teachers we dominate the classroom discourse and present all the examples in a mechanical, perfunctory manner, we rob our students of their best opportunity to really learn something. I believe that we often need to let students figure it out for themselves. If we allow our students to interact and grapple with mathematics as it truly is, we can hope that they will not view mathematics as a shallow collection of problems associated with one another merely because they occur on consecutive pages of the textbook. We should realize that having students understand where the formulas come from and why they are true is a crucial component of any high-quality mathematics lesson, not just a nice aside that we sometimes take the time to address.

Listening to my students gave me a great deal of hope that this type of mathematical teaching and learning is possible and that it can have a positive impact on our teaching, our students' learning, and the mathematical discourse in our classrooms. Against the multitude of forces and voices telling us (me) how to teach, what instructional style to use, how students learn best, and that students cannot possibly figure this out on their own, I ask for a moment of quiet for us to listen, I mean *really* listen, to what Ruth had to say at the end of her interview.

Ruth was in my class both semesters this past year. In her interview, she said that at the beginning of the year, she really did not like my class and that mathematics was harder for her than it had ever been. She said that she was "terrified" when she found out that I would again be her teacher the second semester. I remember that at the beginning of the year, when she was working on an activity, she would become very frustrated with me when in my judgment she was ready to figure out the next piece by herself and I tried to walk away. As the year progressed, she became more comfortable and would interrupt my question to tell me to go away, because she saw what she was supposed to do next. By the end of the year, she was asking me to restate what we were trying to prove as a class and refusing to let me put specific numbers in the problem because she wanted to think about it abstractly a bit longer. She experienced this transition from conventional to reform-based pedagogy more immediately, clearly, and concretely than I have, as I was taught only through a conventional approach. To her, the discussion about conventional and reform mathematics teaching is not a philosophical debate occurring in journal articles, or being talked about at annual conferences removed from any classroom, but *her life,* her real and immediate life in mathematics class for the past year.

So please, fellow teachers, administrators, parents, mathematicians, mathematics educators, a moment of quiet.....

MC: Anything that you'd like other math teachers, or people like myself who are going to be teaching math teachers, to know, or just people who want to improve teaching math?

Ruth: Um, I definitely would just say that, I mean, I don't know if the answer should be withheld all the time, but letting students get to the answer and not just presenting it to them is definitely worthwhile, even if it takes a little longer.

MC: Yeah. Even if your students don't like you at first?

Ruth: Yeah. Just a little bit. But then later on, they'll, I think they'll be thanking you.

Reflecting and Connecting with Practice

- Many external factors influence what and how we teach mathematics. Patty's chapter and now Joe's mention concern with the emphasis on procedures instead of concepts. Joe said that time is a factor in trying to teach conceptually. Are you concerned about "covering" topics in your curriculum to the detriment of teaching conceptually? Joe also began his chapter by describing many stakeholders in mathematics education who try to influence the teaching-learning process: university mathematics educators, mathematicians, administrators, parents, teachers, and students. How does each of these stakeholders influence what and how you teach?
- Consider how your students might answer the following questions: What is mathematics? How would you describe mathematics class? Do you think that you can generate mathematical knowledge? Ask your students to write a journal entry about these questions. How do your expectations compare with their actual responses? How do the responses compare with what you have written in your beliefs mapping? If students responded quite differently from the way you expected, what could you do to facilitate the kinds of thinking about mathematics and mathematics class that would satisfy you?
- The lack of students' contributions that Joe observed in his classroom led him to try to understand his students better. When and how do your students contribute in your class? Have you ever had

students "figure out" a formula on their own? What are the advantages of having students derive formulas? How do you ensure that your students are engaged mathematically? Joe contends that learning mathematics means to speak it, write it, and participate in mathematical thought and conversation. When and how do your students speak, write, and participate in mathematical thought and conversation?

- Write a brief interview that you or a colleague could conduct with a small group of carefully selected students to improve your understanding of your students' perceptions of your classroom activities. How do you think they view your class in comparison with other mathematics classes they have taken? After the interview, consider the following questions: What did you learn about their perceptions? What kinds of processes did they use to describe the activity you engage them in? How will this information influence your teaching?
- Joe ended his chapter by writing about Ruth, a student who clearly disliked his teaching when she first started in his class. In the interview, however, her comments reveal that she came to understand and appreciate what he was trying to do. When you try something novel or push students in ways they have not been pushed before, do you have some "Ruths" in your class? If so, how might you help them understand the value of these kinds of activities?

References

Ball, Deborah L. "With an Eye on the Mathematics Horizon: Dilemmas of Teaching Elementary School Mathematics." *Elementary School Journal* 93 (1993): 373–97.

Gattegno, Caleb. "How Do Children Use Their Minds?" www.atm.org.uk/people/gattegnoclips/ATM-Gattegno-07.mp3.

National Council of Teachers of Mathematics (NCTM). *Curriculum and Evaluation Standards for School Mathematics.* Reston, Va.: NCTM, 1989.

———. *Professional Standards for Teaching Mathematics.* Reston, Va.: NCTM, 1991.

———. *Principles and Standards for Teaching Mathematics.* Reston, Va.: NCTM, 2000.

Schoenfeld, Alan H. "When Good Teaching Leads to Bad Results: The Disasters of 'Well Taught' Mathematics Courses." *Educational Psychologist* 23 (Spring 1988): 145–66.

Stigler, James W., and James Hiebert. *The Teaching Gap.* New York: The Free Press, 1999.

SECTION 6

Conclusions

CHAPTER 11

Synthesizing the Bases of Purposeful Discourse: Reading, Reflecting, and Community

Beth Herbel-Eisenmann
Michelle Cirillo
Samuel Otten

> Writing an afterword can be a delicate task.... As a university-based researcher, my afterword might be construed as an attempt to assess the value of this work, a valuation handed down from the academy: This I did not want.... I was left with the conundrum of how to offer an account of what I think is the very special—in fact unique—value of this work without seeming to offer an unasked-for summative evaluation. I will try to frame my remarks in a way that will show my great admiration for the work of this group, and my gratitude to them for what I have learned.
>
> —Catherine O'Connor
> *Regarding Children's Words: Teacher Research on Language and Literacy*

The contributions made by the teacher-researchers in the previous chapters highlight how thoughtful, reflective, and candid mathematics teachers can be. Much is to be learned by looking across the set of chapters and synthesizing some important points. Like O'Connor, describing her conundrum in the opening quotation, we do not want this chapter to be seen as a summative evaluation of this work. We have learned a lot from being part of this group, and we have great admiration for the teacher-researchers and the work they are doing in their secondary school mathematics classrooms. We are amazed at their willingness to open their practice to us and to the broader community by contributing to this book. And as this chapter and the one that follows it exemplify, this broader community consists of educators of mathematics teachers as much as mathematics teachers. We acknowledge that this synthesis of essential points is based on our reading and interpretation of the work, and we do not claim that it captures the views of the teacher-researchers.

For the sake of clarity and brevity, we decided to organize this chapter along three dimensions. First, the *literature* on classroom discourse influenced not only the ways that the teacher-researchers think and talk about their classroom practice but also what they do in their classrooms. Second, the process of *reflection,* which occurred in the study-group activities and the action research projects, both gave the teacher-researchers opportunity and time to decide what they wanted to change in their practice and helped promote that change. Finally, we highlight the important role that *community* played in supporting the participants throughout this process. Although all these points are interrelated, we treat them as separate sections because each is important in its own right. We expand on each of the three dimensions and illustrate them by referring both to ideas the teacher-researchers described in this volume and to things they have said in interviews. Through the discussions of these three points, we also seek to illustrate the power of doing research *with* mathematics teachers rather than *on* them.

The Influences of Reading Literature on Classroom Discourse

In the third year of the project, Beth gave a presentation at a conference in which the focus was on some of the study-group discussions. One of her colleagues asked her how this work might have been transformative for the teacher-researchers. At the next project meeting, Beth asked the teacher-researchers this question: "If someone were to ask me about whether this work has been transformative for you, how do you think I should respond?" For thirty minutes, the teacher-researchers talked about how the readings transformed the ways in which they *thought* and *talked* about their practice, but that transformation of what they were actually *doing* in their practice was a different level of transformation. We organize this section using the teacher-researchers' distinction about how the readings have been transformative in these two related, but different ways.

Ways in Which the Readings Influenced Thinking and Talking about Practice

Reading and discussing literature on classroom discourse pushed all of us to deeper, more complex understandings of the idea of "classroom discourse." This outcome happened regardless of where we began our thinking about this topic. For example, as Darin and Jeff wrote (in chapters 4 and 6), they initially knew little about what discourse meant but were intrigued by the possibility of trying something that, even though somewhat unfamiliar, could affect their teaching positively. In contrast, Jean, Tammie, and Angie (chapters 7, 8, and 9, respectively) had already started paying attention to their classroom discourse, inspired by professional development activities in their schools, information gathered at professional conferences, and experiences using curriculum materials funded by the National Science Foundation (NSF). In fact, one of them made this comment:

> I think none of us came into the project really expecting to discuss linguistics. ... But it made me really aware of just how big of a topic discourse is. I mean, I came into this with a pretty focused and pretty narrow view of what I thought it was and what I was doing and what I thought I wanted to do. There may have been some articles that I didn't, at the outset, find as interesting. But just the fact that I was reading about it and engaging in a conversation about it opened me up to so much more of what discourse is. (Focus Group Interviews,[1] January 2007)

The literature that we read expanded the teacher-researchers' definitions of discourse from primarily being about talk to including a much broader picture, which included such features as power, authority, and control, as well as such nonverbal behaviors as wait time, pauses, and pacing. The chapters by Lana (5), Jeff (6), and Jean (7) especially illustrate these broader definitions of classroom discourse.

Related to nonverbal aspects of classroom discourse, the teacher-researchers' sense of "time" with respect to their teaching became different. That is, many of our early discussions focused on how much time the teacher-researchers had to cover particular ideas or to get through grade-level expectations and course objectives mandated by districts or departments. As they read about and examined their classroom discourse, the idea of "time" seemed to evolve into considerations of the quality and quantity of talk. That is, how much time they spent talking

1. The quotations from the focus group interviews were completed by a person outside of the regular project work. We do not identify the speakers to maintain anonyity for this additional work. Further articulation of these interviews can be found in Adams (forthcoming).

during a given class period or activity structure and how much time they did *not* talk (e.g., see Tammie's discussion of wait time in chapter 8) became increasingly important to the group. Furthermore, much to their disappointment, some teacher-researchers noticed that they even overlapped student-talk in their attempts to keep the conversation moving (see Jean's chapter 7). They came to realize that, if they wanted students to think through the mathematics, they needed to slow down, pause more, and let students finish talking about their ideas (even when students' ideas were exploratory, partial, or not very well articulated).

In addition to helping the teacher-researchers develop a broader meaning for the word *discourse,* the literature on classroom discourse gave them an entire language that enabled them to talk about their practice in new ways. As mentioned in chapter 1, although the teacher-researchers were amused by the existence of "official" words to label some of their "ordinary" verbal and nonverbal practices, they also found these labels powerful when communicating with one another. In fact, after a year of doing some of this work, their growing understanding of their classroom practices and their new language for their classroom practices motivated them to give formal presentations to other mathematics teachers at regional and national conferences. As some researchers argue, having a language for specific discourse processes is meaningful because the movement from engaging in a process to being able to treat the process as an object of reflection provides an opportunity for a shift in development (for example, Sfard [1995] makes this argument as it relates to the development of algebra and algebraic thinking). Before developing this technical language, the teacher-researchers were not able to identify and talk about specific aspects of their classroom discourse, such as revoicing, hedging, vague references, turn-taking, IRE, funneling, and focusing. Without this technical language, many of these aspects of their classroom discourse would have remained at a semiconscious or unconscious level, as they do for most people. With the language and the information provided by the readings, however, the teacher-researchers were able to gain new insights into their teaching practices and build on a foundation of heightened awareness of the interactions that were taking place in their classrooms.

Ways in Which the Readings Influenced What They Were Doing in Their Classrooms

Reading the literature on classroom discourse reminded us that, in addition to creating an environment in which students felt safe to share, the kinds of tasks that were used could make a difference in the quality of class discussions. Many of the teacher-researchers—especially those who had not been using curriculum materials funded by the NSF—quickly observed that, when given a task of "high cognitive demand" (Stein and Smith 1998), students engaged in different kinds of discourse than when they were given tasks that were more procedural. For example, in chapter 3, Patty wrote that she could "no longer rely solely on the activities provided" in her textbook. Similarly, in chapter 4, Darin wrote about acquiring a used set of NSF-funded curriculum materials and finding that these materials enabled him to engage students in quite different interactions as they tried to make sense of the big mathematical ideas.

Unlike some previous research in mathematics education, in which social aspects dominated a teacher's work on her or his classroom discourse (e.g., Nathan and Knuth [2003]), in this project, the teacher-researchers gained new insights into both the social and mathematical aspects of classroom discourse. This dual focus helped the teacher-researchers work toward their goals of improving the ways in which students engaged with mathematics. For example, Darin, Jeff, and Jean (chapters 4, 6, and 7, respectively) were concerned with aspects of control and authority. Darin rearranged his classroom and began to use a document projector so that his students could more easily talk to and question one another. Jeff established a way for students to take over one of the daily classroom activities, and Jean carefully considered her use of revoicing. All these changes, which could be seen as social, were really concerned with facilitating students' ownership of the mathematical ideas. Patty's focus (in chapter 3) put the mathematics more clearly front and center when she decided to confront and change what she came to see as calculational discourse in her classroom so as to support her goal of having her students see mathematics as a thinking process. Lana (in chapter 5) examined the talk that occurred when using graphing calculators through the focus of improving students' learning of content, and Tammie (in chapter 8) did the same with the process of writing. Almost everyone attended to both social and mathematical aspects of their classroom discourse, but with the unifying goal of empowering students to engage in the process of doing mathematics.

The readings and the discussions of the readings gave the teacher-researchers images of new patterns of classroom interaction; but, as Joe's students indicated in their interviews (chapter 10), classroom practices aimed at moving students toward forming communities of high-level talk (see chapter 2) were difficult to enact because they differed from what students were typically asked to do. Moreover, the teacher-researchers became aware that, even within a single class period, students were expected to participate in myriad ways, depending on the activity structure. To meet the challenges of engaging in new patterns of interaction, some teacher-researchers (like Jean and Angie, see chapters 7 and 9) took time to discuss their new expectations explicitly with their students. They modeled the practices they wanted to see and encouraged students when they did such things as explain their thinking. Angie, in particular, became more explicit about how she wanted students to engage in whole-class discussions as they summarized the big mathematical ideas from their small-group activities. And Tammie (in chapter 8) extended our discussions about making the rules explicit for verbal participation in particular activity structures by making explicit some subtle rules for writing about mathematics.

Having open discussions about these new norms for communication was important in helping students understand both the importance of the practices for their learning and the expectations for their participation. As Jeff pointed out in chapter 6, sometimes students bring discourse practices from home that serve them well in their out-of-school communities but are quite different from the discourse of school. One example of a practice that is valued in mathematics is that of mathematical argumentation. Forms of arguing are different in other content domains, such as literacy or science (see, e.g., Herbel-Eisenmann, Cirillo, and Skowronski [2009] for more information) and are often viewed in negative ways in everyday life (O'Connor 1998).

As the teacher-researchers read literature on classroom discourse, they found ways to pay attention to their students and understand them as individual learners. Paying attetion to the student as an individual is one important way to ensure that all children have equitable opportunities to learn mathematics (Warfield and Yttri 1999). In some instances, the process of attending to students as individuals involved using new tools for collecting data about students' learning, such as adding questions to examinations that focused on what students thought was most interesting; distributing an inventory of students' beliefs (see chapter 5 for Lana's descriptions of these two ideas); making a short survey of how students viewed their participation in the classroom (see fig. 3.3 in Patty's chapter 3); or developing a set of interview questions that would help teachers better understand how students perceive new practices (see Joe's chapter 10). These additional sources of information helped the teacher-researchers make decisions about students' participation and about better supporting students' understanding of, and engagement with, mathematics. More subtle forms of attending to students were also described. For example, Lana's growing awareness of, and attention to, discussions in small groups helped her understand many things about her students that she had not really noticed before reading the literature (see the end of chapter 5). Also, Angie's more strategic decisions to try to engage her students in discussions with one another helped her reduce the number of "ping-pong" interactions that occurred between herself and only one student at a time (see chapter 9). These kinds of awareness, however, did not happen solely as a result of reading literature. Our reflective activities gave the teacher-researchers opportunities to attend to, become aware of, and change their classroom discourse.

The Influence of Reflection

From the outset of the project, the teacher-researchers engaged in many kinds of reflection. Some activities that the teacher-researchers cited as provoking especially meaningful reflection included creating beliefs mappings, juxtaposing their beliefs mappings with classroom videotapes, and incorporating ideas from the study-group readings into their own daily practice. As one teacher-researcher explained, she found the *combination* of these activities powerful:

> I don't think you could have done [these in isolation]. If you just show me my data, I will walk away feeling terrible. Or you can raise my level of knowledge and awareness and have me still thinking I'm doing what I thought I said was important. But if you show me my data and at the same time have me immersed in all these possibilities, raising my level of knowledge and awareness, I mean, it's like you've got to have [all these activities]. (Focus Group Interviews, January 2007)

From this teacher-researcher's perspective, the combination of activities was particularly important. That is, merely presenting data or only offering more knowledge about classroom discourse would not have been enough. She also needed opportunities to consider whether what was occurring in her classroom was aligned with what she declared to be important.

Before beginning this project work, the teacher-researchers had not made explicit to themselves the beliefs that they thought drove their instructional practice. Creating the beliefs mapping (see chapters 3 and 5 for examples) allowed them to try to articulate those beliefs. The beliefs mapping played an important role in the teacher-researchers' reflections because it let them see the existance of underlying and pervasive assumptions that they took to be important:

> I'm not sure that [the experience] changed my beliefs, but I think it changed how I looked at the way that I practice my beliefs. So, what's really important to me is that every student learns math, that I value the student exploring and thinking and talking rather than me telling the student. When you look at my practice, who is doing most of the talking? Me. If a student doesn't get it, do I make sure they're involved in the thinking or do I assist them so that they can bypass the thinking? Do I facilitate thinking, or do I facilitate them getting an answer? But when I looked at my practice, particularly the analysis [of the baseline data], I thought, "OK, this isn't as aligned with what I want to have happen as I would like, so what can I do to facilitate aligning my practice with my beliefs? (Focus Group Interviews, January 2007)

As this quotation highlights, the increased awareness gained from developing a beliefs mapping enabled the teacher-researchers to identify what they *wanted* to happen (and why) and to continually examine whether what they *wanted* to happen was *actually* happening. Because the first section of the book describes the journey over a long period for Patty, Darin, and Lana, readers can fairly easily see how the beliefs mapping continued to allow the teachers to examine their practice. This examination and reflection took place, to a large extent, as the teacher-researchers watched and reviewed videotaped lessons.

When the teacher-researchers first read the analysis of their baseline data and watched themselves on videotape, many realized that they were teaching as they had been taught (see chapters 3 and 4 for explicit realizations of this actuality). The teacher-researchers thought that their countless hours of being students in mathematics classrooms (what Lortie [1975] has called an "apprenticeship of observation") influenced what and how they taught. They also realized that those practices, which worked for them as students, probably did not serve all their students well. This realization, when contrasted with their beliefs mappings, proved to be a powerful impetus for change.

In addition to watching themselves on videotape, everyone watched videotapes of the other teacher-researchers as well as teachers outside the project. For example, when we were recruiting teachers to participate in the project, some teacher-researchers participated in a session that involved viewing a videotape of Deborah Ball's classroom (Ball 1993). Both Patty and Darin (in chapters 3 and 4) said that this viewing influenced their decisions to become involved in the project work. Patty wrote, "As I watched, I knew I wanted my class discussions to resemble the one taking place in that video." Darin's response was more about student involvement: "[Students] were engaged and focused on the task at hand. I wanted to be able to achieve that outcome in my classroom." At one of the project meetings, we also watched Cathy Humphreys teach the Border Problem (Boaler and Humphreys 2005). Many of the teacher-researchers then tried that task with their classes. The ways that the teacher-researchers set up the task and enacted it were clearly influenced by the Cathy Humphreys videotape and chapter. These images of other teachers' practices gave the teacher-researchers another vision of possibilities for their practice and provided some alternatives to the IRE pattern that many of them found dominated their classroom discourse.

When the teacher-researchers began to watch themselves on videotape, they needed time to move past being dissatisfied or hypercritical to honing in on the discourse practices. When we asked them to start sharing their videotapes with one another, they were helped by hearing both what other people noticed in their classroom discourse and alternative interpretations of what we were watching and hearing. Sometimes these viewings provided encouragement for alternative practices; sometimes the teacher-researchers were pushed to provide additional evidence for claims they were making.

As the teacher-researchers progressed through the first year of action research cycles, they grew more and more skilled at, and comfortable with, gathering many kinds of artifacts to better understand what was happening in their classrooms. These artifacts served as an important type of formative assessment of their practice. In addition to videotaping class periods, they gathered information about their practice by developing or adopting surveys from readings; doing brief interviews with students; having students write quick journal entries; and writing journal entries of their own about things they noticed when students worked in small groups. Throughout the cycles of action research, we also revisited many of the readings that the teacher-researchers found particularly helpful. Through these re-readings, we noticed that our understandings changed and developed. In fact, revisiting the readings helped us critique some of the academic ideas from within the context of the teacher-researchers' practice. For example, our discussions of revoicing further developed the conception of this practice by revealing some additional complexities that had not yet been considered in the literature (see, e.g., Herbel-Eisenmann, Drake, and Cirillo [2009] for ways that our discussions contributed to the idea of revoicing).

Throughout the various forms of reflection, the teacher-researchers talked about the changes that they were incorporating into their practice and considering for the action research projects. They talked about how reflection had enabled them to transform their thinking about their practice. They also discussed, at length, how changing their thinking was easier than changing their practice. All the teacher-researchers, however, incorporated changes into their classroom practices, from moving desks to trying new kinds of tasks to turning over activities to students to asking students to revoice one another, and so on. Yet, when they talked about these changes, they described a mix of progress and backtracking and reminded us how hard some of these changes can be. Often they sensed that, without the context of our new community, their progress might have been altogether short-lived.

The Role of Community and Collaboration

Joe's chapter 10 reminds us that classrooms are part of schools, school districts, and broader communities. Other people from inside schools—such as administrators and students—and outside schools—such as parents and community members—are often not as supportive of teachers as we might like them to be (McGrath and Kurlioff 1999; Peressini 1998). In fact, these people may support conventional practices, such as IRE, which Jeff described in chapter 6, or they may oppose newer practices as described by Joe (in chapter 10). (Lana's chapter 5 describes a discrepant situation, in which she described how her administrator's annual evaluation supported the new discourse practices Lana was using.) Sometimes, when teachers want to use practices viewed as different from the "typical," resistance and lack of support from administrators, other teachers, parents, or students can deter teachers from doing what they think is best. As Hiebert and Wearne (2003) pointed out, "Teachers have been encouraged to make mathematics less problematic for students. Parents assume that teachers should make mathematics less of a struggle; a good teacher, says the common wisdom, helps students learn in a smooth and effortless way" (p. 6). The assumptions that parents make, as described in this quotation, can conflict with teachers' goals to have students grapple with challenging, high-level mathematical tasks. It can also conflict with attempts to engage students in forms of classroom discourse that are different from the ones they are used to.

Some of this resistance and apathy is described in this book. The community we created became paramount to the teacher-researchers in many ways, one of which was supporting perseverance in the climate of less-than-ideal support coming in their own classrooms, schools, or local contexts. For Darin and Jeff, who both considered leaving teaching, becoming part of our community kept them in the profession. For Joe, being part of our community supported him in trying to engage students in atypical interactions that pushed them to think and participate in new ways. Finally, the student interviews clearly show that students can grow to appreciate and understand why these alternative practices are important for their learning.

Community played many additional roles in our collaborative work. We list many of these roles here and return to the idea of community in more detail in the next chapter. Our community played an important role as we discussed the readings and as the teacher-researchers reflected on their classroom practices. For example, Darin (chapter 4) shared his experience of getting important insights into the readings from other teacher-researchers, insights that he had not gained when reading the literature on his own. As we watched one another's teaching on videotape, the teacher-researchers also made suggestions about alternative tasks or discourse patterns. We shared struggles and ideas and supported one another through difficult areas. We also provided an important pat on the back when it was needed.

Some teacher-researchers described how their new awareness sometimes led to disappointment. Sometimes new practices that involved engaging students in speaking, writing, and listening were more exhausting than delivering a carefully prepared lecture. In all these contexts, the community was important. Our community revitalized every group member's interest in teaching. It also encouraged members to take risks that they would not have taken otherwise. For example, Jeff transferred from one school to another; began teaching new courses, such as calculus; and explored forms of technology he had never used in his teaching. Joe took a different kind of risk and persevered in teaching in the way that he believed was best for his students. We do not contend that these practices and risks would not have occurred without the community, but we do believe that the community played an important role in these experiences.

Closing Thoughts

In this chapter, we have tried to highlight some important aspects of the group's work in delving deeply into professional literature, reflecting critically on practice, and building a cooperative and productive community. Too often teachers are treated as if worthwhile knowledge about teaching can come only from *outside* the classroom and be generated only by university researchers (Cochran-Smith and Lytle 1993). As O'Connor (2003, p. 152) so insightfully wrote,

> Classroom teachers know this reality from the inside-out, from the first-person point of view. So when they reflect on their experiences, the results can be of value and of interest to many. However, systematic study of their own experiences, pushing beyond reflection to systematic observation, description, and sometimes explanation, is much rarer and more difficult but is of great value indeed.

The work reported here highlights not only how much "outsiders" to the classroom can learn from mathematics teachers' systematic observations of their classroom discourse practices but also how important this kind of work can be to the students in these classrooms. Because we strongly believe that action research is one of the most promising ways to build more nuanced understandings of classroom practices as well as one of the most promising ways to improve teachers'—and ultimately students'—learning, in the next, and final, chapter, we turn to arguing for more of this kind of work with mathematics teachers.

References

Adams, Barbara. "Owning Professional Development: The Power of Teacher Research." Ph.D. diss., Iowa State University, forthcoming.

Ball, Deborah L. *Shea's Numbers.* Ann Arbor: University of Michigan, 1993. Videorecording.

Boaler, Jo, and Cathy Humphreys. *Connecting Mathematical Ideas: Middle School Video Cases to Support Teaching and Learning.* Portsmouth, N.H.: Heinemann, 2005.

Cochran-Smith, Marilyn, and Susan L. Lytle. *Inside/Outside: Teacher Research and Knowledge.* New York: Teachers College Press, 1993.

Herbel-Eisenmann, Beth, Michelle Cirillo, and Kathryn Skowronski. "Why Classroom Discourse Deserves Our Attention!" In *Mathematics for Every Student: Responding to Diversity, Grades 9–12,* edited by Alfinio Flores, pp. 103–15. Reston, Va.: National Council of Teachers of Mathematics, 2009.

Herbel-Eisenmann, Beth, Corey Drake, and Michelle Cirillo. "Muddying the Clear Waters: Teachers' Take-up of the Linguistic Idea of Revoicing." *Teaching and Teacher Education* 25, no. 2 (February 2009): 268–77.

Hiebert, James, and Diana Wearne. "Developing Understanding through Problem Solving." In *Teaching Mathematics through Problem Solving: Grades 6–12,* edited by Harold L. Schoen and Randall I. Charles, pp. 3–13. Reston, Va.: National Council of Teachers of Mathematics, 2003.

Lortie, Dan C. *School Teacher: A Sociological Study*. Chicago: University of Chicago Press, 1975.

McGrath, Daniel J., and Peter J. Kuriloff. "'They're Going to Tear the Doors off This Place': Upper-Middle-Class Parent School Involvement and the Educational Opportunities of Other People's Children." *Educational Policy* 13 (1999): 603–29.

Nathan, Mitchell J., and Eric Knuth. "A Study of Whole Classroom Mathematical Discourse and Teacher Change." *Cognition and Instruction* 21 (2003): 175–207.

O'Connor, M. Catherine. "Language Socialization in the Mathematics Classroom: Discourse Practices and Mathematical Thinking." In *Talking Mathematics in School,* edited by Magdalene Lampert and Mary L. Blunk, pp. 17–56. New York: Cambridge University Press, 1998.

———. "Afterword: Imagining the Classroom." In *Regarding Children's Words: Teacher Research on Language and Literacy,* edited by Cynthia Ballenger, pp. 149–59. New York: Teachers College Press, 2003.

Peressini, Dominic D. "The Portrayal of Parents in the Reform of Mathematics Education: Locating Context for Parental Involvement." *Journal for Research in Mathematics Education* 29 (November 1998): 555–82.

Sfard, Anna. "The Development of Algebra: Confronting Historical and Psychological Perspectives." *Journal of Mathematical Behavior* 14 (1995): 15–39.

Stein, Mary Kay, and Margaret S. Smith. "Mathematical Tasks as a Framework for Reflection: From Research to Practice." *Mathematics Teaching in the Middle School* 3 (January 1998): 268–75.

Warfield, Janet, and Mary Jo Yttri. "Cognitively Guided Instruction in One Kindergarten Classroom." In *Mathematics in the Early Years,* edited by Juanita Copley, pp. 103–11. Reston, Va.: National Council of Teachers of Mathematics, 1999.

CHAPTER 12

An Argument for Taking Up Similar Work

Beth Herbel-Eisenmann
Michelle Cirillo
Lorraine Males

> Because teacher research interrupts traditional assumptions about knowers, knowing, and what can be known about teaching, it has the potential to redefine the notion of a knowledge base for teaching and to challenge the university's hegemony in the generation of expert knowledge for the field. Because teacher research challenges the dominant views of staff development and preservice training as transmission and implementation of knowledge from outside to inside schools, it has the potential to reconstruct teacher development across the professional life span so that inquiry and reform are intrinsic to teaching. And finally, because teacher research makes visible the ways that teachers and students co-construct knowledge and curriculum, it has the potential to alter profoundly the ways that teachers use language and literacy to relate to their colleagues and their students, and it can support a more critical and democratic pedagogy.
>
> —Marilyn Cochran-Smith and Susan L. Lytle
> *Inside/Outside: Teacher Research and Knowledge*

We began this book with an overview of a project undertaken by eight secondary school mathematics teacher-researchers and two university researchers in mathematics education. In this project, the university researchers worked collaboratively with the mathematics teacher-researchers to help them examine and articulate their beliefs about mathematics, mathematics teaching, and learning. Then, with these beliefs as a guide, and with support from the university researchers and one another, the teacher-researchers engaged in cycles of action research related to their classroom discourse. In this book, each teacher-researcher thoughtfully communicates goals regarding his or her action research project and shares some of the insights, struggles, dilemmas, and conclusions that he or she developed as a result of this experience.

Just as the teacher-researchers in this book expressed a desire to empower their students, collections such as this may empower both mathematics teachers and teacher educators. The teacher-researchers' work reminds us that when the context of professional development helps teachers and teacher educators collaborate in supporting teachers' empowerment, we can all learn a great deal. As the opening quotation from Cochran-Smith and Lytle reminds us, collaborating *with* teachers instead of conducting research *on* or *about* teachers can transform knowledge about teaching. Collaborative research can redefine professional development and teachers' learning, and it can transform the relationship between teachers and students into a more democratic one. Moving toward more democratic relationships is inherent in the process of action research, because one of its primary goals is to create equitable relationships among university researchers and teacher-researchers and between teacher-researchers and their students so as to "provide more equal access to challenging curriculum and more engagement in decision making" (Darling-Hammond et al. 2005, p. 170).

With the exception of some chapters in the series *Teachers Engaged in Research: Inquiry into Mathematics Classrooms* (Van Zoest 2006a, 2006b; Smith and Smith 2006; Langrall 2006; Masingila 2006), the literature contains little evidence that action research has been used in mathematics education as often or as long as it has been used in other areas, such as literacy and science education. In another recently published book, Bill Atweh (2004) argued for the importance of having more mathematics educators take up collaborative action research. The three grounds for his argument are similar to the three reasons provided by Cochran-Smith and Lytle at the beginning of this chapter. Atweh proposed that action research, as a form of collaborative work, is important for pragmatic, epistemological, and political reasons. Here we build on Atweh's argument by connecting it with related literature and by supporting the ideas with statements from interviews with the teacher-researchers in this project. In doing so, we hope to convince more people in mathematics education to forge critical, collaborative, and long-term relationships like the ones we describe in this book.

Pragmatic Argument

Atweh argued that people separate knowledge *generation* from knowledge *application* in many different ways. For example, university researchers generate knowledge in the hope that teachers will eventually apply it to their practices. For the most part, university researchers and teachers separate themselves by publishing in and reading different journals, joining different professional organizations, and attending separate conferences. Given the typical separation between university researchers and teachers, it is no wonder that school systems have been plagued by (often costly) failures of various reforms offered by "outsiders." Teachers see most of these mandates as external demands that "force" them to change. The teacher-researchers involved in this book have often felt the same way. For example, in a project interview, Joe claimed that if the goal of professional development is to have an impact on teachers' practice, teachers must be active in this process.

> That's the only way to actually do it ... the only way that it's ever actually gonna have any impact. Like you can go in and try to tell somebody what they're doing is wrong or they should be doing this and this instead ... you're never gonna get anywhere. So ... yeah, [making decisions about what I wanted to do rather than be told what to do] made sense to me and I wasn't bothered by it. Also, 'cause I don't like people telling me what to do. (Interview, 2008)

Here Joe provided evidence that the flexibility of the action research process was a productive way to facilitate change.

The use of action research encourages reflection on, and changes to, teaching practices. Policymakers at the national, state, and local levels repeatedly ask teachers to change the way they teach, but they rarely supply worthwhile data that compel teachers to change. By collecting evidence of their own discourse practices, teachers investigate their goals in the context of their own classrooms. Action research provides the reflective and collaborative opportunity that teachers need to investigate the social influences in classrooms. Reeves (1990) stated that "without the action research, the social dimensions of the role of language in mathematics learning would be difficult to appreciate" (p. 446).

Atweh contended that action research acts as a conduit between theory and practice because it is intrinsically based on bridging the theory-practice gap. Cochran-Smith and Lytle (1993) seem to agree with this point of view, stating that if teachers see the knowledge base for teaching as being constructed only by university researchers, their role is merely "to learn the skills of effective teaching and also learn how to apply them to practice" (p. 88). A premise of the teacher-research movement, these authors argue, is that teachers should participate in forming and using knowledge in education. When teachers participate, inquiry and reform become a natural part of the teaching-learning process.

Epistemological Argument

The epistemological argument for using action research is based on constructivist theories of learning. Drawing on the work of Davis, Maher, and Noddings (1990), Atweh described learning as a process that develops from previous knowledge and experience and involves reflection and negotiation with others. In most models of teachers' professional development, the tacit view is that information is simply transmitted from someone who is considered an expert to others who are considered novices. Cochran-Smith (2006) argued that we must move toward a concept of teacher learning "as a life-long process of both posing and answering questions" (p. xiii).

Although many of the teacher-researchers in this project considered constructivist theory a viable theory of learning, the majority of their experiences in professional development contradicted this theory. In this sense, some of the teacher-researchers seemed to have compartmentalized this view of learning as applicable to their students but not necessarily to themselves. Thus, the project work ran counter to the teacher-researchers' experiences. More specifically, they expressed some surprise when, early in the project, Beth suggested that they might experience uncomfortable dissonance as the project progressed and that this discomfort was a natural part of the learning experience. Jean replied that she thought it was ironic that she expected this dissonance for her students but had not considered how it might apply to her too. She laughed at having overlooked something that seemed fairly obvious. Jeff, in his final interview, described the connections between the ways the university researchers supported his learning and the new practices he was attempting with his students:

> Just like we are supposed to do in our classroom, where we provide opportunities for the kids to discover and to learn, then you're doing that to us, too, and … you provided the resources, you provided the time, you provided the encouragement, the support, to take out of it what we can get out of it. Um, but along with any kind of growth there is going to be frustrations and setbacks. (Interview, 2008)

In addition to making a connection between the ways he was working with students and his experience in the project, Jeff's quotation also reminds us that learning involves frustrations and setbacks. Why, then, might teachers want to continue pushing forward in the face of negative feelings? One reason might be that knowledge is generated on the basis of people's interests or needs (Carr and Kemmis 1986).

To better understand why people might want to continue developing knowledge, many action researchers (e.g., Carr and Kemmis 1986; Grundy 1987) have used Habermas's (1992) theory of knowledge-constitutive interests, which consist of *technical, practical,* and *emancipatory* interests or needs. *Practical* and *emancipatory* knowledge-constitutive interests are relevant to this project. Teachers' *practical* interests in generating knowledge involve needing to understand their own and their students' beliefs, motivations, expectations, and knowledge as well as to understand the context in which they work. This type of interest "may be met by learning about research findings through in-service or reading" (Atweh 2004, p. 191) but may also require substantial engagement with, and deliberation about, research knowledge.

Emancipatory interests are tied to the human desire to be autonomous and free from "dogmatic dependence" (p. 191). These interests grow from the need for empowerment (or "the ability of individuals and groups to take control of their own lives in autonomous and responsible ways" [Grundy 1987, p. 19]), which becomes the motivation for learning. Atweh (2004) posited that action research is one way to build on emancipatory interests and that these interests can be enhanced by collaborations both inside and outside the classroom. Critical reflection is necessary for developing emancipatory interests. Only by raising their own questions about their practice and collecting evidence can teachers take emancipatory interests seriously. Unless teachers develop emancipatory knowledge, they will forever be subject to the agenda of others with "better" knowledge (Atweh 2004). In the next few paragraphs, we elaborate on how the teacher-researchers' practical interests were served by discussing the readings and by creating beliefs mappings. We then explain how the project meetings acted as a catalyst for igniting the teacher researchers' emancipatory interests.

Practical and Emancipatory Interests Served by the Project Work

In this project, the teacher-researchers' practical interests seemed to be served by reading and discussing professional literature and by creating the beliefs mapping. The teacher-researchers found the ideas in the readings to be a useful lens for examining their classroom practices. They read the ideas, grappled with them in the discussions, and began to use the language and ideas as a new way to talk about what they were doing in their classrooms. The beliefs mapping served as another way to build on their practical needs: it provided a way for them to make explicit what they believed was at the heart of their practice. The teacher-researchers described an increasing awareness as they constantly revisited their beliefs mappings throughout the project. Reconsidering their beliefs became a way for them to think about how to change their discourse practices. It also became a way for them to challenge their own beliefs. In her chapter, for example, Patty explained how her mapping changed over the course of the project:

> Looking at my mapping now, I cannot explain why I placed the note about skills at the very center of my mapping (i.e., "It is important for students to know their skills before they can move on to more difficult mathematics"). If I were to create a new mapping today, that note would not be anywhere near the center.

As Patty engaged in project discussions, watched herself on videotape, and reconsidered her beliefs mapping, she decided that she placed too much emphasis on mathematical skills and not enough on big mathematical ideas and mathematical processes. In her chapter, Lana did not describe a change in her beliefs. Rather, she focused on how her mapping became increasingly useful to her reflective process over time:

> Initially, I did not consider the mapping of what was closest to my heart in mathematics teaching and learning to be terribly important or useful. I have changed my mind about the usefulness of this mapping, and now I draw heavily on what I profess to believe to guide planning and make decisions.

In her final interview, Lana also said that reflecting on her beliefs mapping seemed more manageable than trying to concentrate on the large set of discourse readings we had done:

> For me, I would say ... the mapping being like a big part of the reflection piece initially and compared to all the discourse readings that are big, [the beliefs mapping's] just like one piece of paper. That artifact is easy to go back to so it's easy to keep it in the forefront a little bit and to watch how that has evolved and the reflection has evolved with this new information coming in. (Interview, 2008)

Eventually, this mapping helped Lana select a focus for her action research project.

As their understanding of classroom discourse grew and they explicitly articulated their beliefs, the teacher-researchers valued having time to reflect because it allowed them to write journal entries, review their own videotapes and the videotapes of other teachers, and discuss the literature. Reflecting in the project meetings helped the teacher-researchers develop their own agendas and foci for their action-research projects. This process ran contrary to their previous professional development experiences and served emancipatory needs. In the final project interview, when asked how they felt about not being told what to do for their action-research projects, most of the teachers responded that it was different from any of their other professional development experiences. For example, Lana said,

> Oh, it was incredible. ... I mean, the part that made it so uncomfortable is that it was so different than other professional development, like in terms of quality and expectation. We're just never, ever, ever, ever, ever treated with autonomy or to think that what we think would be best or to think about what's important and do it for a long time or to be supported in what you think is best over a long time. ... That structure was so foreign. (Interview, 2008)

In contrast with her experience with more conventional professional development, Lana associated the project work with empowerment: She felt that she was finally treated as if she were able to make decisions about what was best for her students. The teacher-researchers found continuing support from peers and critical friends in the group to be crucial to their development.

Lana also used the word *uncomfortable* to describe the work she did in this project. Several of the teacher-researchers discussed the challenges of participating in this kind of professional development. For example, one of the teacher-researchers said,

> Here's the funny thing—we sat here and complained about professional development in our schools and how it's very scripted, and now we're all sitting here realizing that this action research component is so wide open and it's totally up to us to figure it out. It's that openness that's so scary. (Focus Group Interviews,[1] January 2007)

Just as this teacher-researcher said that the openness of action research was "scary," another teacher-researcher described this open approach as being "without a net" (Focus Group Interviews, January 2007).

---

1. The quotations from the focus group interviews were completed by a person outside of the regular project work. We do not identify the speakers to maintain anonymity for this additional work. Further articulation of these interviews can be found in Adams (forthcoming).

As constructivist theory suggests, the teacher-researchers, who had previously been treated as though they simply needed to apply information given to them (often by an "outsider"), found the autonomous nature of action research to be both empowering and a little daunting. Epistemology does not focus only on *what* and *how* someone comes to know something, it also involves *why* someone might want to learn something. Meeting the teacher-researchers' practical interests through study-group readings, discussions, and creating beliefs mappings provided a starting place for igniting their emancipatory interests as they reflected on and changed their discourse practices through action-research projects.

Political Argument

Teachers' descriptions of their feelings about how they are treated in most professional development experiences support Atweh's argument against separating knowledge generation from knowledge application. His political argument for increased use of action research recognizes that an underlying assumption of this separation is that it serves the view of teaching as not being a profession. The separation and valuing of knowledge production by university researchers "diminishes respect for [teachers] to understand and theorize their practice and to talk about their practice and defend it publicly" (Atweh 2004, p. 192). To support this third argument, Atweh drew on three relevant characteristics of a profession, as proposed by Noddings (1993). He argued that action research would help elevate mathematics teachers to the status of professionals:

1. Because professionals are viewed as having specialized knowledge, action research provides a way not only to improve their practice but also to develop an understanding of it.
2. Because professionals work in an atmosphere of collegiality, action research not only contributes to the development of collegiality within groups of teacher-researchers but also develops relationships among teacher-researchers, university researchers, and teacher educators.
3. Because professionals enjoy a degree of autonomy in their work, action research can develop a sense of agency and control because teachers raise their own questions and generate knowledge.

The chapters in this book clearly illustrate the first point. Each chapter describes the ways that the teacher-researchers developed an understanding of their practice, then used these understandings to improve it. We believe that the specialized knowledge that the teacher-researchers drew on and developed in their work is also apparent in their chapters, so in this chapter we expand only on the importance of the second and third factors: collegiality and choice.

Collegiality

Teachers in the United States work largely in isolation. The pathology of this isolation in schools can make action research collaborations difficult (Cochran-Smith and Lytle 1993). Despite the fact that teachers believe that other teachers are the major source for improving and maintaining their practice, they usually have little opportunity to work with, observe, or receive feedback about their teaching from their peers (Clarke 1994). In the final project interview, Jeff talked about the camaraderie that formed as the members of the group learned about one another, their respective settings, and their beliefs about teaching. He did not find the same kind of community in his own school because he often did not have the time to have substantive conversations: "So many times we've said in your meetings—we don't have these kinds of discussions with people in our buildings. So that's been very refreshing" (Interview, 2008). In Jeff's quotation, we do not see his colleagues as preventing him from having substantive discussions. Rather, we believe that the structures in U.S. schools do not allow such discussions to take place. Yet we would argue that engaging in such activities as reading professional literature, watching videotapes of oneself and others teaching, and participating in a long-term project like the one described here gives teachers support and time to reflect on their practice.

As with our group, having regular project meetings can combat the isolation teachers often feel and help them develop strong bonds with their colleagues. Weissglass (1994) suggested, "Teachers need to meet regularly with the same people in order to develop the trust necessary to talk meaningfully about important issues" (p. 77). He also warned against single professional development sessions: the purpose of support groups is to develop trust among the members of the group and to enable each member to work through issues and feelings and set goals. In his final interview, Joe spoke about the ways that the group supported the changes that he was trying to make:

> [H]aving somebody else affirm my belief that it was very difficult to actually do this in practice. ... it's one thing to do the readings ... and it's another thing to actually go to your classroom and ... try to actually do it. So the fact that I thought it was hard and that other people thought it was also hard ... just to know that other people were trying it, and it was hard for them too. That was really helpful. (Interview, 2008)

As the teacher-researchers so articulately expressed in their interviews, enabling and pushing their students to engage with problem solving and inquiry challenged both teachers and students and might not have happened without support.

We believe that at least two important features of our group's makeup contributed to the collegiality described previously by Jeff and above by Joe. First, the teacher-researchers were from different school districts and were at different career stages. We found that the purposeful diversity of the group (e.g., grade-level certification, experience with professional literature and organizations, etc.) added to everyone's experience. Each member of our group made unique and important contributions. Throughout our time together we found, for example, that more experienced teachers could sometimes give teachers at earlier stages of their careers wise advice, and the early-career teachers charged the group with productive energy and enthusiasm to try out different strategies. Some teacher-researchers brought healthy skepticism to the work; others brought a sense of humor. The diversity itself seemed to add power to the ways that we worked together. Professional respect is often a theme in groups that engage in action research (Van Zoest 2006). Another factor that may have contributed to the productive, long-term relationships was the commitment to give the teacher-researchers the kinds of choices that we were never given in our own professional development.

Choice and Autonomy

Another powerful aspect of this experience for the teacher-researchers was the experience of "servicing-in" (Meyer 1998) instead of being inserviced. That is, the teacher-researchers took on a second job in which they not only taught but also systematically studied their own teaching (Meyer 1998). This kind of approach assumes that teachers are professionals and are, therefore, capable of making thoughtful, intelligent, and productive choices about what they want to improve in their practice and about how those improvements can take place. This view is important because ultimately the fate of any professional development program depends on the decision of the user—the classroom teacher (Doyle and Ponder 1977).

In treating the teacher-researchers as professionals, we attempted to offer as many choices about the project work as possible. From our collective experiences, offering choice does not seem to be a typical component of district-level professional development. But choice is very important to the professionalization of teaching:

> When individuals are free to choose, they are more likely to think about the choices and decide what is the best choice among the alternatives. When teachers are told what to do, they do not think; they just respond. Since the activity was not of their choice, they do not find it personally meaningful—that is, it does not connect with their previous knowledge in a way that makes sense to them. Individuals who do not experience choices in teacher education programs are more likely to view theory, research, and practice as fragmented and disconnected. Individuals who actively choose are more likely to see connections and engage in practice that reflects a cohesive view of the relationship of teaching to learning. (Castle and Aichele 1994, p. 5)

The personally meaningful activity referred to by Castle and Aichele is embedded in the process of action research because teacher-researchers use issues that they find compelling to select the focus of the project. In fact, research shows that professional development is more likely to achieve significant change in classroom practice when teachers view the professional development as being responsive to their needs (Clarke 1994). Giving teachers choices about what to change and how to change it ensures this kind of relevance.

After the teacher-researchers signed on to participate in this project, we found many ways to include choices in the project work. For example, the project meeting schedule was negotiated by the group and allowed for the teacher-researchers' personal and professional commitments. The teacher-researchers selected their focal class period each year and selected the dates for the visits when we collected baseline data. When we offered the library of discourse readings, the teacher-researchers decided which readings from each section they would read for the next project meeting. And, most important, when it came time to engage in action research, the teacher-researchers decided what their projects would focus on and how they would make the changes they thought they needed to make. As Atweh pointed out, however, *total* autonomy is not desirable. The collaborative, critical, ongoing relationships that developed between the university researchers and the teacher-researchers gave the teacher-researchers the support and resources they needed to accomplish their goals. All professional development programs should enable participants to gain a substantial degree of ownership by involving members in making decisions and regarding the members as "true partners" in the change process (Clarke 1994).

Working toward Professional Development That Is Empowering

In this chapter, we draw extensively on the ideas proposed by Bill Atweh to make the argument that this kind of work is important for pragmatic, epistemological, and political reasons. Although we use his reasons to structure our argument, we would be remiss if we did not highlight the fact that a primary goal of this chapter is to illuminate that argument with examples from the work of these diligent teacher-researchers, who articulately reflected on the work done by our group. We do so to suggest that, although we find the university researchers' arguments compelling, we should also take the voices of teacher-researchers seriously.

In the pragmatic argument we advocate that teachers be part of the knowledge-generation process in education. Current theory on how people learn indicates that students in classrooms should not be treated as passive recipients of knowledge. Similarly, teachers should not be treated this way in professional development. Through the epistemological argument, we advocate that teachers' practical and emanicipatory interests should be taken into account in professional development. The teacher-researchers in this project found the beliefs mapping to be a practical lens that helped them engage with the literature and further their understandings of classroom discourse. And although the teacher-researchers found the action research process to be challenging, they felt that the process empowered them and their students. Finally, drawing on Atweh's political argument, we discuss the value of engaging in this kind of work with a collegial group. Choice and autonomy proved valuable and helped establish a professional development context in which critical, long-term collaborations were developed.

As people who work with mathematics teachers, we need to consider carefully the pragmatic, epistemolocal, and political assumptions embedded in our professional develoment plans. Responsible forms of professional development must integrate long-term collaboration into the work of empowering teachers and teacher educators to better support student learning.

References

Adams, Barbara. "Owning Professional Development: The Power of Teacher Research." Ph.D. diss., Iowa State University, forthcoming.

Atweh, Bill. "Understanding for Changing and Changing for Understanding. Praxis between Practice and Theory through Action Research in Mathematics Education." In *Researching the Socio-Political Dimensions of Mathematics Education: Issues of Power in Theory and Methodology,* edited by Paola Valero and Robyn Zevenbergen, pp. 187–206. New York: Kluwer Academic Publishers, 2004.

Carr, Wilfred, and Stephen Kemmis. *Becoming Critical: Education, Knowledge, and Action Research.* London: RoutledgFalmer, 1986.

Castle, Kathryn, and Douglas B. Aichele. "Professional Development and Teacher Autonomy." In *Professional Development for Teachers of Mathematics,* 1994 Yearbook of the National Council of Teachers of Mathematics (NCTM), edited by Douglas B. Aichele and Arthur F. Coxford, pp. 1–8. Reston, Va.: NCTM, 1994.

Clarke, Doug M. "Ten Key Principles from Research for the Professional Development of Mathematics Teachers." *In Professional Development for Teachers of Mathematics,* 1994 Yearbook of the National Council of Teachers of Mathematics (NCTM), edited by Douglas B. Aichele and Arthur F. Coxford, pp. 37–48. Reston, Va.: NCTM, 1994.

Cochran-Smith, Marilyn. "Series Foreword." In *Teachers Engaged in Research: Inquiry into Mathematics Classrooms, Grades 9–12,* edited by Laura Van Zoest, pp. ix–xix. Greenwich, Conn.: Information Age Publishing, 2006. Available from the National Council of Teachers of Mathematics.

Cochran-Smith, Marilyn, and Susan L. Lytle. *Inside/Outside: Teacher Research and Knowledge.* New York: Teachers College Press, 1993.

Darling-Hammond, Linda, James Banks, Karen Zumwalt, Louis Gomez, Miriam Gamoran Sherin, Jacqueline Griesdorn, and Lou-Ellen Finn. "Developing a Curricular Vision for Teaching." In *Preparing Teachers for a Changing World: What Teachers Should Learn and Be Able to Do,* edited by Linda Darling-Hammond and John Bransford, pp. 169–200. San Francisco, Calif.: Jossey-Bass, 2005.

Davis, Robert B., Carolyn Maher, and Nel Noddings, eds. *Constructivist Views on the Teaching and Learning of Mathematics. Journal for Research in Mathematics Education Monograph No. 4.* Reston, Va.: National Council of Teachers of Mathematics, 1990.

Doyle, Walter, and Gerald A. Ponder. "The Practicality Ethic in Teacher Decision-Making." *Interchange* 8 (1977): 1–12.

Grundy, Shirley. *Curriculum: Product or Praxis?* London: RoutledgeFalmer, 1987.

Habermas, Jurgen. *Postmetaphysical Thinking: Philosophical Essays.* Translated by William Mark Hohengarten. Cambridge, Mass.: MIT Press, 1992.

Langrall, Cynthia W., ed. *Teachers Engaged in Research: Inquiry into Mathematics Classrooms, Grades 3–5.* Greenwich, Conn.: Information Age Publishing, 2006. Available from the National Council of Teachers of Mathematics.

Masingila, Joanna O., ed. *Teachers Engaged in Research: Inquiry into Mathematics Classrooms, Grades 6–8.* Greenwich, Conn.: Information Age Publishing, 2006. Available from the National Council of Teachers of Mathematics.

Meyer, Richard J. "Implications: What's Next for Our Group and Yours?" In *Composing a Teacher Study Group: Learning about Inquiry in Primary Classrooms,* edited by Richard J. Meyer, Linda Brown, Elizabeth DeNino, Kimberly Larson, Mona McKenzie, Kimberly Ridder, and Kimberly Zetterman, pp. 204–13. Mahwah, N.J.: Lawrence Erlbaum Associates, 1998.

Noddings, Nel. "Professionalization and Mathematics Teaching." In *Handbook of Research on Mathematics Teaching and Learning,* edited by Douglas A. Grouws, pp. 197–208. New York: Macmillan, 1993.

Reeves, Noelene. "Action Research for Professional Development: Informing Teachers and Researchers." In *Transforming Children's Mathematics Education,* edited by Leslie P. Steffe and Terry Wood, pp. 436–47. Hillsdale, N.J.: Lawrence Erlbaum Associates, 1990.

Smith, Stephanie Z., and Marvin E. Smith, eds. *Teachers Engaged in Research: Inquiry into Mathematics Classrooms, Prekindergarten–Grade 2.* Greenwich, Conn.: Information Age Publishing, 2006. Available from the National Council of Teachers of Mathematics.

Van Zoest, Laura. "Introduction to the 9–12 Volume." In *Teachers Engaged in Research: Inquiry into Mathematics Classrooms, Grades 9–12,* edited by Laura Van Zoest, pp. 1–18. Greenwich, Conn.: Information Age Publishing, 2006a. Available from the National Council of Teachers of Mathematics.

Van Zoest, Laura, ed. *Teachers Engaged in Research: Inquiry into Mathematics Classrooms, Grades 9–12.* Greenwich, Conn.: Information Age Publishing, 2006b. Available from the National Council of Teachers of Mathematics.

Weissglass, Julian. "Changing Mathematics Teaching Means Changing Ourselves: Implications for Professional Development." In *Professional Development for Teachers of Mathematics,* 1994 Yearbook of the National Council of Teachers of Mathematics (NCTM), edited by Douglas B. Aichele and Arthur F. Coxford, pp. 67–78. Reston, Va.: NCTM, 1994.

Additional Resources on Communication in the Mathematics Classroom

Readers wishing to further explore the vital topic of communication in the mathematics classroom may want to add one or more of these valuable NCTM publications to their repertoire of resources:

- ***Getting into the Mathematics Conversation: Valuing Communication in Mathematics Classrooms,*** edited by Portia C. Elliott and Cynthia M. Elliott Garnett, 2008. This outstanding compendium offers readings on the broad subject of communication in the mathematics classroom. It spans all grade levels and targets all communication forms—listening and speaking, reading, writing, and multiple forms. It is organized around nine topics: the need for conversation, the nature of mathematics, sociocultural perspectives, classroom management, curriculum, learning context, learning environment, pedagogy, and assessment. Handy four-color matrix inserts offer at-a-glance identification of the articles that target a teacher's needs by three dimensions—grade level, topic, and communication form—to instantly guide the reader to the desired content. Stock #13292
- ***Exploring Mathematics through Literature: Articles and Lessons for Prekindergarten through Grade 8,*** edited by Diane Thiessen, 2003. These collected articles and lessons exemplify how to use children's literature to effectively teach mathematics in grades Pre-K–8. The articles involve communication, problem solving, representation, reasoning, and connections. Helpful teacher notes, lists of materials needed, discussions of the mathematics, and blackline masters of student recording sheets are all included in this useful volume. Stock #12581
- ***Math Is Language, Too: Thinking and Writing in the Mathematics Classroom,*** by David J. Whitin and Phyllis Whitin (copublished with the National Council of Teachers of English), 2000. This book describes how to build a mathematical community that honors all voices and uses writing and talking to uplift those voices and enrich mathematical ideas. The stories relate events that took place over a four-year period in a fourth-grade classroom in which students of varying abilities were encouraged to develop a spirit of inquiry through writing and talking. Stock #723
- ***New Visions for Linking Literature and Mathematics,*** by David J. Whitin and Phyllis Whitin (copublished with the National Council of Teachers of English), 2004. This book contains a wealth of ideas for integrating literature and mathematics in grades K–6, including criteria for evaluating children's books, strategies for introducing books to children, discussions of the use of problem posing and book pairs to engage all students, and connections to both mathematics and English language arts standards. The book also includes extension activities and an annotated bibliography of the best mathematics-related literature available. Stock #12777

Please consult www.nctm.org/catalog for the availability of these titles and for a plethora of resources for teachers of mathematics at all grade levels.

■

For the most up-to-date listing of NCTM resources on topics of interest to mathematics educators, as well as on membership benefits, conferences, and workshops, visit the NCTM Web site at www.nctm.org.